SLIDING INTO REVOLUTION

A doctor's memories of
life, love and revolution

M.S. KIA

M.S. KIA

Sliding into Revolution

A doctor's memories of life, love and revolution

First published by Printed by Lulu 2024

Copyright © 2024 by M.S. Kia

M.S. Kia has no responsibility for the persistence or accuracy of URLs for external or third-party Internet Websites referred to in this publication and does not guarantee that any content on such Websites is, or will remain, accurate or appropriate.

Second edition

ISBN: 978-1-7385174-1-1

Cover art by Sanam Hayati

This book was professionally typeset on Reedsy.
Find out more at reedsy.com

To Jaleh, Maryam and Nargess without whom life would lose its meaning

Contents

Foreword — v
Preface — vi
Acknowledgement — viii

1 Chapter 1 — 1
  Light through clouds darkly — 1
2 Chapter 2 — 4
  Love in the courtyard — 4
3 Chapter 3 — 7
  Roots — 7
4 Chapter 4 — 12
  The chequered blanket — 12
5 Chapter 5 — 16
  Moving house — 16
6 Chapter 6 — 23
  Growing up — 23
7 Chapter 7 — 28
  Politics and theatre — 28
8 Chapter 8 — 33
  nineteensixtythree — 33
9 Chapter 9 — 37
  Intermission — 37
10 Chapter 10 — 39
  On route to Iran — 39
11 Chapter 11 — 42
  First days in Shiraz — 42
12 Chapter 12 — 47

	Silence of the cemetery	47
13	Chapter 13	52
	The new communist movement	52
14	Chapter 14	59
	Private party for the world elite	59
15	Chapter 15	63
	Baq Namāzi	63
16	Chapter 16	65
	Congress of traditional medicine	65
17	Chapter 17	69
	The revolutionary tide	69
18	Chapter 18	77
	Sa'di Hospital under attack	77
19	Chapter 19	85
	Death to gomunist	85
20	Chapter 20	91
	The academics join in	91
21	Chapter 21	99
	Hafteh hambaste and the final sprint	99
22	Chapter 22	104
	Go martyr yourself!	104
23	Chapter 23	108
	The fat man	108
24	Chapter 24	114
	The iron gate	114
25	Chapter 25	119
	Rainbows over chaos	119
26	Chapter 26	126
	Masjed Habib	126
27	Chapter 27	136
	Reflections	136
28	Chapter 28	142
	Āshurā-Tāsuā': University and the Mosque	142

29	Chapter 29	152
	The Sa'di village plot	152
30	Chapter 30	162
	Unreality of reality	162
31	Chapter 31	164
	Invading SAVAK	164
32	Chapter 32	172
	Citadel and television	172
33	Chapter 33	179
	Heady days	179
34	Chapter 34	189
	Digging deeper	189
35	Chapter 35	196
	Glimpses of the basement	196
36	Chapter 36	200
	The Cultural Revolution	200
37	Chapter 37	208
	Mojahedin headquarters	208
38	Chapter 38	213
	War	213
39	Chapter 39	218
	The night they came for me	218
40	Chapter 40	223
	Solitary	223
41	Chapter 41	232
	Ich liebe dich	232
42	Chapter 42	240
	The doctors room	240
43	Chapter 43	247
	Andalibi	247
44	Chapter 44	250
	Jān-e Maryam	250
45	Chapter 45	256

Niriz and Jahrom	256
46 Chapter 46	262
Living with tavvābs	262
47 Chapter 47	270
Last months	270
48 Chapter 48	277
The return	277
49 Chapter 49	280
Lost flowers, a reflection on the past	280
50 Chapter 50	288
Hiding	288
51 Chapter 51	298
The escape	298
52 Chapter 52	309
24 General Yazgan	309
53 Chapter 53	316
Revolutionary court	316
54 Appendix 1	320
55 Appendix 2	322
Main opposition parties and groups to the Shah and Islamic Regime	322
56 Appendix 3	326
Bibliography	326
Afterword	332
Reflections	332
About the Author	337
Also by M.S. Kia	338

Foreword

Farsi names and words

There are various ways of transcribing Farsi words into Latin text. With proper names, I have simply converted the words as they are pronounced in a Tehrani accent into Latin text. I am aware that many English texts use different vowels. Thus *Sheikh Fazlollah Nuri* is sometimes written as *Fazlullah* and his town of birth as *Noori*. I have chosen the most common usage in literature.

As to letters of alphabet not present in English:

I have used 'q' to represent the guttural sound produced by making a 'g' sound using the back of the tongue. In much of English language literature they use 'gh' to represent that sound. Thus the holy city of *Qom* has also been written as *Ghom*.

The letters 'kh' make a sound like the 'j' in the Spanish word jamon.

An apostrophe represents the deep 'e' sound particularly at the end of names - such as *Tabātabāi'*. In the English language literature this is sometimes written as an 'ei' as in *Eid Noruz* to describe the new year celebration in Iran or *Eid Fetr* that ends the month of Ramadan.

I have used the accented *Ā or ā* to represent the 'a' sound in 'hall' as opposed to the 'a' sound in 'sand' as in *Āshurā*. In the above example of *Tabātabāi'* both types of 'a' sound are present as well as the guttoral 'e' at the end.

Preface

This is the memoir of an Iranian doctor and University teacher. It aims to show how life's unpredictable trajectory is determined by a combination of chance and choice, and how one can literally slide into a revolution without at any moment being able to foresee the ultimate consequences of one's decisions. And of loving and living with the consequences of those decisions.

It is above all a story of a revolution as it was witnessed from below; a worm's eye history of the Iranian Revolution as it appeared to me, a minor participant, in one corner of the country. The bigger players are only sketched in so far as they relate to the narrative. It is also an attempt to redirect the observer to the crucial role played by those whom the ultimate victors of the Revolution have tried to erase – the secular democratic forces, the left, who in many ways ignited the revolutionary fire. Even though the Revolution in the end disgorged an autocratic theocracy, they were not the only participants, nor even the inevitable winners. The tactics adopted by the ultimate losers, the secular and left democrats, were as much to blame for this.

This is a selective memoir because it focuses on the events that led to the Revolution. And being a memoir, some element of the personal life is interwoven. It was impossible for me to be passionate about the Revolution without a love for my family. The two are, for me, part of the same battle. To preserve a love for humanity through adversity can only come through a love for those within immediate touch. Those who may be only interested in the Revolution could skip the earlier chapters.

Because the Islamic regime is still in power, and who knows what other trials are facing the people of Iran, I have changed the names of virtually all the people who are alive. Those who have died are remembered in all their glory. I have used tape recordings and notes I made when I arrived in exile and memory was fresh. I have tried as much as possible to corroborate all the events I describe though whatever source I could find - including interviewing survivors. I accept full responsibility for any mistakes and apologies for any omissions. The bits that may be incorrect remain in the spirit of experience, or in Daniel Defoe's words, 'lying like truth.'

Acknowledgement

I thank my wife J, my daughters Maryam and Nargess, J's brother Massoud, Afsaneh, Azar, Charles Fox, Dewi Johns, Daniel Low-Beer, Diviya Kapur, Fazlollah, Humphrey Hodgson, Kamyar, Martin Hartog, Mehdi, Richard Olver, Said, Shirley Hodgson, and Solmaz for their criticisms on this document. In particular the honest critique of Solmaz, Azar, Dewi, Daniel, Charles and Richard have made me rewrite huge sections. I am deeply indebted to J's niece, Sanam, for the cover design and for Ffion and Michael Williams for copy editing the text. I have deliberately omitted the surnames of all my Iranian friends and family. Let my efforts encourage other participants to enrich the living history of a people in revolt.

1

Chapter 1

Light through clouds darkly

Walking down Munich's Ludwigstrasse it suddenly dawned on me, 'all's for the best even in this worst of all possible worlds', though Pangloss may or may not have agreed. I had been snatched from the firing squad by a combination of luck and family ties. I had survived imprisonment with its ever-present threat of being betrayed. Then there was the fear of hiding, of being caught, of not knowing if the weekly signing in with the Revolutionary Guards was going to be my last, each time making sure that the key to whatever house I was hiding in was safe somewhere so no links could be made were I to be detained, not to return. Living from moment to moment, moving from one hideout to another, hanging on the love and sacrifice of friends and relatives. And then that cold mountain peak when I used my shivering body to protect the girls.

Now the end was visible. I was about to fall off the end of the earth plate. I was loved unreservedly. Undeservedly. It was half Pangloss I muttered, half to myself half to an invisible audience. I was used to talking to myself as if I was addressing a large crowd, finding, trying out the words to convince them – me. That collective that is within each individual – what makes us a social animal I thought. Ten minutes on I rediscovered the site of my first trauma.

The night I became an adult.

The outside world was always there. As far back as memory stretched, I sensed that there is something more important out there, beyond the walls that separated the small courtyard from the narrow alley with a gutter pitted with little pools of foetid, tarry, stagnant water running down the middle. That courtyard was my world and seemed huge until I went back years later and saw how it had shrunk.

In the basement my maternal grandfather, *Āqā-joon* to me, took visitors all morning, ranging from humble petitioners to politicians and clerics both local and foreign. Some came to pay their respect. Most came to get a letter of recommendation for a job or a plea of some kind, an introduction to one or other bureaucrat. *Āqā-joon* would never refuse to write a recommendation for this or that petitioner in his unreadable miniscule almost parkinsonian handwriting. In the first elections after the allies invaded Iran and deposed the old Shah in 1941, he had been elected to the Majles (parliament) from Varamin, a village south of Tehran, one of the few who had been elected without bribes or coercion. Ebrahim Āshtiani, to give him his full name, had cast the only negative vote to the new Shah Mohammad Reza's first bid to give himself greater powers. He was alone in refusing a tie when the Majles (Parliament) deputies went to see the Shah, or to bow. 'Only God gets my bow' was his retort, with a twinkle in his eye. That gentle looking face hid a mind of steel. He was not re-elected. Now my maternal grandfather was powerless and without influence, but people came anyway, and he obliged.

Later politics became physical when, while attending a primary school in Fallowfields, Manchester, prime-minister Mosaddeq nationalised the oil[1] and I was regularly beaten up by the class above, as if I had a hand in 'stealing our oil', as they put it. Or again, when on June (28 *Mordad*) 1953 with the family on our summer vacation on the slopes of the Alborz mountain, a servant ran breathlessly into the *bāq* (orchard) in Dezashib we had rented for the summer and brought news of Mosaddeq's overthrow by a coup, and of gangs of thugs roaming the streets shouting pro-Shah slogans, "the same ones that had shouted 'either death or Mosaddeq' a week or so before" she added with a chuckle. The coup was organised and financed by the CIA with help from pro-British agents in Iran.[2]

Or in 1956 when we entered Istanbul the day after the pogrom of Greeks orchestrated by the Turkish Prime Minister, Menderes. I can still see the hotel room in the curve of Meşrutyet Street in Şişaneh strewn with broken glass from the shattered window which looked down on the normally blue waters of the Horn, grey under the cloudy sky. Greek shop windows smashed or boarded up in a city roamed by ghosts and the wind. Politics had scattered, shattered lives.

[1] see Christopher de Bellaigue.
[2] See Stephen Kinzer, and Christopher de Bellaigue.

Chapter 2

Love in the courtyard

I was born into love, a love that grew in a rocky barren soil parched of water. My unhappy grandmother, *Mādar-joon,* my father's mother[1] - sent off to marry when still a child, marooned and alien in Arāk, a town in central Iran - had been trapped in an unhappy, loveless arranged marriage. Her mother's death opened the window of escape and she travelled to Tehran with some of her children including my father Ezzeddin. The journey took three days by *delijān* (carriage) to the holy city of Qom where they stayed for six months. Two of his fellow travellers died of what was said to be typhoid. Later that century Ezzeddin - Ezzy for short - was to fly non-stop to California. He and his generation jumped several centuries in one lifetime, true vertical invaders as John Berger was to say of the Andalusian Picasso leaping a century into Paris. Understanding this is central to understanding the roots of the Revolution. On the way to Tehran Ezzy saw his first train, *māshin doodi,* literally a 'smoking car' as it was known to everyone, which linked the southern village of Shah-Abdol-Azim to Tehran - a distance of 70 km; at the time it was our sole railway. He alighted in the house of his mother's oldest brother uncle Ziā– oldest son of the eminent Shi'a cleric Sheikh Fazlollah Nuri (of whom later). It was the first time he saw electricity

CHAPTER 2

– one of Tehran's streets, unimaginatively called the Electric-Lamp Street (Cherāq Barq), had recently been electrified. Uncle Ziā', a Majles deputy, owned one of the few cars in Iran – a Ford 28. This was 1924.

On that first day in Tehran, when he was dipping his hands in the little pond of the central courtyard of his uncle's house, Ezzy looked up. As in most old Iranian houses the courtyard was surrounded on all sides by a veranda leading to a circle of rooms. There he saw a young girl, his cousin Ensieh – Ensy to everyone. Their mothers were sisters. She was dressed in clothes that he had never seen in provincial Arāk. He had never set eyes on anyone so beautiful. Their eyes met. For him it was love at first sight. He was seven. They had been born 400 km apart. He never lost that love.

When my father was in the ninth grade, his parents returned to Arāk and he moved in for a year with his aunt Anis, the third daughter of Sheikh Fazlollah, who lived in relative poverty with her solicitor husband and their only daughter in an old house in a narrow alleyway named after the solicitor-cleric, deep in old Tehran. The elderly cleric was obviously respected. The alley became muddy after rain.

They were not allowed to marry until Ezzy finished his education at Dār-al-Fonun – the first higher education school in Iran - and qualified as a railway engineer. They were married by his aunt Anis's husband in a very private ceremony. His own parents did not approve of the marriage and did not attend. The same day he packed his few belongings in a small bag and moved to Ensy's parents' house where they were given a room. Right up to the end of his life he maintained that Ensy's parents - his aunt and my *Khānum-joon* and *Āqā-joon* - were his true mother and father. He certainly gave them more love than he did his natural parents.

He started work in a copper-smelting factory, in South Tehran, Qaniābād, on a miniscule salary of 32 tomans a month. The factory was closed after the allies invaded Iran in 1941 as it was supplying the army with copper. With the help of influential relatives, he joined the railway and his salary ballooned to a more manageable 104 tomans, but still not enough for independent living. The railway had recently been built by the Germans linking the Persian Gulf port of Bandar Shahpur to Tehran and then north to the Caspian port of Bandar Shah. While the southern section had an obvious economic purpose, allowing imported goods and oil to get to the capital, the northern route through the spectacular Alborz mountain range, with its absurdly steep inclines needing heavy locomotives, had little economic function except to link up with the ill-gotten landed estates of Reza Shah, the founder of the Pahlavi Dynasty; land that he had accumulated by forcibly evicting its previous owners. The line did not even link the major population centres of Māzandarān Province. After the Allied invasion, the north-south railway was used as a conduit to supply the beleaguered Soviet army in the war and was dubbed 'the bridge to victory'.

I was born a few months after the allies invaded Iran - and cried non-stop for the next 6 months. I was hungry. Much as Ensy pleaded with her Russian paediatrician Dr Turkia that she had no breast milk, he would chide her - 'You Iranian women never want to breast feed' - and would squeeze her breast, which would produce a gushing stream of milk. One day Ensy gave up and bought formula. They say I never cried after that and was the most smiley good-natured child in the family.

[1] A family tree is at the end to guide a non-Farsi reader through a maze of names.

3

Chapter 3

Roots

Who am I? Who were my roots and where were they planted? No one can totally escape their roots. We are attached to our roots by invisible threads. No one is a puppet of history, nor totally free of that personal history. The roots constantly reach out to entice you, involve you, mould you, suck you in. I was born into a political family. Sadly, the only thing I have in common with Marx is that all our ancestors were clerics – rabbis in his case and mullahs in mine. Mullahs with *sharia'* in one hand and politics in the other. Perhaps that explains my fascination with history from the moment I could read.

Both my grandmothers were daughters of Sheikh Fazlollāh Nuri. The Sheikh, I kept being reminded, was an important player in the Constitutional Revolution of 1906 where an alliance of clergy and the bazaar merchants mobilised large sections of the population, including women, to demand an end to the absolute monarchy. The autocratic Qājār king Mozaffar al-Din Shah was forced to agree to an elected parliament, the *Majles*, on his sick bed, a turning point in contemporary Iranian history.

An eminent cleric in his own right, the Sheikh at first supported the Revolution, but had switched sides when the newly crowned Shah, Mohammad Ali Shah, tore up his father's signature on the Constitution. The battle lines were drawn when the new Shah ordered field guns to shell the nascent parliament (Majles) building. Like much of history, why the Sheikh changed sides is open to interpretation. Was it, as historian Kasravi believed, jealousy of the other mullahs who were more prominent in the eyes of the revolutionary forces, or was it objecting to the increasing British orientation of the Revolution and its leaders, who had taken sanctuary in the British embassy? Or was it ideological, as his grandson the poet Dr Tondar Kia put it: 'a martyr on the rule of *sharia*"? The Sheikh's political views were distinctly authoritarian.

Whatever the reason for his defection, and I go for the ideological-authoritarian version, he called for *mashrua'* rather than *mashruteh*, a religiously legitimised government rather than a constitutional monarchy. Over half a century later, Ayatollah Khomeini expanded the doctrine into a call for an Islamic government, shorthand for a government by the mullahs. Khomeini acknowledged his intellectual debt by renaming the central square in Tehran, Meidāne Sepah (formerly Tupkhāneh) the square the Sheikh was hanged, as Meidāne Sheikh Fazlollāh and placed the Sheikh's face on one of the most used post-office stamps. It was like putting Nelson on Trafalgar Square, or on a second-class stamp. It was but a fleeting memorial. On Khomeini's death the square changed names once again to Meidāne Emām Khomeini. The stamp stays.

The Sheikh was born into a prominent family of Shi'a clergy from the northern village of Nur, on the shores of the Caspian Sea. There are some small places that seem to be fertile soil for nurturing intellectual development. [1] Āshtiān was another such village, birthplace to my great, great grandfather, and another political mullah, Mirza Hassan Āshtiāni who gave out the *fatwa* from Tabriz which banned the use of tobacco after the entire Iranian tobacco crop, its distribution and export, was sold for a pittance to a British business man, GF Talbot, by the Qājār king Nāsser al-Din Shah (1848-1896). The *fatwa* gave rise to riots in Tehran and other cities and a boycott of tobacco smoking by the entire population – the first anti-imperialist uprising in Iran. It was also the first time Iranian women, including women in the Shah's household, entered the arena of mass politics and a dress rehearsal to the Constitutional Revolution of 1906.

CHAPTER 3

Years later I was caressed by one of those teasing nudges of history. In what people call fate, but is no more than the chance meeting of a fish the same colour as oneself if you happen to swim in a small pond that was the Iranian middle class, I met and fell in love with J. Her maternal great great aunt, Anisdowheh, had been a favourite wife of the Qājār king Nāsser al-Din Shah. I wondered if Anisdowleh was party to the boycott of tobacco by the Shah's wives in the *andarun* (women's quarter) in what is believed to have delivered the final blow to the tobacco monopoly by the British? The Shah withdrew the concession.

The Constitutionalists, having survived and then defeated the Imperial Russian Army that occupied Tabriz in support of the despotic new king, Mohammad Ali Shah, marched on Tehran and overthrew the Shah with little opposition. Sheikh Fazlollāh was arrested and later hanged in the central square that later fleetingly bore his name. They say one of his sons, Sheikh Mehdi, danced at the foot of the scaffold. Later Mehdi's son, Kianuri, led the Central Committee of the Tudeh (communist) Party at the time of the Islamic Revolution.[2] Politics is infectious.

Sheikh Fazlollāh, like his disciple Khomeini, was always a politician as well as a cleric. He himself had married the daughter of Seyyed Mohammad Tabātabāi', a prominent pro-constitutionalist mullah, an ally at the time, and had married off one of his sisters, "dear auntie Arab' to us" (*Khāleh-jan Arab*) to Sayyed Mohammad Hassan al-Sadr, head of the prominent Sadr family in Iraq and a senior *Shi'a* cleric who was briefly prime minister in Iraq (1948) and served as President of the Senate during the reign of King Feisal until deposed by Abdol-Karim Qāsem's coup that overthrew the Iraqi monarchy in 1958. The Sadr family was another *Shi'a* clerical family of huge influence in Iraq, and Lebanon then, and now.

During his flirtation with the Constitutionalists, the Sheikh had betrothed one daughter Zakkieh (my mother's mother – *Khānoom-joon*) to Ebrahim Āshtiāni, the son of another prominent constitutionalist and the grandson of the man who had given out the anti-tobacco *fatwa* inside Iran. After the political split, the betrothal was put on ice for many years until after Sheikh

Fazlollāh's execution (for a family tree see Appendix 1).

Another daughter of the Sheikh, Ehterām (my father's mother), was sent off at the age of 8 to marry Mohammad Bāqer, the grandson of a wealthy cleric-landowner in the central city of Arāk, Haj-āqā Mohsen Arāki. This too was a political marriage. Haj-āqā Mohsen had risen from an obscure mullah into one of central Iran's biggest landowners using his power as a local cleric, and perhaps by other means, to obtain land given over as a religious endowment (*vaqf*). The family is notoriously evasive about how he got to where he was, a major feudal landlord and the despotic Mohammad Ali Shah's principal supporter in central Iran. Kasravi, in his seminal history of the Iranian Constitutional Revolution, describes how local revolutionaries took refuge in the telegraph station in protest at the persecution at his hands. In those days the mosques, the foreign embassies and the telegraph stations were safe havens. Seven decades later, and another revolution which involved and enveloped me, the universities and hospitals were to take their place. In Islamic Iran today there are no safe havens. But of that, later. Ehteram had seven children, my father Ezzeddin being the fourth.

Ehterām-Sharieh, her full name, but *Māder-joon* (dear mother) to me, was an unhappy soul. She never felt at home among her husband's huge family in Arāk. Hāj-āqā Mohsen had over thirteen known wives and his eldest son, Ahmad, was even more drawn to women. My father later recounted how Ahmad would be seen every morning trudging down to the public baths with his servant in tow – it being a religious ritual to have a post-coital absolution bath, the *qosl*. His steward (*pishkār*) would sometimes find him at one of the villages he owned showering particular attention to one or other child. 'He or she is born of the master' the *pishkār* would whisper in his ear. Ahmad had thirty-seven children that I know of, my grandfather, Mohammad Bagher, being his oldest son.

Entering this vast family in a strange town at such a young age must have been traumatic for my paternal grandmother, *Mādar-joon*. She felt very lonely there in that village – Kahrizak – which was her husband's share of an inheritance. She certainly never loved her husband. But she gave him four boys and three girls that survived the first few years. There were favourites.

CHAPTER 3

Fakhri the eldest was the real ruler of the household, in charge of the education of his siblings. He could do no wrong. And ultimately when he went to France with the first wave of students sent by the new king, Reza Shah, to study in Europe, all resources were diverted to his education. Sadri, the second son, was later sent to Germany. Both were stuck abroad when the Second World War broke out.

I was effectively the first born for both grandparents - my older cousins were born in France to uncle Fakhri's French wife and were permanently absent, and anyway 'foreign', and uncle Sadri never married after his German sweetheart, Marichen, 'little Mary', failed to join him in Iran. I was precious and under pressure.

[1] Nur was one, giving birth to Nima Yushij, father of modern Persian poetry, among others. The village Āshtiān was birth place of Qavām Saltaneh, five time prime minister, and his brother Vosugh-al-Dowleh who signed the notorious 1920 pact with Britain which divided Iran between the spheres of influence of Russia and Britain. Finally there was Mosaddeq who was born in Tehran but his father was from Āshtiān.

[2] The Tudeh (literally 'mass') Party was Formed in 1941, with Soleiman Mirza Eskandari as its head. It replaced the Communist Party (founded 1920) which had been outlawed by Reza Shah.

4

Chapter 4

The chequered blanket

Looking back, childhood has no narrative, merely a series of snapshots. They may or may not represent what was. But then, 'what was' is that which one recalls as 'what was'. Memory is part of reality. We reinterpret history to illuminate the present. This is how I see my childhood. The closer we get to now the more the images coalesce into a narrative and the more that narrative approaches reality. But you cannot understand that narrative without the childhood images.

Sometimes important people came to visit my grandfather, *Āqā-joon*. There was Mousa Sadr, a distant cousin through marriage of Sheikh Fazlollāh's sister into the great Iranian-Iraqi-Lebanese Sadr family. Mousa Sadr, who later took on the title of Imam, went on to create the Shi'a Amal movement in Lebanon, financed by the Shah as a counter to the Palestine Liberation Organisation (PLO). He was tall, erect, with blue eyes (were his eyes really blue?), with an amazingly white, almost ethereal, skin who would give me a smile. He was to disappear on a flight to Tripoli after the Revolution and his fate remains obscure to this day. The reach of the offspring of the Shi'a clergy spreads far and wide – from secretary general of the Tudeh party, Kianuri, to Muqtada al-Sadr, the scion of US-occupied Iraq. Both are cousins.

CHAPTER 4

A few flashes of what appears as lucid reality but may be fabrication. Does it matter? They are as real as reality. Such was the chequered blanket. There is the little-boy-me looking through a door half-ajar at a red chequered blanket on a bed. Mina my sister is being born. The image is vivid as if I am seeing it now, but Ensy, my mother, later corrected me. Mina was born in hospital and not at home. What do I remember then? Is that image totally fictitious or is it related in some way to Mina's birth. She was born by Kianuri's sister, a midwife who charged them a 400 tomans, a hefty sum, which I can only guess was intended for the Tudeh party coffers. Why else charge your cousin many times his monthly salary? The image of Akhtar imprinted in my mind is of a beautiful woman with grey hair, tightly bound in a bun at the back of her head, and piercing eyes, a poster image of a Soviet party woman. She was married to Abdol Samad Kāmbakhsh, one of the most mysterious figures in the history of the Tudeh party and the Iranian Left movement.

The childhood I remember is idyllic. Summer in Damavand where the whole family, aunts, uncles, grandmothers, cousins all live in large tents in a huge orchard that was the inheritance of Sheikh Fazlollāh's three daughters. The Sheikh had left this fruitful orchard adjoining the Damavand River to his beloved daughters leaving bits of barren land north of the capital to his sons. He was not to know how the latter would become prized real estate property bordering one of the most prestigious boulevards of the capital, Boulevard Elizabeth (now Fatemi). It was in that idyllic setting in Damavand that I nearly died of severe dehydration. A 'doctor' had diagnosed gastroenteritis and stupidly advised water restriction to stop the diarrhoea. Someone apparently came into the tent, took one look at me and shouted at my mother that I am as dry as a tree. Water saved my life. The central place occupied by thirst and water deprivation in Shi'a mythology in the martyrdom of Imam Hossein, which we will come back to again and again in this story, make me question the accuracy of the dehydration coda. But water almost drowned my sister Mina one day as we played 'who will come up last for air?' in the small pond in my grandfather's house. I came up first, no sign of my 3-year-old sister, only a frog next to me in the water. It took me some seconds to realize the frog was Mina. She had lost her grip. I pulled her out. Were it not for the frog, my sister would have been reified into the image of that chequered blanket.

In those days, the equivalent of keeping up with the Joneses was to have your child in a class a year or two above their age. My father Ezzy had done his own somersaults unaided by anyone. I had Ensy. She worked with me at home on the three R's from the age of five and I entered second grade at the age of six when all my classmates were two years older, starting school, as they still do in Iran, aged 7. 'We are going to school tomorrow and they may ask you to do the first form end-of-year exam', mother said casually. That morning I woke up particularly early, anxious, as any child would be, to face the new unknown. There on the table was an electric iron standing on end. I wondered if it is hot, and in a spontaneous thoughtless act that I was to repeat again and again to this day, tested my theory with my right palm. My entire right hand was aflame. I could not, dared not, did not say anything to anyone. If I cried, I made sure no one saw it.

She helped me dress in my best suit, took my right hand, her soft grip feeling like the embrace of burning charcoal and we went to see the headmaster of Neshat primary school. Writing the exam with that burning hand was how I entered the new phase in life by a trial of fire to join a class where I was the baby. It was the start of 10 years of unhappy schooling – with a brief happy interlude in Munich. No one ever heard me complain of the bullying, of the threats, of the constant fear which was my lot, partly because I was smaller and weaker than the rest. There was no way I could complain to parents who so unequivocally did what they thought was best for their children, often at huge sacrifice. Ezzy, often so funny in company, so charming and so in love with Ensi. Such a good father. And Ensy, her smile, at once soft and insecure, reflecting a childhood of fragile health, a beautiful face that not even small-pox could scar. How could I upset them with my petty woes?

So fragile a thing is memory –
  sunlit flashes
  on the dark hill.[1]

[1] Claire Holtham (who incidentally had also learnt Farsi), Road From Herat,

CHAPTER 4

Five Seasons Press, 2011.

5

Chapter 5

Moving house

The new middle class was on the move northwards towards the Alborz mountains. Slowly at first, then inexorably as oil bankrolled their ever-expanding numbers and lifestyle, it was like an avalanche in reverse. Social mobility was exteriorised in the creeping colonisation of the barren desert and emerald-green villages north of the capital. As Garry Shteyngart said about Manhattan, everyone in the city became a real estate whore. Houses spread like an oil spill to cover every bit of earth north of the city. If it were not for a mountain-wall blocking this external show of affluence – the capital would have slid into the Caspian by now. As it is the slopes of the Alborz mountain range became disfigured by the jagged scratching of high rises, poking upwards in random bunches of grey, white and yellowed concrete reaching out for the perennial snow line. The concrete-moss was slowly devouring the beautiful *bāq* (orchard) gardens of the many villages that dotted the slopes of Alborz, transforming them into one huge maze of high walls, haphazard blocks and exhaust-fuming metal, that has all but obliterated the view of the mountain. The conical Mount Damāvand, the majestic dormant volcano, now weeps for its lost solitude as the brick and concrete mangrove has crept eastwards towards its slopes and my childhood idyllic Damavand

CHAPTER 5

and westwards merging with the city of Karaj, transforming Tehran into another monstrous metropolis.

When I was born both my grandparent's houses had opened to narrow alleyways, *koocheh,* not far from the nerve centre of the old city, the bazaar. A *joob,* a water channel, would meander in the middle, usually filled with foetid water and bits of discarded rubbish, thick watermelon skins with the juicy-red carefully scraped off, paper-thin cucumber skins expertly peeled, vines with a few rotten grapes hanging on – the food of rich and poor alike - and newspapers that were mainly bought to know who died and which funeral to attend. In winter your rubber galoshes sank in mud. Later, the *koocheh* was asphalted which showed up the rubbish in the *joob* more grotesquely. Even rubbish looks better in natural surroundings.

Once a week or month, depending on the *mahalleh* (neighbourhood), water from the Alborz mountains would flow down this *joob,* usually in the middle of the night. A *mirāb,* the mysterious man of the night who controlled the supply of water in any neighbourhood, would then allow each house in turn to fill up their water tank deep underground – the *ābanbār.* He was a man of power and no one questioned his authority. We children would look down the steep steps that led to this subterranean cave but would never, ever, muster the courage to step down. Somewhere beyond, as the last steps disappeared into a terrifying darkness, was the cool water that was delved out in tin buckets or watering cans or later miraculously sprouted out of the taps. That water was not for drinking though; donkey carts would bring spring water, *āb-e shah* (water of the king) that was stored in earthenware pots in the courtyard. Scores of nannies, servants, cooks and other dependents who occupied the basements of every house I had visited warned us of the *jinns* down there in the depth. I never saw a *jinn* but Ābji (literally sister) and Sārā servants in grandmother *Mādar-joon's* house, old even then and in Ābji's case totally bent over like a bow by ankylosing spondylitis, said they had. I never tested that out.

The *koocheh* (alleyway) in those early days was a multi class environment. You would have those titled by the Shah, the *dowlehs* and *saltanehs,* living on the same alley as the carpenter, the steward, the servant, the grocer. There would be the large houses of the rich, the landowner or the minister next to that of his servant and also next to his stables. Geography did not define your social standing. And each neighbourhood (*mahalleh*) would have its own culture, have its own column (*dasteh*) in the *Āshura-Tāsuā* marches to mourn the martyrdom of imam Hossein,[1] and compete for the best banner – somewhat akin to the Caribbean carnivals, but with tears and self-flagellation instead of dancing, laughter, drugs and sex. The contrast speaks volumes of the differences between the two cultures.

The early moves were cautious keeping the extended family close. The first to move was Ezzy's mother, *Mādar-joon*. Sadri, her second son and an engineer bought a house a little north at Gorgān Street with his parents and his two unmarried younger siblings. There, the neighbours would blurt out popular songs (*tasnif*) from seven in the morning till very late. That move was clearly a statement of his success in the new Iran. In the 1970's, uncle Sadri slipped further northwards and built a large five-story house in Jordan Avenue, whose name is not really Iranian. Another daughter, aunt Aqdas, leap-frogged over him and bought land in what at the time was desert but was closer to the Alborz Mountains. There it sat, a beautiful, large, two-storey house with a garden and a swimming pool, the first in the family, lonely, surrounded by high walls, vulnerable in the barren desolate landscape. With that move she had declared to everyone where she stood socially. Her husband taught at the Medical School, but more significantly, owned a private medical laboratory. Soon the plots around her were built with similar homes. It was clearly labelled an upper middle class, professional neighbourhood, modern, imitating California. Houses with blue blobs on the outside and expensive-looking garish metal gates. Wealth had to be displayed to be envied. Unlike the British. No traditional families as neighbours. No loud radio's either. Aunt Aqdas was our most northern-residing relative then. An expression of her superior status.

Soon after I was born Ezzy moved out of his aunt-mother-in-law's house into a rented house in Aramaneh Alley close by where Mina was born. But he took seriously ill with brucellosis and was admitted to the Railway Hospital

CHAPTER 5

where he lay for three months. One day in semi coma, he overheard the senior doctor telling his assistant that he would not make it till morning, in French: *il va mourir dans vingt quatre heures*. He survived the medical pessimists and was sent to Belgium to supervise five railway engineers for training. It was one way of getting him out from under their noses. As deputy chief of the north-west railways in the early post war years, Ezzy kept discovering massive thefts by colleagues and others. Once he exposed to the authorities train loads of loot which the Shah's army, along with its Zolfaqāri tribal allies, had plundered that freezing, snowy winter from the city of Zanjān and transported with the help of railway colleagues. Zanjān was gateway to the Azarbāijan provinces, the last station on the north-west railway and the jumping point for the invasion and crushing of the short-lived Soviet-backed Autonomous Government of Azarbāijan. Ezzy was summarily removed from his post and sent home to stew. My father was and remained too honest for the Iran the Shah was building. With his departure to Belgium the house proved too costly and Ensy moved in with her mother once again, in Borhāndowleh Alley off Amirieh street. It was the spring of 1948.

It was a two-storey house surrounded by a relatively large courtyard. One side had a blue tiled pond which is where I saved 'the frog', my sister. As you came into the house there were rooms on both sides and a central stairway which then branched both ways to the first floor, a poor copy of Hollywood movies, you could almost see Gloria Swanson coming down them, where my unmarried uncle Fazl and aunt Tāhereh had their rooms. We were put up in the visitors' room, the most precious room in any Iranian house, never opened except for special guests. At the end of the cul-de-sac alley was a tall blue wooden gate set in a domed frame - almost like the gate to a city - that was the door to large house beyond. Flowing over the high white-chalked brick wall that went out on either side for what to a child seemed an endless expanse, branches of wisteria would pour their purple grape-like flowers in the spring interspersed with leaves that were as light as insect wings. I never saw the gate open and never saw what was inside. It was the home of our landlord, Borhandowleh, a titled gent who gave his name to the alley.

Opposite us on the other side of the alley aunt Tayyebeh, my mother's other sister, lived with her husband, two children and the cook in a two-story rented house which like ours also abutted on the main road, Amirieh Street – one of the few tree-lined streets which began south at the railway station and went on to end up in Shemirānāt on the foothills of Alborz mountain, 37 kilometres to the north. Walk into Amirieh and life exploded into view. Pedestrians sharing the pavement with cyclists skilfully swerving round you, often with a passenger or two on the cross bars. Buses whizzing by the driver's mate, the *shāgerd shofer*, hanging out the door and shouting out the destination – Toopkhooneh-Bāzaar or Rāhe Āhan, refering to Toopkhāneh – literally the home of the field-gun - the square at the heart of Tehran close to the bazaar whose name, chameleon-like, changed with the political tide first to Sepah to honour Reza Shah (no one on the streets called it by that name), then changed to Sheikh Fazlollāh after my great grandfather after the Revolution, and now Imam Khomeini. Rāhe Āhan at the other end of the number 2 bus was Tehran's only railway station.

The northward migration of the middle classes speeded up in the 70's. Aunt Tāhereh, who had 'married north' into a home off the fashionable Shahreza avenue, hopped further northwards three times in the next four decades, with a detour west to the fashionable *Kākh* avenue a little further up from the Shah's main palace. We camped in a room in that house for a year when Ezzy was once again out of favour with the current railway chief and out of a job. Later aunt Tayyebeh also moved north, having been given land to build on by her father-in-law-cum-uncle in another desert neighbourhood, lower down and thus less prestigious than aunt Aqdas. Even Ensy's mother, grandmother *Khānom-joon* moved twice, each time a few hundred metres northward along *Amirieh* avenue. She declined the more secular suburbs. She was more at home in the traditional areas within easy reach of the bazaar. And anyway, money was tight.

And so the migration went on and on. Every time I visited home from the UK during my studies and later when I returned to Iran to work, I was shocked by the concrete oil slick, slowly devouring the beautiful *bāqs* with their mud-bricked low walls separated by winding alleys along which flowed clear

CHAPTER 5

mountain streams. The slow death of the numerous villages that constituted Shemirānāt, Vanak and lately the picturesque mountainside villages Ushum and Fasham which sank into concrete. The less traditional half of the middle layers of society, were upward moving socially and migrating physically – the new nomads. They camped in one spot only to migrate further north as cash flowed into their pockets. The city became, by and large divided into a poorer and more traditional south and a pseudo-modern north. And there they built the new symbols of modernity – the cinemas, the shopping malls and the leisure centre, Radiocity. The dividing line at the time of the Revolution was Shāhreza now called Enqelāb (Revolution) avenue. Moving house was a mirror of social change.

Not all our family followed the northward migration. The more traditional sector, the Ashtiānis, mostly stayed in the southern parts of the city many around in the old town near the central bazaar. Here we witnessed the early schism between the traditional and the nouvelle petite bourgeoisie and bourgeoisie which played such an important role in the trajectory of the revolution-to-come.

But the new post-revolution Islamic regime is also a north-migrator. Underneath the patchwork of villages that made up Shemirān, which was invaded by concrete, each village had retained some of its old inhabitants and traditional societies. It was thus that the fashionable high class and overtly secular Farmanieh, to which my parents eventually moved in their own northward migration after I had left Iran, was cheek by jowl with very traditional Chitzar where they did their day-to-day shopping. Someone persuaded the aesthete Khomeini to reside in Jamaran, on the mountain slopes, a muezzin-cry from the ex-Shah's Niāvarān summer palace. Soon the neighbouring villas, many with swimming pools, were taken over by turbaned clerics. Some confiscated from exiled rich Tehranis, some bought. In an interesting twist, the underground opposition, especially after the revolution, also used the northern suburbs to hide out. The large houses often within large walled gardens offered security from prying neighbours and Revolutionary Guards.

There they now live, the traditional and the new, side-by-side seemingly in disharmony. Parties, alcohol, drugs, dancing, massive exposure of skin, and more drugs, all those markers of 'modernity' in today's Iran are there, in proximity to the devout, the turbaned, the veiled. The young cruise in cars and pick up phone numbers by the handful for potential later use. The 'price' for non-interference, to be left in peace, is determined by the local Revolutionary Guards in the local *komiteh*. It is an accommodation convenient to all but those that want more from life than drugs, booze and sex. Soon the offspring of the new rulers of the country, nicknamed *aqazadeh*, having engorged themselves in newly plundered wealth, began to adopt the hedonistic habits of the secular middle class, those that is who had not gone abroad.

[1] See Chapter *28, Āshura Tāsuā: The University and the Mosque* for a more detailed description of some of these ceremonies.

6

Chapter 6

Growing up

School. The images that come to me are a mixture of wonder, fear and despair. After two years of school under the protection of an older cousin the family was off to Europe, a trip that was like walking into a book. The entire family came to see us off at Mehrābād airport. You walked up to the plane on the tarmac with the family standing behind a fence. They waved goodbye to the plane as if it was alive until it vanished over the horizon, perspective being lost in the blue sky as in a miniature painting. This ritual, as well as showers of presents, pistachio, sweets and one occasion a large sack of fresh pears, handed over in the airport, was to be repeated until the late 60's, when taking the plane to London became like boarding a train to Mashhad. The KLM flight attendants gave us children chocolate and colouring books. Cut price flying was almost half a century in the future. Milano, Lausanne, Paris then a week in London's Park Lane Hotel overlooking Green Park and a frock-coated butler bringing us breakfast on silver ware and a trolley. The entire trip was way beyond our means. But Ezzy, whose intrinsic romanticism belonged to another century and another world, the poetic world of Lamartine, was recreating the visit he had made to Belgium three years previously when he was recovering from his near fatal case of Malta Fever (brucellosis) for his beloved Ensy. It was 1951

By the time we arrived in Manchester he had spent the £300 he had brought and was left with nothing. Churchill who had replaced Atlee as British premier, fought it out with Iranian Prime Minister Mosaddeq over who was to pay our salary, not helped by the fact that Ezzy had reported home that the Brits were charging post-war prices for locomotives, he discovered, that had been manufactured before the war. We moved to a small hotel in Fallowfields. For the next eight months, mother would hide some bread and butter from breakfast for our lunch, while they both went without. We ate at the hotel and walked everywhere and somehow, Ezzy fobbed off the hotel owner in deferring payment.

Pre-smoke-free Manchester was grim and some of that grimness must have rubbed off on everyone, young and old. The sky was grey, the fogs were grey, people were grey, clothes were colourless, teachers were colourless, school kids were in grey flannel shorts. Under that pan-greyness every paper, from Daily Mail to The Observer were caricaturing Mosaddeq as a fanatic, a Frankenstein, a latter-day histrionic Hitler in pyjamas. Mosaddeq had nationalized the Anglo-Iranian Oil Company and was regularly vilified in the popular press – Left and Right. He did a lot of his work from his bed, in his pyjamas and was prone to faint at convenient moments. Not sure who was more histrionic, the British press or the old man simply demanding that Iranians get a fair share of their oil.[1] At the local primary school I got used to being beaten up in morning break by the class above for 'stealing our oil'. In the absence of television, kids were more political, more aware of news. The entire family listened to the BBC news on the Home Service and discussed it over dinner. I learnt to run away - a trick which served me well later - only to be clobbered by my only friend Dennis for stealing 'his oil'. He took personal possession.

A year later, we moved to London, Hotel Regina, Cromwell Road and I boarded at a school in Watford. Mina went to the local primary. Rationing in the early 50's meant one egg a week, slices of beef so thin that light shone through and every Friday running to the local tuck shop, the news kiosk by Cromwell Road Station, clutching the family ration card for a few pieces of

CHAPTER 6

chocolate. Two memories stand out.

The Colonel, bushy grey-white moustache, green hand-knit jumper, a bit frayed at the elbows and sleeve ends, permanently perched, like a mobile statue by the radio in the lounge of the hotel, waiting for the end, alone. Coming from a country where the family was omnipresent the loneliness of *The Colonel* still haunts me. Then there was Miss Liyusha on the top floor of the hotel. A refugee from somewhere in central Europe, ageless in my image, with an accent and holes in her shoe which she covered with newspaper, who laughed and played with Mina and me and occasionally gave us a sweet. One day she borrowed some money from Ezzy and disappeared. Weeks later, she rang up Ezzy and asked to meet him somewhere. Don't tell the hotel owner that you are meeting me, she said. I believe she gave back some of what she owned and then vanished into that post war void. She too haunts me. London was full of people living in the shadows. A new brother Ali was born that January in St Mary Abbots's Hospital. Now there were five of us.

Back to Tehran, a room in my grandparents' house and sixth form in a new school where during morning breaks the entire school encircled me and my only friend Faramarz in the yard, jeering in unison: *"landani, landani! tonboon kandani!"* (Londoner, Londoner, your pants are down). I was the first person they had seen who had been abroad. The novelty had worn off by the second term.

Seventh grade was in Sari, in the northern province of Mazandaran, where Ezzy had become head of the northern railways section. I came under the protection of a thug in our class, a much older boy who limped on a right leg shrunk by polio and carried a large knife tucked in his boots. His story, which he kept repeating, was that he was knifed 37 times by Tudeh Party gangs after the first failed coup by the Shah and left to die. In 25 Mordad, (16 August 1953) the Shah had sent colonel Nasiri, head of the Imperial Guards, with a written order removing Mosaddeq as prime minister. Nasiri was promptly arrested and the Shah fled on his private plane to Baqdad. Iran erupted as the people tore down his statues everywhere until the CIA-organised coup overthrew Mosaddeq three days later. My classmate was a Shah fanatic and took me as his protégé, his ward, and even gave me his book of poems, every one in praise of the Shah. One day a friend whispered in my ears that my classmates had decided to invite me to a picnic out of town and then gang rape me. I was a pretty boy. I declined the offer and ran home. The same threat was made a few years later by a group of boys we were playing football, when we returned to the Sari railway station during a vacation. Again, a friend's whispers saved me. Childhood was full of sexual threats. Eighth grade in Hadaf high school Tehran, where a classmate, Faramarz Ismail Beigi, was to be my immediate boss in Shiraz twenty years later and briefly share my prison.

And in September 1955, we moved to Europe again. Istanbul, our first stop, was wind swept, cold and in tatters caused by the anti-Greek riots officially sanctioned by Turkish Prime Minister Adnan Menderes. Ensy spent the first day clearing the broken glass from the floor of the hotel room, in Şişana, that faced the park, a stone's throw from the British and US embassy. It was a cold, overcast autumn,. Grey images of destruction and deserted streets. The Orient Express was bedbug-infested and when we arrived in Vienna we were in an agony of itching. And then our destination Munich, with me sitting in the co-educational class in that school in the suburb of Gräfelfing with the boys on the right, not taking in a single word of what the history, geography or literature teacher were saying, I would furtively eye the girls on the left. Spring came and that day of Wandertag in the Bavarian forest, Ursula with her straight black hair and blue eyes coming up to me with a few words that I did not understand linguistically, but understood biologically. The vivid dreams that night tumbled over me like a tsunami. Hormones transcribed as dreams. They say a person inherits a certain number of heartbeats, beyond which it simply stops. Passion, on this interpretation, cuts years off one's life. Another bad statistic concocted by desiccated men who know nothing of love, or lust, or teenage hormones on the rampage. 1955 was the best year of my life yet. It was another nine years before the green dress opened a more lasting door.

The next phase was a disaster. I boarded at Grenville College, Bideford which sold itself to my parents by its beautiful buildings and the promise of making me into an English gentleman. I was studying for O levels. Sexual predators again, only this time in the form of the headmaster and the English teacher. They never got beyond repeated caning and fondling my shorts-covered bottom for what seemed like an eternity, although it could not have been more than a few minutes. Those were the same years as the hushing-up of paedophilia in the Catholic Church in Ireland and more. And then the bullying by classmates, the looted tuck box, the tears all poured out in a diary and in a dialogue with 'god'. God and religion preserved me as *'Me'* and like the tuck box, gradually faded and vanished entirely over the first years of university. First to go was religion as I faced its absurdities and was confronted by diverse, divisive and vehemently held interpretations of the same thing. God followed soon, no longer necessary to explain anything. Boarding school prepared me well for prison.

I was offered a place in Medical School at Edinburgh and at St Thomas' Hospital. It was unusual to gain two acceptances. Foreigners were taken on as tokens. They were not the money earners for universities then that they are now. My tuition fee was £80 per annum. I accepted London to be close to friends. We moved into Flat 1, Queens Court, Queensway. It was 1960 and swinging London was about to be born. It leap-frogged over me.

[1] Between 1913 and 1935 the Anglo-Iranian Oil Company grossed profits of US$ 3 billion, but a mere US$ 624 million remained in Iran. The royalties paid to Iran in 1947 was half the tax paid to the British government.

Chapter 7

Politics and theatre

As in most things, you gravitate to what you know and I knew the *Jebhe Melli* (National Front- NF) founded by Mohammad Mosaddeq.[1] I became a supporter. Years later I noticed entire families joined one or other political grouping, so much so that it sometimes looked like a family gathering at the top. In the Second year of medical school in London, I moved into a flat with Khosrow. Khosrow had recently arrived from the US with a degree in political science. Thin, with a shock of black hair and a beard that failed to cover a large scar from leishmaniasis (kala-azar), this son of a carpet merchant was active in the National Front. Very active. In fact, perpetually active - running around, ringing people, scheming, planning, arguing as if he thought he was not going to live long. He was crunching a lifetime into as few years as he could. He had a leaky aortic valve that was already limiting his ability to breath. Always an alarm bell. He was discovering Marx. It was 1962.

The flat became a den of political activity. Khosrow had registered in the London School of Economics and was one of the more active members of the NF.[2] Egypt's Jamal Abdul Nasser, who had inherited the mantle of nationalism from Mosaddeq, provided the NF with radio time beamed at Iran. I once tried to record a piece for broadcast but failed dismally as I kept

CHAPTER 7

jumbling the words.

Some of the early meetings leading up to the formation of the world-wide Confederation of Iranian Students[3] – Confederation or CIS for short - took place in our flat. The student movement abroad was galvanized into activity after anti-government student protests in autumn and winter 1960 ultimately resulted in the removal of Sharif Emami as prime minister, to be replaced by Ali Amini. I joined the Iranian Students Association in London, now under the control of anti-Shah students. Things were moving fast. First the European branch of CIS was born in Heidelberg uniting all the local branches. Next year's attempt to unite the Students on both sides of the Atlantic in Paris with those of Iran failed. Tehran University delegates were refused exit visas and delegates from Tudeh and 'Third Force', a breakaway group from Tudeh, walked out because of a dispute about delegate numbers from the US. A year of mutual recrimination followed, much of it taking place in our flat. Then, finally the CIS reunited in the 'Unity' Congress in Lausanne in 1963 and went on to play an important role in mobilizing public opinion against the Shah during those black years of repression, despite a number of ideological splits in the mid 1970's.

After the Revolution some members of the Confederation returned to Iran and tried to influence events. But ours was a homegrown revolution: both the Islamists and the main Left organisations grew from within the country. Many of the boys and girls arriving from Europe and N America never really understood its dynamics and their interferences, were just that – intervention without real roots or substance. I will turn to one or two examples later.

There were some fascinating characters going in and out of our flat. There was the flamboyant Jamshid Anvar, (whose French wife Francoise belonged to the French Communist Party) sporting a Fidel Castro beard and even emulating his way of public speaking, waving his arms about. Anvar later chaired the CIS and had a distinguished career in the United Nations as High Commissioner for Refugees (UNHCR). There was the dour Mohsen Rezvani, who later played an important role in the Maoist split from the Tudeh Party, a Lenin look-alike – complete with goatee beard without the smile.

The strangest of them all was Hassan, a delegate to the Heidelberg CIS conference, who dressed like an Oxford Don complete with leather, elbow patches and an accent to boot, who pretended to be a doctor without having ever set foot in a medical school. One day three of us, Hassan, Ali Dowlatdad, friend, and ex-flatmate, and I were sitting in a cafe drinking coffee when Hassan launched on a lengthy tale, in total seriousness, of how he had seduced two nurses simultaneously in the bar at St Bartholomew's Hospital Medical School, where he was a final year student, knowing full well that both myself and Ali were current medical students in the same University and knew personally every one of the handful of Iranian medical students studying at the time. A few years later Hassan married a girl from a prominent Iranian family, still pretending to be a doctor. Every morning he would take his stethoscope and go to 'work' and once a week would stay away overnight, being 'on call' in the hospital. He was convincing. He would write sick notes for work for my future wife. His father-in-law was so happy at her marriage to this promising physician that he bought a 2000 square-metre land in Tehran to build a hospital. Year later, she woke up to the lie having given birth to two children.

One particular student stands out, Parviz Nikkhāh, a Tudeh delegate to CIS. On *Eid Noruz*, the start of the Iranian calendar in March 21, 1963 we went *en mass* to the embassy's annual reception for Iranian students. Nikkhāh, shortish but handsome, with sharp penetrating green eyes, an engineering student in Manchester, stood erect on a chair and as if addressing a huge crowd slammed the monarchy in an impassioned speech in front of the ambassador Ardeshir Zahedi, the Shah's son-in-law, close friend and advisor.

Nikkhāh's story illuminates the relationship between the student movement abroad, the global historic background and the anti-Shah struggles taking shape within Iran. After the Sino-Soviet split, Nikkhāh broke from the main Tudeh party and joined the pro-Mao Revolutionary Organisation of the Tudeh Party. He returned to Iran and took a university teaching post, hoping to set up revolutionary cells among the peasants, following Mao's policy of encircling the cities from the countryside. They were still reconnoitering when he was arrested along with six others from his group

CHAPTER 7

and accused of being behind a plot to assassinate the Shah. On April 10, 1965, one Reza Shamsābādi, a conscript soldier handpicked as a guard in the Marmar Palace fired shots at the Shah. The Shah escaped but two of his bodyguards and Shamsābādi were killed outright. A major international campaign organised by CIS forced the Shah to commute their death sentences to ten years. Nikkhāh made a courageous defiant speech in court condemning the Shah and spent five years in jail. Somewhere along the line he converted to the Shah's 'White Revolution' and was released early. Why he changed his mind we will never know.

On his release Nikkhāh became an ideologue of the regime and was put in charge of the radio-television station. His conversion from Maoism to the monarchy may have as much to do with the way that his fellow prisoners treated him as it was to an ideological somersault. The prison is a small crucible where you develop along lines totally divorced from the world outside. He paid for this when he was shot by the Islamic victors of the Revolution almost as soon as they took power. Was this the continuation of the prison enmities? Many of those who now led the new government, and indeed like Lājevardi, were put in charge of the prisons, had been fellow prisoners. In that post Lājevardi was responsible for organising the systematic torture across the country that resulted in the creation of the *tavvāb* (the repentant), someone who has been stripped of all that made them what they were and transformed them into the eyes, ears and even the arm of the authorities. We will come back to the *tavvabs* later. Lājevardi was assassinated by the Mojahedin in his shop in the Tehran Bazaar. There were many more people who ought to have been higher on theexecution list than Nikkhāh. Like another victim of Lājevardi, Taqi Shahrām, who led the Marxist split in the Peoples Mojahedin,[3] Nikkhāh was more a casualty of a personal vendetta than a political execution. For me he will remain a man with immense courage and a touch of arrogance. It was the latter that, I believe, led to his demise. But there may be other explanations.

Meanwhile within Iran a guerrilla movement was taking shape with the Marxist Fadāi' and the Islamic Mojahedin being the main players. Abroad, the Confederation, now divided up into a number of separate organisations each with its own ideology, managed to work together in confronting the regime. The highpoint came with the huge demonstration in USA and Europe during the Shah's visit that culminated in the death of a German student at the hands of the Berlin police in June 1967. The mass protests, embassy occupations and other activities of Iranian students across Europe and North America was one of the inspirations for the international revolutionary upheavals of May 1968.

But after 1965 my tiny dalliance with the student movement ended. Medicine and J took over my life. But Khosrow had interested me in Marxism, and I read widely the secondary texts, avoiding the somewhat dense original texts. Just like my involvement with student politics, my dalliance with Marxism was also on the periphery.

[1] The National Front (*Jebhe Melli*) was founded in the late 1940's and included the Iran Party, the Toilers Party, the National Party, and the Tehran Association of Bazaar Trade and Craft Guilds. After the 1953 coup the NF became one of the two main anti-Shah opposition groups.

[2] Cosroe Chaqueri (to use the Frenchified way he preferred) author, historian, and political activist, became active in student politics in the 1960's. Later he created Mazdak publications to document the history of the Left which he uncovered, among others, from archives in Moscow and Baku and translated himself, having mastered Russian and Azari which he added to English, French and German. His many publications include: *The Soviet Socialist Republic of Iran, 1920-1921: birth of the trauma; Origins of social democracy in Iran; The Left in Iran 1905-1940, and 1941-1957.* Cosroe was a pioneer of modern, evidence-based historical narratives, referencing every statement. His history of the Jangal uprising in Gilān Province (1915-21) *Milād Zakhm, Jonbesh Jangal,* Akhtarān Press 2007 (in Farsi) is the most documented history of this important event in the aftermath of the Constitutional Revolution of 1906. He died in Paris in 2015.

[3] See appendix 2 for a summary of the opposition to the Shah and the Islamic regime.

8

Chapter 8

nineteensixtythree

Sexual intercourse began in 1963, Larkin sang somewhere. It was far too tough for me, I whispered elsewhere. That first and only effort in the Munich darkness had left a deep hole full of guilt and shame. Guilt that only religion can induce. Shame that only those in the shadow of maternal love can feel. A transparent light green shadow that glanced its soft embrace and enveloped me. Like her smile. But it stretched across Europe and across time. Guilt is a stone, an apparition, a spider's web, a continuous hum, a recurring nightmare, a constriction, an intermittent asphyxia, a revolving door. It permeates and oozes from every pore. Guilt knows no divorce, no separation no escape. A partner for life. Unlike morality, not amenable to reason, to logic, to experience, more like a growth. And above all it is so closely intertwined with love, that beautiful, gentle, soft maternal smile and unconditional love. How can one ignore unconditional love? And anyway, where would I have ended that virginal night were it not for the charm, good looks and utter confidence of uncle Fazl. The Fazl who had introduced me to Gogol, and the Fazl who had pulled and pushed me into the garden. Fazl had reached for the apple.

Yet I had lost the door and had no key. I did not know how to get back to the garden. Thirst and so much water. It was nineteen-sixty-three, and the grapes were hanging over a wall which I knew not how to climb. And I was not proud enough to cry sour.[1] I sat in my square Battersea bedsit, a beautiful machine-woven carpet full of colour on a white background spilling onto the walls, too big to fit, and pined. For love, for sex or preferably for both. The Beatles were singing 'can't buy me love', and I yearned and yearned without knowing the way through the labyrinth of sex even when it was offered. Oh, where was Fazl? London is so lonely for the shy and the incompetent. And then there was that light green shadow.

She was wearing the same green dress, cut low, at the meeting of students. The top of her breasts moved gently as she laughed. She sat with the Tudeh Left. I sat with the nationalists. She asked straight out, are you Mina's brother. I flushed scarlet, burning, burning. Her confident brown eyes burning into mine. Later that summer, at the Serpentine Lido, there she was again in a dark blue bikini, the same beautiful figure, soft to the look. The confident brown eyes, no coquetry here, just pure joy at being young. Then came her 21st birthday in October. Her cousin Fariborz had come over from Germany. As a child the family had assigned them to each other, as you would the family jewels. I danced with her and the firm push of her right hand on my chest left a mark like a footprint on fresh concrete. She was wearing a black dress with lace on the outside. It was low cut. She said she had bought a Mini and was driving without licence or insurance. Last week she had run out of petrol in the middle of Piccadilly Circus and had calmly called over a policeman to look after the car as she went to get petrol. Her unflappability was yet another facet of her total self-confidence. Was it possible for me to sit beside her as she prepared for her test?

Love proves one of the laws of dialectic. One minute you are not in love and a minute later you are. The fire simply flares up as if a match is thrown onto a pile of straw and in what feels like a blink the entire forest of the self is ablaze. I remembered the exact moment quantity turned into quality and sexual attraction turned into wild, passionate love. She was driving with me sitting on the passenger seat of her light blue mini. Turn right, turn left, I was instructing and put my right hand on her shoulder. It was an unconscious move – totally uncalculated. I love this girl, my fingers cried out. I do love

CHAPTER 8

this girl, my entire being answered back.

A day later I was walking round the block in Brompton Road, where she shared a room with a girlfriend, hoping to meet her, 'as if by chance' when she returned from dinner and clubbing with cousin Fariborz. Round and round the block I walked, expectant, rehearsing the words I would use to make it appear as a chance meeting. It was a cold rainy night in late October. I gave up when it became clear even to my desperate longing that she must have slipped in as I was circling the other side. It was 4 am and I had been circling my Kaaba[2] for six hours. She had gone to the Swiss Club and was in bed by one, oblivious of the gyrations outside her window. It was a cold and wet night in October. My heart burnt for a glimpse.

In the new year I asked her. She was unsure, not of herself but of me. She let it rest. Another black dress, half undone on the bed on the top floor of St Thomas' House. Ashkenazi was tying up two souls in a web of passion and love as he played the Rachmaninoff's second piano concerto. Those opening chords promising life and then sliding into the lilting tune remained with us forever as the symbol of the web of love. And of the moment of its interlocking into a unity. What had started as smiles and food and talking eyes and soft breasts had metamorphosed into something much deeper. She had become a person and you can only love a person not a smile. Her undoubted beauty had melted into her complexity and oneness. J and I had become one. That was love, and not the flash in the mini. The smile suddenly radiated the freshness of a mountain spring, fresh and life-giving every spring, until springs come to a close for us.

We announced our engagement on my birthday right in the middle of a game of *hokm*, the poor man's version of bridge, childishly, dramatically, as I trumped a card and took a hand. Farhād, my school friend, later took J aside and warned her how difficult living with me had been. She was warned. But if that policeman in Piccadilly did not intimidate the girl with no licence or insurance, an innocent child-man was unlikely to.

And even the shadow smiled a wide smile, slipped right out from the inside of me and melted into history.

Life began in Nineteen-sixty-four. (It was a green dress beyond the door).

[1] One day Mr Fox was walking along an alleyway when he saw a bunch of grapes appetisingly poking over a garden wall. He jumped and jumped but the grapes remained tantalisingly out of reach. Ah, they are sour grapes, he muttered to himself and walked off (*Aesop fable: Fox and the Grapes*).

[2] In the *hadj* pilgrimage to Mecca, Muslims walk round the Kaaba, reputedly built by Abraham, seven times.

Chapter 9

Intermission

We married in Tehran. Inside the new nest back in the UK, the first months were a strange mixture of intense passion and a battleground. Skirmishes, both partners skirting each other, establishing new lines and new barriers, engaging one moment in battle one moment entangled in intense lovemaking. New rules were being established. Habits that were integral to me were being questioned. Irrationality tumbled with rational thought. It was a hard time. It was a wonderful time. Then gradually the love matured into something deeper, still passionate but I began to see things that I had been blind to. She became more of a person and less an object to admire. And paradoxically she became more beautiful.

Later in life I understood why a painting becomes more beautiful, and strangely more mysterious, the more you look at it. Knowledge in mysterious ways enhances the mystery. People who pray say they have the same experience. The familiar becomes a new discovery each time. Her face was that painting and that mystery, and that prayer. I began to know those tiny changes of contour, not physically measurable, which expressed deeper emotions. I saw how not just the eyes but how the skin radiates different light reflecting different emotional states. How the colour of her high cheekbones changes with the light inside and the light shining on it from outside. The human face is like an encyclopaedia. It contains the face of the entire human race in one contour. An entire history, a passage through space-time of an entire species in one living landscape. I had to learn to read this history at the same time as being thrown into clinical medicine for which the medical school had not prepared me at all. I was growing up very fast. And stumbling here and there.

The next ten years were normal, or more accurately, conventional. Bristol was a last unreal interlude before the return home in 1975. We both had always wanted to go back. And we burnt our bridges. The house in Cotton was sold, but not before J gave a party where she gave gourmet food to over one hundred guests. That was to be a farewell for ever. That 'ever' lasted 8 years.

10

Chapter 10

On route to Iran

The trip was leisurely. We meandered through Europe in a slow plod. The specially bought left-hand drive Peugeot estate, whose light blue leather interior was indelibly imprinted in Nargess's memory, was packed with an obsessive attention to detail. Every space, every small volume, had its own occupant. No air was permitted in this car, except at mouth level. The roof rack was over-packed with the same precision, wrapped in transparent plastic specially fortified like a wired corset. The unloading process in one camp site after another was systematic and obsessively supervised. I drove. Massoud, J's younger brother, sat beside me and shared the wheel. J and the children sat in the back. It was July 1975. Maryam was seven and Nargess five. Throughout the five weeks of continental drift J hardly spoke.

She became increasingly apprehensive and sullen as arrival time drew near. She had escaped from a restrictive society against her father's wish when 18. It was her flight, in both meanings, to freedom. Now she was going back having burnt all the bridges behind. No house, no bank account, and the certainty that we could not leave Iran for five years. Promise to work in a university for five years and you can skip military conscription, the Shah had bargained with students abroad to attract them back. She feared she would

SLIDING INTO REVOLUTION

lose the freedom that for J was, and still is, the most treasured possession. I was elated. I could not wait. The kids were so used to travel not a squeak came from them. J ruminated in the back seat. Silent.

The Iranian border was utter chaos. Brand new 'tax-exempt' cars piled alongside kilometer upon kilometer of lorries queuing to get across. It took 5 hours of pushing, shoving, being squeezed, shouting, and angst, to extricate ourselves. In Tabriz the post-price-hoist oil boom hit us again. In this city of half a million there were no hotel rooms available, and we slept in a *karavānsarai*,[1] with sheets that may have been white in their day but now let out forensic odours from patches of greying dirt of dubious origin. On the doorstep of the Shah's 'Great Civilization'[2] where we were 'about to rival Japan in prosperity' we still had not got used to using soap. Whatever happened to the soap made in my grandfather *Āqā-joon's* hometown of Ashtiān, with its super-soapy smell and its uneven chunky shapes? We slept fully clothed, defecated in a toilet where it was an acrobatic feat to avoid the mounds of excreta and left at dawn for the final exhilarating trip to Tehran arriving at father-in-law's home in the early evening.

My encounter with the booming consumer-mad country took place when I went to pay the drastically reduced tax on the car. No one had warned me, but half of Iran seemed to be at the gates of the customs office in Tehran, which was situated in a gigantic parking lot, surrounded by high walls. I sweated under the summer sun all day, and the next, until someone taught me to do it the Iranian way. The gatekeeper to the car depot looked up giving me that look Iranians reserve for the *farangi* (European). Was he expecting someone with blond hair and blue eyes who had crudely pushed two 100 toman notes (about 30 dollars) into his hands? Another two days of pushing, shoving, cursing, bribing, and more pushing and I drove out with a taxed car and expertise in slipping in the cash.

Just before we had departed Bristol, my last abode in England, I had gone to the local 'intellectual' bookshop. I guess you will be writing your travelogue, John, the proprietor sneered in that peculiar English way. No, I replied curtly, sensing his distaste for the chattering, champagne-socialists, he thought us. 45 years down that road, I am fulfilling his prophesy, without the champagne.

CHAPTER 10

[1] *Karavānsara (or caravansarai)* – literally home for caravans - were inns that were originally built on routes as stopping places for caravans of trade or pilgrims. They are cheaper and more basic, than hotels.

11

Chapter 11

First days in Shiraz

Our arrival in Shiraz was greeted by two days and nights of earthquakes. The city of poets, the city of Hāfez and Sa'di,[1] of wine, of love, of gardens through which ran crystalline streams, the emerald jewel enclosed by a ring of golden-brown hills, was shaking. One of these hills, facing west has the profile that had an uncanny resemblance to Reza Shah. Maybe that was what enamoured the city to his son. To us new arrivals it was also a city of youth with its superb university. That night the city showed its youthful vigour through quivering walls and floor and woke us up in a jerk. We panicked, grabbed the kids and rushed into the alley. Since nothing happened for a couple of hours, we went back to bed only to be woken up again and another wait under the beautiful star-lit night – this time for an hour or so. Further aftershocks, we just ignored.

    The next few weeks were difficult for both girls. They enrolled to a school on the city's main street – tree lined Zand Avenue, the pride of Shiraz. Maryam went to the first class and Nargess enrolled in the kindergarten. Their Farsi was a bit staccato and came out with a distinct foreign accent, like an Armenian Maryam's classmates mocked. Morning roll call was standing in rows in the cemented courtyard singing the anthem to the monarch, which

CHAPTER 11

they had to learn pretty quickly. Maryam and Nargess never complained. But their young black eyes talked.

They hated that school with its didactic dry teaching by dry teachers, in large dry classrooms, an unfriendly alien world, which they could scarcely relate to. Maryam, a front tooth missing from that that first week withdrew into her imaginary world of witches. Five-year-old Nargess painted and painted. Only a few friends. Nargess's first, a neighbour's daughter, was run over a few months later and instantly killed on the main road outside our flat, another casualty to the rapid transition from donkey-cart to car. The children only settled in once we moved to Namazi compound and they changed school to Ardevan. Maryam went on her regular trips to witchland, through the walls of the bathtub, as she explained to her friend Kamran. One day, when Kamran bathed in our flat, the children found him frantically pressing the sides of the bath, looking for the secret trap door. Nargess's pictures became more colourful.

But J settled in no time, lost her initial foreboding, rapidly adapted to Iran and within a few weeks was well known in the Bazaar where she went regularly for antiques and carpets and soon became an expert on *Qashqāi'* tribal rugs. There she met a young film-maker who used her for a short film he was making. It took him some time to teach her how to hold a *chador,* that particular Iranian veil, covering head to foot.

In that first spring I climbed the hills behind our house, the golden brown apparently barren hills that surround the green jewel of the city. There we picked fifty-two different species of wildflowers, one with such an iridescent blue that only nature can produce. The barrenness was fertile with colour and variety. You just had to look, just like the rest of Iran. Shiraz was alive with life despite the apparent death of politics.

Shiraz was pleased with itself, basking in indolent slumber.

I was working in the Department of Medicine of Pahlavi (later renamed Shiraz) University as associate professor of medicine, when the Shah announced the new, imperial, calendar starting with the accession to the throne of Cyrus, the Archimedean king of biblical fame. It was to be the year 2535. And a year earlier in March 1975 he had given birth of the Rastākhiz (resurrection)

Party which all Iranians had to join. We were on the frontiers of the 'Great Civilization' which was all form, and little content. And not being particularly imaginative, he opted for a one-party state that was the vogue in Africa and Asia those days. The new calendar, though, was his very own idea – and it backfired. It lasted just over a year. Rastākhiz replaced the two indistinguishable Mardom and Melliyun (renamed Iran Novin) parties, both also created from above to alternate in office, not unlike Tweedledee and Tweedledum. All civil servants, employees, university staff, teachers, indeed anyone on a state payroll was ordered to join the new Rastākhiz party. This was a confirmation to the world that there is no longer any opposition in Iran. When asked by foreign correspondents what would happen to those who did not want to join, the Shah graciously replied they were free to leave the country. The country had truly become an island of security with hundreds of young people who had taken up an armed struggle in the Fadāi' and Mojahedin and other armed guerrilla organisations were either killed in combat, in prison, regrouping, or abroad (see appendix 2). Everyone I met advised me to sign up, as apparently all had done so.

Yet appearances were deceptive. Soon after my arrival I heard an explosion and next day we found a blown-up white Peikan car [2] in Baq Eram Boulevard outside the American Consulate. It was the work of Parvis Zarqāmi, son of Mohamad Khan Zarqāmi, head of the Khamseh Bāseri tribe. Parviz had been in Egypt with Bahman Qashqāi', himself a legend in the anti-Shah movement. Bahman, the son of a Qashqāi' chief Sohrab Khan whose uncle, Naser Khan, was the head of the Qashqāi' tribe, had studied medicine in the UK and later joined the pro-Mao breakaway group from Tudeh, Sāzman Enqelābi, the same organisation to which Parviz Nikkhāh, my youthful hero of the embassy speech, had belonged. On returning to Iran, Bahman was arrested by SAVAK, but later released and secretly slipped into Fars Province, rallied some of the Qashqāi' tribes, and tried to get a coalition of other tribes. A year later, abandoned by most of his followers, and with his mother and sister arrested, he gave himself up after Alam, Shah's closest adviser, promised him immunity. The assurance proved worthless. Bahman Qashqāi' was executed on November 8, 1965.

CHAPTER 11

That particular Qashqāi' rebellion came to a bloody end, but the Qashqāi' who had rebelled against central authority throughout the century, continued their resistance in different forms. In order to placate and tame them the Shah set up a special tribal school (*Madreseh Ashāyeri*) in Shiraz, opposite Sa'di hospital. It was the brainchild of Bahman Beigi and was to teach, and 'civilise' the *ashāyer* (tribes). It certainly taught them well, but as I witnessed later during the Revolution, the students joined forces with us across Zand Avenue, swinging their *falākhān* (special catapults) round their heads, raining stones at high velocity and with deadly accuracy on the heads of soldiers hundreds of metres across the avenue during the many sieges of Sa'di hospital. But I am running ahead. Later an explosion in the university student dormitory, in Sa'di street near Chāhār-Rāhe Zand (Zand cross road), killed three students, apparently as they were constructing a bomb. No mention was made on the news.

On a personal level I decided to just let the issue of Rastākhiz Party pass by, and no one seemed to have noticed. The bogy SAVAK either did not see or did not care. When a few months later the Shah visited the University, I just played sick and stayed away, and again no one saw, or cared, even though SAVAK had checked all our files the days before for security reasons. We had moved initially into an empty flat near the historic Qor'ān Gate that had been rented by my parents in anticipation of our arrival. We had no furniture as the lorry carrying our luggage had crashed and overturned in Turkey. It was a double good luck. Firstly, because the crash had occurred next to a police station, which miraculously meant that through the winter snows it was not looted even as the driver gave up waiting for rescue and went back to England. More significantly, the impression of a simple unostentatious life it gave to the medical residents and students who came to us as guests was in marked contrast to other professors. Even though they knew the reason for the barren flat, they took us to their heart as a '*mardomy*' (one of the people). This was to have important consequences when the Revolution started.

[1] Hāfez (1326-89) and Sa'di (1184-1283) are two of the most revered poets in Iran. Hāfez is held in almost mystical ecstatic reverence. Virtually every

urban home contains a copy of his *Divān* (collected works) that is consulted for most important decisions (*fāle Hafez*) – a divination.

[2] Hilman Hunter, built on license by Iran National.

12

Chapter 12

Silence of the cemetery

The Shah will never fall, uncle Fazl answered me as if that was a self-evident truth. We were sitting by the pool in the exclusive Imperial Club (Kloob Shāhanshāhi) in north Tehran. We are an island of stability, he added. I had said that a revolution was inevitable. I had blurted this out blindly. There was no intellectual thinking behind my statement, no real knowledge of any revolutionary movement, no political analysis. It was a gut feeling, purely a statement of disgust, a disgust at the Iran that glared at me when I got back after 20 years. In each visit I had seen the ostentation, the shallow pretensions, the vulgarity of a new middle and upper class with no roots. The new houses mushrooming everywhere with glossy outside – the facade dotted with blue slabs, blue blobs with no aesthetic logic, displaying windfalls of wealth. Yet their toilets reeked as in the houses of my childhood. Wealth had to be on view and damn the details. There were the trappings of modernity – Radiocity, many new cinemas mushrooming north of Shāhreza (today's Enqelāb) Avenue, 'the Green Line' separating affluent 'modern' north and traditional south Tehran, and the fashionable Safavieh shopping mall on Shemirān (now Vali Asr) Street en route to the Alborz foothills. The rising new middle class was jubilant. A middle class that was secular, looked to the West for its models and appeared supremely optimistic. You saw that in *Shahrefarang*, the flashy shops, the gaudy new architecture, showy cars. But it was shallow. The writer, Jalāl Āl-e Ahmad, had called it westoxification (*qarbzadegi*) – like a disease. As the new Tehran kitched, the traditional sectors seethed with resentment and some of the young, both traditional and modern, fumed.

I was on the opening day of the new Shāhanshāhi park in Shemirān Avenue, with virtually the entire population of north Tehran in attendance. Make-ups were crude and vulgar, the gaudiness was like grease that you had to claw through. The petro bourgeoisie – a class of freeloaders who, in the words of Ryszard Kapuscinski 'produce nothing and unbridled consumption makes up its whole occupation,' were on display in all their crudity. I went home with an intense feeling of nausea. My naïve assertion of the inevitability of a revolution was a manifestation of that nausea and an expression of blind hope. If I felt like vomiting on this state, sooner or later most Iranians would too. But my uncle Fazl was of course right. Iran was particularly quiet then. Yet the petro-bourgeoisie sat on suitcases already packed, exported money and bought homes in London, Nice and LA. They too were instinctively aware of their short life span. Unlike the French aristocracy, who were face down and did not see the end coming, they did.

We had just come back from an opening ceremony of aunt Tāhereh's kindergarten. There had been the expected, speeches, with mention of Shāhanshāh Ārayamehr (king of kings, light of the Aryans, the puffed-up title the Shah gave himself) cropping up here and there for no other obvious syntactic or logical reason than prudence and sycophancy. J and I had made sure that a plate and glass filled each hand allowing us to avoid the customary clapping at his name without risk. It was 1976, the height of repression. The year before J and I burnt our bridges and went to Shiraz. The Shah was riding high on the suddenly ballooning oil income after the OPEC price increase in 1973. Any dissenting voice had been savagely crushed by the SAVAK. As Thomas Freedman noted, the first law of petropolitics is that the price of oil and pace of freedom always move in opposite directions. The following year, Khosrow Golesorkhi, poet and filmmaker, had defiantly defended his

Marxism in open court and been executed along with Kerāmat Dāneshian. The Shah, who under international pressure had allowed foreign observers into his trial, would never again make the same mistake.

I had instinctively felt a revolution was brewing in the depths of society. It was both a secret wish and a gut feeling. For a century people in my country had been denied their two basic demands: the quest for freedom and for independence from foreign interference. The Constitutional Revolution of 1906 with the same two demands had ended in the dictatorship of Reza Shah. The brief interlude of relative freedom during the premiership of Mohammad Mosaddeq and the nationalization of the oil industry was beheaded in the British-US engineered coup of 1953, and now we had the graveyard upon which the Shah built his 'island of stability'.

The Tudeh party had disgraced itself in the eyes of the people of Iran after its disastrous policy of initially opposing the nationalisation of oil and the government of Mosaddeq and even more ruinous dithering during the three days of the CIA-engineered coup that toppled him. The defection of ayatollah Kāshāni and other senior clerics from the nationalist camp a year before had already weakened public support for Mosaddeq. Damaged by this defection and that of many others in the National Front coalition, and faced with the inactivity of Tudeh, Mosaddeq was left virtually defenceless. On that hot August day of 1953, with thugs marching and tanks rolling, he declined to leave his home until the last minute telling Kianuri, an important member of the Central Committee of the Tudeh Party, on the phone 'Sir, everyone has betrayed me'.

Mosaddeq was arrested. His foreign minister Fātemi, who on the day the Shah had fled Iran had made a fiery speech to cheering crowds in that central square with a chameleon-like revolving name, went into hiding. He had written a number of scathing attacks on the Shah in his paper, *Bakhtar Emruz*. Fātemi went into hiding on the day the coup. He had been arrested a few days earlier with the first coup attempt and released when that failed. A couple of years earlier he had been shot in the stomach in a failed assassination attempt while giving a speech on the funeral of an assassinated journalist that necessitated numerous operations. He was in hiding for nearly six months when he was arrested. The Shah took his revenge. On the way to the army prison, he was attacked by thugs in a prearranged encounter and had at least eight knife wounds. His older sister was also knifed trying to protect him. He was later dragged from his hospital bed to the military court still suffering from his wounds and with a raging fever. Despite this he stood his ground throughout the court hearing and defended Mosaddeq and his policies. He was sentenced to death by the military court and was executed while having a raging fever. He refused a blindfold.

As an 11-year old, I had followed the last months of Dr Mosaddeq's premiership in the daily papers that Ezzy bought. I had read of the abduction, torture and murder of Mosaddeq'a Minister of the Interior, General Afshārtous described in gory detail in the papers. I had been shocked by the pictures of the bleeding Fātemi immediately after the stabbing that appeared in the afternoon papers. The image was there to show the people what to expect if they crossed the monarch. The coup regime then proceeded to effectively destroy Tudeh. They shattered forever the entire trade union movement Tudeh had taken years to build up, and its military organisation which had infiltrated the heart of the army. Of the 466 Tudeh members in the military 429 were arrested, some shot, and a large number spent many years behind bars. Across the country anything between seven and twenty-one thousand Tudeh supporters were arrested without a whiff of opposition and its network within the country was torn apart. The rump remaining in Iran was heavily infiltrated by SAVAK and over the next decades used to entrap new opposition groups, such as the emerging Fadāi'.

Tudeh was only to fully recover from this blow after the Revolution, but its demise left a bitter aftertaste. The left had been shown to be a stooge of Moscow and for a nation with nationalism deep in its veins this was unforgivable. The Tudeh party, which in the period after the war had become the largest and most influential political party in Iran, which had been instrumental in introducing modernism into Iran, whose cultural influence extended in every artistic field and to virtually the entire intellectual life of the country, was in tatters.

CHAPTER 12

Exiled to Eastern Europe, the Tudeh Party went on to half-heartedly semi-approve the Shah's 'White Revolution' in 1963, the cornerstone of which was a land reform modelled on the US-sponsored Alliance for Progress in Latin America. The 'White Revolution' broke the back of feudal landlords and jump-started Iran into a predominantly capitalist economy with very close ties to the USA and deeper dependency on the sea of black gold. The 'White Revolution' also targeted the power structure of the Shi'a clergy by depriving them of their substantial income from endowments (*vaqf*). It was their turn to be crushed. An urban revolt against the Shah's reforms in June 1963 organized by the clergy and their natural allies in the Bazaar was savagely put down and their leader Khomeini exiled to Najaf in Baathist Iraq. The uprising was to be a dress rehearsal of the tactics used by the clergy in the lead-up to the 1979 Revolution.

The island of stability, a social desert, was being built on crushed bones. The Tudeh leadership abroad gave up any hope for change, and encouraged by the 'brother' communist party of the Soviet Union, proceeded to woo the Shah into democratising his regime and becoming a 'constitutional monarch' – a policy of despair. A silence descended on the country. On the surface it was all smiles. Glory and smiles. Sycophantic grovelling and blood. Grease-paint and foreign imports. Tin-shack shantytowns, *halabi ābad* and *hasir abad* straw-shack townships, and marbled mansions. The silence of the grave. But the graveyard was stirring, and it was the new homegrown left that led this reawakening. To understand the rebirth of the left and the road that led to Revolution we need to make a historic digression.

Chapter 13

The new communist movement

It was midwinter of 1971. I was immersed in my very busy job as medical registrar in the Department of Medicine at Bristol. Five thousand kilometres to the east deep in the snowy jungles of Gilān province bordering the Caspian Sea, a group of young men calling themselves the *Jangal group* launched an attack on the Siāhkal police outpost. Even though virtually all the people involved were either killed or captured, it was the opening salvo of eight years of armed struggle in what came to be known as the New Communist Movement (*jonbesh-e novin comunisti*). They delivered the first cracks in the outwardly impregnable armour of the monarchical regime.

The *Jangal*, which later morphed into the Fadāi', was originally formed by the amalgamation of two smaller groups, the Jazani-Zarifi and Ahmadzādeh-Puyān groups. Bijan Jazani and Hasan Ziā'-Zarifi had both been in the Tudeh Youth Organization earlier and were looking at securing arms through old contacts in the Tudeh. What they didn't know is that a key member of the Tudeh's Tehran Organisation, Abbās Shahryāri, had been recruited by SAVAK. They were arrested, along with some other comrades when meeting their contact in Tudeh. Jazani and Ziā'-Zarifi were savagely tortured and given long prison sentences. The remainder of the group went ahead anyway and attacked the Siāhkal police outpost.

With Siāhkal the Fadāi'[1] had broken into new ground. Theirs was a response by a new generation to the supine state of the left after the CIA-engineered coup against Mossadeq in 1953. The post-coup regime had all but destroyed the nation-wide Tudeh organisation, including their large clandestine network in the armed forces. The porous rump was widely infiltrated by SAVAK. Dedication, discipline and self-sacrifice were to be a reply to the flabbiness of the Tudeh leadership, who had fled abroad, although many in the Tudeh rank and file had demonstrated a heroic dedication and stance, and many were executed or received long sentences. Now disaffected youth coalesced into small groups to discuss, read and debate, searching for a way out of the impasse. Mostly students, with a sprinkling of working class and professionals, they were influenced by what was happening in China, Vietnam, Algeria, and in particular by the Cuban Revolution and the Latin American urban guerrilla movements. Some, like Jazani and Ziā-Zarifi had left Tudeh in frustration. The armed struggle was their vision of breaking the wall of silence and showing up the regime as vulnerable. Cuba had given a model of how a handful of selflessly dedicated revolutionaries could trigger a more widespread rebellion. Their courage, and blood, they argued, would be the motor for social upheaval. With the Fadāi' a new Left had arisen from the ashes of the old.

Siāhkal paved the way for another large group, the Peoples' Mojahedin Organisation of Iran (PMOI)[2] to take up the armed struggle. Set up in 1965, the Mojahedin, with Islamic roots but also influenced by Mao and the Palestinian and Algerian Revolutions abroad and the Islamic thinker and preacher Ali Shari'ati at home, was gaining adherents among religious youth but was unsure of how to proceed. Siāhkal offered them a model. Many other groups followed the path of the armed guerrilla struggle, all made up of highly dedicated men and women ready to die for their beliefs. To paraphrase Edmund Wilson on the Narodniks of Tsarist Russia, the Shah's obduracy and cruelty made the courageous fierce, and the general fear and futility caused them make themselves felt as individuals or in small devoted groups at the risk of their own annihilation.[3] And annihilated they were. In the first year I was in Shiraz starting from December 1975, through to December of the following year, and including in the death of the entire leadership of the Fadāi' in June, there were almost weekly reports of raids, clashes and deaths between security forces and the urban guerrillas. This in addition to the hundreds tortured, incarcerated and executed. Yet, every time the regime thought it had destroyed the Fadāi' it would re-emerge, phoenix-like. New recruits would appear, gel into cells, and link up with the remnants of the old guard.

When the attack on Siāhkal took place I was only obliquely aware of what went on in my country. The job left little time for life let alone much else. The attack on Siāhkal had exploded into the student community, galvanising the Confederation, but J and I were no longer students and had no part in the student opposition to the Shah. Our response was pure emotion, full of admiration for the courage and sacrifice, though deep down I was unsure that the armed struggle would get anywhere. I had read Richard Gott's sympathetic account of the guerrilla movements in Latin America and Regis Debre's highly influential *Revolution in Revolution* which generalised the experience of the Cuban revolution into a new theory of revolutions. But Che Guevara's death in the Bolivian jungles in 1967 had already dented Debré's theory. I read Franz Fanon, and found the glorification of violence difficult to swallow. I was a doctor. When the Tupamaros of Uruguay, perhaps the most successful urban guerrilla movement in Latin America, was all but annihilated the following year, my doubts were strengthened. We argued with close friends, two doctors from Shiraz, Rahmān and Āzādeh on a scholarship from Pahlavi University as postgraduates. Both were to play a large part in our life later. Rahman with his well-groomed silver hair and erect, almost stiff, posture and Āzādeh, a pathologist and former wrestling champion with his brown bushy dervish moustache covering his lower lips had been childhood friends and both were sympathetic to the Fadāi. I too was entranced, from afar, but with increasing clouds of doubt. Our heated debates were precisely that, intellectual rumination. We felt the warmth of the fire without touching or even seeing the flames.

CHAPTER 13

A few months after my return to Iran, the Venezuelan Carlos[4] took OPEC leaders hostage in Algiers on 21 December 1975, Bijan Jazani, Hassan Ziā'-Zarifi and seven others were taken out of their cells and shot in the hills overlooking Evin Prison "trying to escape", to prevent them being exchanged. They had been in prison for over 4-years serving long sentences. In prison Jazani, perhaps the most profound thinker in the new Left had written what at the time was the best analysis of the effects of the Shah's 'White Revolution' on restructuring Iranian society. In an interview with the BBC in that last bloody month of 1976, the Shah proudly admitted to there being 3,300 political prisoners, all Marxist – which like almost everything he said was not entirely true as there were some Islamists as well. He then went on to execute another eight on Christmas Eve. These were the human sacrifices to the 'island of stability'. But despite the blows, and prospect of truly mediaeval tortures, including SAVAK's version of the rack - the dreaded Apollo - which sometimes went on for weeks and even months, the guerrillas regrouped and continued their fight against the regime until its demise, dealing the final death blow to the Shah's military at the climax of the Revolution. The Left kept the struggle against the Shah alive in those dark days, a fact even the ultimate victors of the Revolution were to admit.[5] On my first days in Shiraz I had witnessed some of their work.

Outside Iran, the Confederation of students were winning vital international public opinion for the opposition inside. Earlier the Confederation had a martyr when the West German police shot dead a German demonstrator against the royal visit to West Germany in 1967. Faced with the Shah's US trip ten years later, the fragmented Confederation had put aside all differences. A group of the most militant, among them Said and Afsaneh who later became close friends, gathered in the *Mianeh* (middle) section of the Confederation ('middle' to designate their support for both the armed guerrilla struggle in Iran and China in the Sino-Soviet split) had done their research well. They built placards made of the same material used by the police, layers of acrylic, with detachable wooden handles and distributed them to a handful. In a re-incarnation of the Spartan Phalanx, they attacked the centre and split the mounted police lines in two. The subsequent cloud of tear gas swept over the White House lawn, rolling, enveloping US president Carter and his royal guests, weeping gaseous tears as they greeted their weeping supporters. This image captured the zeitgeist. The Shah, his wife Farah jewelled in a long white dress, guests of Jimmy Carter, standing on the steps of the White House, shedding chemical tears, televised, full frontal, visible to the entire world. Back in Houston they returned the two yellow school buses they had hired, and being students with little money they had fiddled the mileage reader and pretended to have gone out on a local picnic. "Picnic my ass!" exclaimed Mr Goodman, the owner, in a Texan growl and grinned. "I saw you on television". You could fool the mounted Washington police, but not a Texan. They paid up.

Misguided and ultimately futile though their tactics of urban guerrilla warfare was, a conclusion that Jazani had already reached in prison before being murdered, the Fadāi' had shown that it is possible to fight at a time when all protest appeared stifled at the throat. More importantly, they were the first radical reawakenings of the left in Iran, which had been totally discredited in the eyes of the post 1953-coup generation. The Tudeh Party's reformist policies, its bungling of the nationalisation of oil, its inaction in the face of the CIA-engineered coup against Mosaddeq, its permanent genuflexion to Moscow, and its internal corruption revealed in a series of memoirs of ex-Central Committee members, had turned Communism into an indefensible ideology. The cynical support for the Shah's White Revolution as being 'on the whole progressive', at the instigation of Moscow which was trying to woo the Shah away from its US allies, confirmed the general distrust of the Left, seen as a stooge in the service of Soviet foreign policy goals. The joke was when it rained in Moscow, Tudeh members opened their umbrellas in Tehran. It clashed with the deep and historic nationalism of Iranians. It required a home-grown left, clearly independent of foreign governments, to resurrect it. That was the most important legacy of the Fadāi' movement, which resonates to this day and it was something I had failed to understand in that far corner of England.

CHAPTER 13

The Shah's White Revolution had a number of consequences that its instigators had not bargained for. The land reform released millions of surplus labour that migrated into the cities. Iran's urban population rose from 38% to 48% within 10 years and went on growing. For some of those arriving in the cities to work, the experience must have had the same transforming effect as it had for peasants arriving to work in the new industries in Tsarist Russia.[6] Yet the new industries, such as those assembling parts manufactured in advanced industrial countries (such as the Hillman car manufactured as Peykan by Iran National) did not offer enough work to absorb the migrant labour that camped in belts of shanty towns, euphemistically called 'tin', or 'straw' townships (*halabi ābad and hasir abad*). Millions were living precariously on the margins in either seasonal, semi-permanent work or in the informal sector. These people, as we will see were to become the battering rams of the Iranian Revolution. The oil wealth separated state from society to an extent where it is difficult to find any parallels in human history.

Meanwhile in 1975 all youth was suspect. In large urban areas, SAVAK, in addition to following up leads, would randomly arrest young men and women who looked suspicious in the street, torture them, compile lists of all their acquaintances, seek common threads. The system was savage, but seemingly effective, random terror that occasionally hit a target – like birdshot. It was a technique that had been developed by the CIA in crushing the urban guerrilla movement in Latin America. Brutal, inefficient, bloody. The technique remains in use today in the random stop-and-search by the police in London and other urban centres –without the torture. It is difficult not to concede that for a brief moment in time – perhaps two to three years – it appeared at ground level that the Shah had pulled it off. Iran was on the surface an island of security in an area of turmoil. The Shah felt secure enough to send 22,000 troops to put down a Maoist-nationalist uprising in Dhofar province of Qatar, which was in turn supported by some of the Iranian guerrilla groups. A proxy war. The conscript army proved remarkably useless, not venturing from the main road or population centres. The Shah did not draw the obvious conclusion, though those with eyes to see did.

The monarch felt comfortable enough to celebrate the 2500 anniversary of the monarchy. He arbitrarily chose the reign of the Archimedean king Cyrus of Old Testament fame, who had freed the Jews from Babylon, as the point of departure - totally ignoring the Medes for reasons that I guess had no other logic but the magic number of 2,500 which became the start of the new calendar starting on March 1976 at the beginning of the Iranian year of 1355. The calendar lasted just over a year and was ignored everywhere but in official documents. The fragile edifice began to crack and finally collapsed through its own internal fissures.

[1] Their full name was Organisation of Iranian Peoples Fadāi' Guerrillas - *Sāzmāne Cherikhāye Fadāi' Khalq Iran.*

[2] See Appendix 2 for a brief summary of the main political groups in opposition

[3] Edmund Wilson, *To the Finland Station* New York, 1940.

[4] Illich Ramirez Sanches, alias *Carlos, The Jackal*, was at the time attached to the Popular Front for the Liberation of Palestine (PFLP) who carried out the attack on the OPEC oil ministers in Algiers.

[5] See *The Student Movement in Iran (jonbesh daneshjui' Iran)* vol 1, by Emadeddin Bāqi, Tehran, 2002 ISBN 964-5925-03-7 (in Farsi).

[6] See for example: A *radical worker in Russia. The autobiography of Semën Ivanovich Kanatchikov,* edited and translated by Reginald Zelnik. Stanford University Press 1986.

14

Chapter 14

Private party for the world elite

The earliest rumbling of discontent arose out of the celebrations for the 2,500 years of monarchy. These took place in the fields around *Takhte Jamshid* within sight of the ruins of the palace of Persepolis, unusually for its time constructed entirely by paid labour and burnt down by Alexander of Macedonia in a drunken stupor. The celebrations were very much a family affair with the Shah inviting heads of states to the lavish tents, fed by food flown directly from Maxim's in Paris and the army, dressed up in ancient fancy dress, performing a march-by. It was all like a schoolboy's fantasy of a birthday party. The people of Iran, who were presumably blessed with two and a half millennia of monarchy, had absolutely no part to play. They were not even invited as bystanders to cheer the king. They were simply forgotten. But they did not forget their money being poured down the throat of foreign dignitaries as the post-1973 oil boom began to fade.

The Shah had a soft spot for Shiraz, perhaps because he saw himself in the lineage of Cyrus and Darius whose tombs were nearby. Certainly, his increasing megalomania began to look grotesque. Interviews with Oriana Fallachi, and later Lord Chalfont, bring this out. Farah, his wife, saw herself as a guardian of culture – after all she had studied in the Paris Ecole des

Beaux Arts. She particularly championed the Shiraz festival of arts that was held annually in the autumn. She lavished large sums of money and hence attracted a motley crew of international talent. Stockhausen came once and performed the electronic piece *Sternklang* in the *Vakil Bazaar*. I can only imagine the reaction of the *bazaaris* as I purposefully stayed away. In 1971, Peter Brook had premiered his play Orghast in the hills above Persepolis, beneath Darius's grave dug into the cliff face, in part spoken in a totally made-up language. I had until then great respect for Brook and could not understand what made him come to the political and cultural desert that was Iran. And help legitimise the Shah's rule.

In my second year, through friends in the arts I was invited by Shiraz radio to act as their reporter in the Shiraz Festival. I had earlier turned down the request to take control of the hour-long late night classical music program. I did not want to be identified with any part of this regime, but this assignment might allow me to make some satirical comments on what I felt was an extravagant and pretentious attempt at 'culture' to ape the West and to pretend that Iran was the Japan of the Middle East, a boast the Shah had made. That year Maurice Béjart's ballet company from New York alongside other pieces, premiered the ballet "Heliogabalus", based on a poem by Artaud, with the Archimedean king Darius's tomb as backdrop. I can still see the lead dancer spinning and rotating her arms like a gracious propeller, or wings of a dragonfly about to fly off into the starry, moonless night. I melted at the beauty of her dance and remained mesmerised while I interviewed her. I can't recall her name.

Next day, Morton Feldman gave a concert in the same venue, and refused to answer my question as to what he thought of the audience in Iran, so totally without any background in European music, would make of his relentlessly quiet, composition, *pianissimo* all through. I rubbished him in my report. Hatred of the monarch and traces of socialist realism, a legacy of Tudeh on the left as a whole, fogged my judgment. Of this, and other sad legacies of Tudeh, I will have more to say later.

The next, and last, Shiraz festival in 1977 was even more disconnected from the popular mood. The revolutionary tide was already on the move. A

Hungarian-American troop performed a play with a scene apparently feigning sexual intercourse. Rather stupidly, instead of choosing a venue with only the elite as witness, they performed in a shop front, in Ferdowsi Street in central Shiraz. Word of mouth got out that they are having sex in public. There was an outcry in the mosques. It should be recalled that Shiraz houses Shah Cherāgh, the third most holy Shi'a shrine in Iran. Hence its clergy were particularly powerful headed by the three ayatollahs, Mahallāti, Dastqeib and Rabbāni-Shirazi. Mahallāti was the most senior but quite worldly, corpulent and close to the regime. Dastgheib was his rival, imprisoned by the Shah, and had a fiery son, Seyyed Ali Mohammad, today a senior cleric. Rabbāni was the most political and had also been imprisoned by the Shah, giving him some street credibility among the devout youth. He projected himself as a confidant of Khomeini. The sex-in-the-window episode was certainly a welcome weapon. Who knows what Rabbāni would think of his grandson's fatal crash in his yellow Porsche speeding at 120 miles-an-hour, a beautiful south Tehrani girl at the wheel, thirty eight years later?

I saw Tadeusz Kantor's *Dead Class* in the town theatre. The play was a satire, which admittedly did not really come across in Polish, directed against the communist regime in Poland. In one scene they were part naked with prosthetic, and rather droopy, genitals, no more offensive than much that was produced in the West. But we were not in the West. The play received an ovation, though I doubt if most of us understood much. To a put on a play, even hinting at sexual intercourse, out on the street showed graphically how the ruling elite had lost touch with the majority of the population. Most the students I talked to found the entire festival offensive.

Pahlavi University was unique. It was the only English language university in Iran. All students, including medical students, did three years in the Faculty of Literature where they essentially learnt English. The medical school was probably the best in the country. It was able to appoint not only faculty who had trained in the USA or Europe, but also used visiting professors extensively, mainly from English-speaking countries. The department of medicine, which I had joined, was particularly well staffed with some outstanding teachers like Khosrow Nasr, Farāmarz Ismail Beigi and Asqar Rastegār[1] to name just a few among many. A recently developed residency program attracted the best graduates from across the country. The University, and particularly the Medical School, was favoured by the Shah and his US allies. It was rumoured that in the 60's the Americans had formulated a contingency plan in the event of a Soviet invasion of Iran to move the capital to Shiraz, using the Zagros mountains as a natural defensive barrier, and to create a wasteland north of this barrier with nuclear weapons. Hence, they developed the University and the associated Namāzi hospital (paid for by one of Fars province's most wealthy family) as the field hospital for the potential war.

Whatever the credibility of this theory, the Shah had favoured the University which bore his name by appointing one of his favourite henchmen Hooshang Nahāvandi, subsequently minister of court, as chancellor. Initially Pahlavi only took in the children of the elite. Mixed sex parties were encouraged and girls wearing mini skirts walked the campus. Uniquely, the dormitories were mixed. But after the 1973 OPEC heist the doors were opened to a new class of students from more traditional middle-class families. So, when I arrived there was an interesting contrast of ultra-modern, fashion conscious boys and girls and those with more conservative attire and tastes. Within a short time, the mini skirts had become knee length or trousers but there were still only very few girls who wore headscarves.

[1] All three had trained in the US. Nasr was a great organiser with an amazingly creative brain. A man with vision, he essentially built up the Pahlavi Medical School into a world-class institution. Ismail-Beigi, my old schoolmate is a real scientist with an original brain, and today is in receipt of multi-million dollar grants in the US for research on diabetes. Rastegār is a great teacher and organiser with wide interests and a unique ability to relate to people and gain their loyalty. The last two created the residency program. Rastegār went on to take charge of the residency program and then become Chief of Medicine at Yale Medical School. Later he created the Yale global health department. There were many more eminent faculty members. Khosrow Nasr, sadly died in the US in January 2020.

15

Chapter 15

Baq Namāzi

After a year in the apartment near the Qor'an Gate we were offered an apartment in Bāq Namāzi, a gated compound which housed the Namāzi Hospital a number of single or double storey villas, a new block of flats with six apartments, and the nurses' home, all in a *bāq* (orchard) full of tall, sycamore (plane) trees, pomegranate trees, persimmon trees, grass, flowerbeds, a swimming pool and a tennis court – California-in-Fars. It was late summer, and the branches of persimmon trees were groaning under their huge orange-red load of fruit, which miraculously never snapped. Pomegranates glowed intense red against the bright green leaves, but too sour to pluck. Right at the end of the *bāq* lived Naneh Ali with her one cow and her coveted mulberry tree, our version of the old woman who lived in a shoe. Where she came from and what she did, I never asked - perhaps a mirror to why three years later our side of the Revolution lost. Our furniture arrived after eighteen months.

When I went to release it from the customs, the SAVAK man was only interested in the boxes with books. He made me unpack the first two and spread them on the tarmac like unchaffed wheat ready to be trampled with the ox-drawn *gāvāhan* grinder of my childhood days. He picked one up, a book on modern French history. "What is this?" He asked unsmiling, clearly not good on English. "Modern French history" I replied shyly. "Are they all like this?" he gestured at the large number of boxes of books piled high. I nodded or said something. He was clearly not going to open them all and with a disdainful wave dismissed me. Years later I was to have a totally different reaction to my library.

Most of the children in Bāq Namāzi went to the English-speaking International School. We had always decided on an ordinary school, and the girls moved to Ardavān School not far from the *bāq*. So, Maryam and Nargess developed two sets of friends – those in the *bāq*, and those at school. Just like Āmeneh and Zahra, daughters of Dr Mohsen Mahluji who was to play an important role in my life. Āmeneh was the younger and was crystalline in her views, not unlike her father. Zahra was more reserved, perhaps more thoughtful. In Ardavan, Nargess befriended Āzita and dropped her after she stole her Pez collection of sweet dispensers with Disney cartoon heads. The friendship with Āmeneh-Zahra, imagined and expressed always in that order, was to last with the usual ups and downs of all friendships, till today. Inside the *bāq* the children inhabited a totally idyllic world, unencumbered by parents, the only dark shadows were the, sometimes savage, battles for the conquest of the 'red hill' between the boys' gang and the girls' gang.

We soon moved into villa seven with its beautiful veranda. The girls started art classes with Karimi, a young man with light brown hair and a scraggy beard, looking so European. He would let them do whatever they wanted with paint, to express, to be free of the constraints of margins and lines that define and confine. Until one day, when he failed to show up and they expressed the freedom he had taught them by graffiting the entire studio wall. He banned them for several weeks. Karimi's freedom stopped at painting the walls of the studio he was renting. All freedom has a boundary.

They also did theatre workshops and were encouraged to write their own scripts and even did a show on local television. Ballet was more formal, and the piano teacher was wooden. Both owed more to our ideal image for a broad education, than reality. But the teachers became household friends and villa seven slowly morphed into a home to many of the Shirazi artistic and musical community.

16

Chapter 16

Congress of traditional medicine

In March 1977, a two-day Congress of Traditional Medicine was opened in the medical school. Spring blossoms were sending out signals and the reborn light evoked vague yearnings in me, as it did every Spring. The brains behind the congress was Mohsen Mahluji, a neurology professor trained in Leeds who had long abandoned teaching neurology, or indeed medicine. Medicine, as it was taught in Pahlavi and elsewhere, had failed to link ill health and poverty, he said. Look up 'poverty' in the index of any medical textbook, he would say, and you won't find anything. Mohsen came from a prominent family in Kashan, and his wife Jaleh was a daughter of the khan from the Arab-Sheibāni tribe, belonging to the Khamseh (five) tribes of Fars province.

Mohsen's religion had deepened sharply after a pilgrimage to Mecca shortly before my arrival. He grew a beard, dropped alcohol and became interested in traditional medicine. Mohsen combined the radical anti-clerical Islam of Ali Shari'ati with the pedagogic views of Ivan Illich and Paolo Frere.[1] Most of all he articulated a radical anti-Marxist populism that was a reaction to the autocracy of the Shah and the sycophantic, bureaucratic mendacity represented by Tudeh. His virulent hatred of the Tudeh Party may have also had a more personal twist, in the attachment of some family members to the party, which he expanded into a bitter hatred of Marxism. He was surrounded by a number of young students, also devotees of Shari'ati. It is difficult to understand the radical non-communist movement in Iran without understanding the role of Shari'ati, who the Shah had allowed to preach and publish, as a counter to the mounting attraction of Marxism to the young. A whole generation of youth came under Shari'ati's influence that intellectually nurtured both Khomeini's powerbase and that of the radical Muslim movements exemplified by the Mojahedin and the Ārman-e Mostaz'afin. The latter were a small, but influential, Islamic group who even more than the Mojahedin tried to marry Islam and Marxism. For example, they believed that the Qurā'n embraces the dictatorship of the proletariat.

On the slow march to the Revolution two different world-views had come to dominate society. Marxism had nurtured the bulk of the Iranian intelligentsia, writers, poets, filmmakers, playwrights, and had its militant manifestation in the armed struggle of the Fadāi' and other left groups. Marxism even affected the thinking of the Islamic Mojahedin. Between them they had lost a large number of men and women in armed clashes or executions or languishing in prisons in the months leading up to the Shiraz Arts Festival the previous autumn. The other, was exemplified by Shari'ati's return to a purified Shi'a Islam, and also by Jalāl Āl-e Ahmad who in his book *Qarbzadegi* (Westoxification) yearned for a return to a mystical Islamic-Iranian past and denounced the 'betrayal' of Iranian intellectuals to Western and Eastern (meaning Marxist) cultural values. The different world views were to coalesce into a temporary and prickly marriage of convenience in the face of the common enemy a year or so later. It was a bit like the marriage of a porcupine and a fox. The spikes came out into the open at the Congress. The incompatibility of the two world-views was to lead to much bloodshed once the Shah had been overthrown. There was also a subsidiary battle surrounding this Congress which had to do with its sponsors and their ulterior motives.

One young man, thin, rather tall, wearing a pistachio-green jacket somewhat clashing with the general attire in the hall, stood up. Ā'in, a third-year medical student, later to become the head of the Revolutionary Guard Corps

CHAPTER 16

in Jiroft, a town in South-Eastern province of Kerman, and who was to die under mysterious circumstances. While sympathetic to the idea of promoting traditional medicine, Ā'in attacked Mohsen in his Kermani accent for dallying with some of the intellectual cliques surrounding Queen Farah, who had sponsored the Congress. These were a number of formerly left intellectuals who had congregated around the Queen's court hoping to modernise Iran from above, just as Dāvar, Teimur Tāsh and others had done during the reign of the previous Shah. Then Behruz (not his real name), a final year student, rose and savagely mauled Mohsen for pulling the wool over the eyes of the students with unscientific unproven nonsense and using every opportunity, including the present Congress, to attack Marxists. A skillful orator and polemicist, with a wealth of anecdotes and immense charm, Mohsen with his short grey beard and dark shadows under his eyes was a bogey for the left-leaning students. Mohsen never forgave 'this shit' Behruz till he died. But he did take note of Ai'n. He visibly moved away from the orbit of people like Rahnema and others in the Queen's entourage and moved closer to the radical Muslim students over the next three years.

Over the next year the authority of those above us was eroding. I rarely made rounds in Namāzi, and preferred the more earthy Sa'di hospital. On the one occasion when I was consulting in Namāzi I noticed a 4th year student standing a few steps behind the throng of students, interns and residents around the bedside of the patient. With his close-cut black beard, big black eyes with a mischievous twinkle, hands behind his back holding a *tasbih* with modest-sized beads, a sign of devotion, he reminded me of the imaginary portraits of Shi'a imams adorning the walls of coffee houses, bazaar's open-fronted *hojrehs* (open-fronted shop) and the popular *chelo kabāb* (white rice with kabab roasted on charcoal) restaurants. Taqi Soltāni made a few remarks relating to the social content of disease that I found refreshing and surprisingly outspoken. Later in the graduation ceremony for the medical school, held in the beautiful Bāgh Eram gardens in front of a huge mound of fruit and a veritable banquet of food, Taqi, made a speech severely critical of the University for its absurd extravagance and compared it to the wastages of the government. It was the first open dissent I had heard in the University. Without exchanging many words, a friendship developed between us that was to flower later when we shared prison cells and survived until his suicide in 1983. Still later that year, someone took me to a mosque, *Masjed Ātashiha (Qobād)* where I heard a sermon attacking the government, without mentioning the Shah, for its corruption, using the Shiraz festival and the 2500-year birthday party as an example. The congregation echoed their approval with cries of *allāh akbar*.

In the spring of 1977 the interns, the same university intake as Behruz and Taqi, went on an indefinite strike for demands that I cannot recall. Two of them, including Hātef with whom I later developed a life-long friendship, came to ask my advice. I suggested that an indefinite strike would make them hostage to the most timid, and in a class as mixed as theirs it was better to go on strike for a limited period for specific demands and then give the University a chance to address the grievances, with the threat of going out again for another limited, but longer period. The class rejected my advice and continued to stay away for another week when one by one the weakest links cracked. They did not achieve any of their goals but were not punished either. We had entered a new era – the Revolution was taking shape in the Medical School.

The rulers failed to see it coming because they were face down.

[1] Ivan Illich, priest, theologian, philosopher, social critic, and author of *Deschooling Society* etc, and Paulo Freire, a Brazilian educator and philosopher author of *Pedagogy of the Oppressed*, among others.

Chapter 17

The revolutionary tide

It was January 1978. US president Carter had come to the country, praised the Shah for his wise rule over the 'island of security and peace in a turbulent area', and was gone. Nine days later, a tornado hit the island of peace and security, fatally as it turned out. A demonstration in Qom protesting at an article in *Ettelā'āt* newspaper lampooning Khomeini, was fired on by the security forces.[1] They went on to the clerical seminaries and beat up young mullahs with some deaths. This was the beginning of the Revolution on the asphalt. The streets became the main battleground. A chain of demonstrations was unleashed on the 40th day of the previous killing, *chehelleh*, the traditional day for commemorating a death. More deaths would trigger another *chehelleh* march, and more deaths. In between, more protests on the streets and in the universities, like snacks between main meals.

That first *chehelleh* demonstration was in Tabriz and lasted two days. The city was set ablaze. Seventy-three banks were attacked, seven cinemas and four hotels were burnt down. Officially there were 6 killed, 125 wounded and 608 arrested. There were simultaneous demonstrations in the capital and all major cities. Over the next months there were demonstrations almost every week and sometimes daily. Here was the Revolution as it appeared in the media, the journalists' revolution, photogenic and dramatic. Yet this image misreads, or deliberately misrepresents, the final sprint to the touchline for the entire race. The world was, and is, led to believe that this was revolution for Islam, fought in the streets, and won after a general strike. This was an image the Islamists also desire to impart.[2] It was not as simple.

Even though it ultimately ended with the victory of the Islamists, they were not the only, or even the main players in all its various stages. A peoples' uprising against tyranny and foreign domination was slowly metamorphosed into an Islamic regime and ultimately into an Islamic dictatorship. There was always a plurality of voices, secular and religious, that was only finally ended by the bloody defeat of the secular and democratic section six years later in 1981. The same battle lines have re-emerged and are being waged again three decades later as I write these lines. Underlying the widespread rejection of the tyrannical king, corruption and foreign domination, there were, and still are, two contrasting visions of the future – the secular republic and a religious caliphate encapsulated in the rule of the clergy. They shared the first two parts of the central slogan of the Revolution "Independence! Freedom! Islamic Republic" (*esteqlāl! Āzādi! Jomhuriye Eslāmi*) but differed on the third. Differed on the manifestation, the solution the effector of their longing for independence and freedom.

The Revolution had been brewing for a long time before, and away from the mosque. The armed struggle by the Fadāi' and other left groups and the Mojahedin, which had begun in the early 70's, was on the surface brutally crushed by the second half of the decade. Even if they did nothing but rekindle the spirit of the left after the coup d'état and keep alight the beacon of hope, they would have done enough. But they did more, much more. They pulled an entire generation from hedonistic self-indulgence to caring for the future of their fellow men and women. *'Remember the flight, the bird is mortal'* is how the young poet Foruq Farrokhzād wrote, prophetically. They had jump-started a revolution.

But the remains of the Fadāi' had regrouped and were actively extending their network in the universities and factories. Throughout 1976 and early 1977 street battles between the Fadāi' and Mojahedin and the security forces

CHAPTER 17

continued. In May the police attacked the Polytechnic and wounded some students. Then came the open letters, the first by National Front members and intelligentsia to the Shah protesting at the lack of political freedoms. SAVAK responded by leaving bombs in their homes or doorsteps as a way of intimidating them. One or two were bundled into cars and left severely beaten. There followed protests in Tehran University commemorating the June 1963 uprising and the death of Ali Shari'ati in London. Shari'ati had an enormous influence among the religious university students and the Shah had allowed his dissenting lectures in the Hosseinieh Ershād Mosque, partly because of Shari'ati's virulent anti-Marxist views. There followed open letters from the association of lawyers, *Kanun Vokala*, protesting at torture by SAVAK and by Ali-Asghar Haj Seyyed Javādi, a journalist sympathetic to Bāzargan's *Nehzat Azadi*, and others warning of impending disaster and advising the Shah to rule as constitutional monarch. Haj Seyyed Javadi later helped set up the Association to Defend Freedom and Human Rights in Iran. The fact that they went unpunished showed how the wall of fear was melting. In August there was a large demonstration in Tehran University where a number of students were wounded and arrested. But all these were still cocooned within institutions, such as universities, and therefore relatively protected by walls. Then in July and August bloody mass protests took place in Khāk-e Sefid and other squatter townships when bulldozers came to destroy their homes. This was the first example of mass open protest, and it was in those *halabi ābāds* – literally, tin towns.

The event that decisively widened the cracks in the atmosphere of fear that was already cracking was the week of public poetry readings. Called by the Writers Union (*Kānoon Nevisandegān*), a group of mostly secular writers on the left, many of whom had been in trouble with the authorities, and some of whom had tasted the Shah's prisons. It was held nightly over one week beginning October 10, 1977 in the Goethe Institute and became increasingly vocal in its criticism of the regime.

The role of intellectuals in virtually every upheaval in the recent Iranian history has been downplayed by both the Islamists, and paradoxically the left, even though most have had overt or covert left leanings. A random searchlight will pick out a few: Tālbof, the creator of modern Iranian theatre; Malkam Khān, who introduced the concept of law; Heydar Khān Amu Oqlu, the great revolutionary ha bast during the Constitutional Revolution of 1906; Nimā Yushij, the father of modern Farsi poetry; Taqi Arāni, the first independent Iranian Marxist thinker; the impresario Bāqchehbān, who introduced Brecht and Shakespeare to the stage; Mahmud Dowlatābādi, who wrote *Keleidar*, considered by many as the greatest novel in Farsi to date; and Bijan Jazani, Mas'oud Ahmadzādeh and Amir-Mas'oud Pouyan, who between them gave birth to the new radical left movement in Iran, Sai'd Soltanpur who used street theatre as a political tool. All but Malkam Khān were on the left. The Iranian cinema was crucial in keeping alive the spirit of criticism and social awareness at a time when the written word was tightly censored. Such films as The Cow (*Gāv* by Dāriush Mehrjui), Kimiyāi's The Antelopes (*Gavaznhā* – a sympathetic picture of urban guerrillas) and Bahrām Beizā'i's Downpour (*Ragbār* – which openly showed illicit love) were landmarks that for a time eluded the censor's scissors. Similarly, poetry, with its unique ability to use metaphor, expressed ideas that went over the head of SAVAK censors. The poetry of Ahmad Shāmlu, Said Soltānpour, Mohammad Zohari, Esmail Khoi', Sohrab Sepehri, Fereidoon Moshiri, Hooshang Golshiri, the plays of Qolām Hossein Sā'edi, the children's tales of Samad Behrangi and many others galvanized a generation which went on to ha bast and lead the Revolution. The iconoclasm of Foruq Farrokhzād, who not only spoke of revolution, but openly expressed the sexual and emotional passion of a woman for the first time, shattered taboos.

Everyone is afraid
  everyone is afraid, but you and I
  joined with lamp and water and mirror
  and were not afraid
  ....
  I am talking of my fortunate locks
  with the burnt poppies of your kiss
  and the intimacy of our bodies,

CHAPTER 17

and the glow of our nakedness
like fish scales in the water.

Adapted from the 'conquest of the garden' 1962 – by Michael C Hillman [see Bibliography].

So there they were, our writers and poets, in the Goethe institute, declaiming their poems and discussing censorship. Ahmad Shāmlu was abroad, Foruq Farrokhzad was dead and some like Dowlatābadi were absent. But most the other major poets and artists were there. They were told to avoid politics. But that was not to be. Starting cautiously with calls for removal of censorship, the readings became increasingly radical over the next few nights. On the third night, film director Bahrām Beizā'i, widened the criticism of censorship to include some sections of public opinion. And when on the fifth night Sa'id Soltānpour, just out of prison, read his poem condemning the Shah's despotism with his fiery words, the thousands of people in the Goethe institute and the streets outside rose to a tumultuous standing ovation.

What has become of my country,
what has become of my country,
where prisons are crammed with tulips,
and dew drops,
and survivors from mounds of martyrs
now shed tears for charred tulips.

What has become of my country
that flowers still mourn.

The patient eyes of men are filled with tears
for so long.

The heart of love itself is fractured in the depth of prison
for so long.

From the crypts of captivity we sang
of the suffocating cage
for so long
that lacerating wounds block our throats

Oh, the fist of revolution!
the mighty fist of people!
the fiery fist of the sun!

What had become of my country![3]

He completely transformed the atmosphere. The head of the Goethe institute stood up and warned that things could not continue in this vein. But the tone had changed and the wild reception by the audience of anything that smelled of revolution set the pace. Sa'edi and others went out to mingle with the crowd standing in the pouring rain. Aslān Aslāniān summed up the days ahead:

shab ast o chehreye mihan siahe.
barādar qarqe khooneh,
barādar kakolash atashfeshooneh[4].

In the end, 60 writers and poets spoke. Only three women. Heavily censored reports of these meetings were published in the papers. The regime became fearful. And an attempt to extend these readings in *Kārvānsarāi Sangi* was broken up by commandoes wielding sticks and chains. One student was killed and 70 were wounded. That was the same place where in May 1971 the Shah's paramilitary forces had gunned down striking workers from *Jahān Chit* textile factory marching on Tehran, killing three.

The revolution had been ignited by the secular half of society – something ignored by most published histories of the Revolution that tend to be sympathetic to either the old or the new regime. Four years later, Soltānpour was arrested on his wedding night during the massive wave of arrests and a few days later he was shot. It was June 21, 1981. Thousands joined his fate. The short window of freedom began by his speech was closed by his death.

Revolutions are built in layers, almost like a renaissance painting. The intellectuals had laid the foundation. Three days after the poetry reading the son of Khomeini, Mostaphā, was found dead in bed. Like the death of Shari'ati in London, people saw the hand of SAVAK. The Shah had deliberately exaggerated the reach of his eyes, ears and sword. The deliberately implanted rumour that one in eight Iranian was a SAVAK agent now ricocheted back. The memorial services which began in Ark Mosque and spread across the country became a focal point. Khomeini saw the extent of the nationwide demonstrations over the next weeks and upgraded his demands to demand an end to the Pahlavi dynasty (see BBC's Story of the Revolution – an oral history).

The summer heat was fading. We were driving back from our annual holiday by the Caspian in September 1978 when I heard on the news of the massacre of 'thousands' in Jaleh square in Tehran. That night I told my father-in-law that the Shah 'was on the way out' and drank through a bottle of whiskey. As on the previous occasion my immediate family thought I was out of my mind. This time, however, I arrived at this conclusion objectively. Two weeks earlier, 600 people had been burnt to death in Cinema Rex in Abadan. Once again everyone blamed the regime, particularly as the police chief was the same as the one who had supervised the Qom massacre in January. In fact, evidence collected by students in Ahwaz implicated Islamists.[5] But with the asphalt of Jaleh square still wet with blood, the bloodied mud stuck on the hated monarch. The Shah would either have to keep on slaughtering or give in. Although a few of his military advisers, including generals Khosrowdād and Oveissi advised him to do precisely that, continue slaughtering, he did not have the will. His regime did not have the will to survive. It was more hollow than appeared from outside, like a battery that was empty but still looked good.

The ten days of poetry reading had galvanized us too, as had the demonstrations in Qom and Tabriz. Early in 1978 Bahrām invited us to form a Marxist study group. It consisted of me, J, Mani and his wife Parvin. Bahrām led the discussions. They began with Dialectic Materialism, choosing Maurice Cornforth *The First Principles of Philosophy* as the text. A sad choice this turned out to be. Hundreds of left-leaning students got their ABC of Marxism from this set textbook used for the Worker's University in France, to fall flat on their face on their first encounter with the Islamists. Mao, with all his naïve explanation of such concepts as contradiction was sophisticated compared to Cornforth. We developed a knowledge of dialectic as wide as a sea but only a few millimetres deep. The other bible of the Left was *Historical Materialism* by the same author, a cartoon-like exposition of the deep insights of Marx and Engels into class and history – shallow, one dimensional, misleading and inaccurate, an equally inadequate weapon in our Marxist education.

We were still discussing the transformation of quantity to quality a year later when we heard that people were planning to attack the SAVAK offices. Bahrām ridiculed us for petit-bourgeois impulsiveness for wanting to join in the excitement. We stayed back and discussed Mao's oversimplification while the rest of Shiraz was making history

[1] The article was published in *Ettelā'āt* on January 2, 1978.

[2] Huge institutions have been set up to rewrite the entire modern history of Iran and to rub out all but its own people– *The Centre for Investigating Historic Documents of the Ministry of Information* or *Institute for Political Studies and Research* are but two. Also to use SAVAK interrogation files obtained under torture to rewrite the history of the Fadāi'.

[3] My translation modified from http://www.middleast4change.org/what-has-become-of-my-country-said-soltanpour-poet-of-revolution/.

[4] It is night and my country's face is black/ brother is drowned in blood / brother's locks are a volcano.

[5] The cinema fire doors were locked. Subsequent independent investigation by students at the Jondishāhpour University, Ahwaz pointed the finger at the clerics and Ayatollah Tāheri. Dr Esmā'il Narimissā, a medical resident in Ahwaz, who was instrumental in collecting the information was later executed by the same mullah who conducted my court – see later.

18

Chapter 18

Sa'di Hospital under attack

Memory does not make films, it makes photographs (Milan Kundra, Immortality). Or images on a shattered mirror. My first splintered memories are of Sa'di hospital under attack, one of the first places in the city to be assaulted by the military. Throughout the spring and summer of 1978 Sa'di, and the adjoining Medical School linked to it by a corridor and a shared courtyard, were the beating heart of the Revolution in Shiraz. What I remember from those months are a series of snapshots which I have linked into a narrative. Accurate or not they make sense to me. As Nabokov wrote in Ada (or Ardor), reality is always 'a form of memory, even at the moment of its perception'.

Sa'di was the poorer of the four main teaching hospitals. Its wards were large, open spaces with thirty or so beds lining the walls on either side, a bit like the wards of my medical student days in London. Bare. No privacy. Suspended over the beds was their very individual smell, non-pungent, non-urinary, unique to Sa'di I thought, until I met it again in Kampala's Mulago Hospital four decades later. It was the smell of the truly sick. The hospital was a two-story, bland horizontal building facing Zand Avenue, the broad boulevard linking the airport to the east to Namazi hospital at its western end. The Department of Medicine offices and library were on the second floor. Behind Sa'di, towards the dry river, so called because most of the year it was just a stony bed, were a number of prefabricated wards – what we called Bimārestān-e Sahrāi' (field hospital) – acting as overflow beds. An elongated shallow courtyard with a central flowerbed separated Sa'di from Zand Avenue. The emergency room, at one end of the courtyard, was always filled to capacity with patients lying on stretchers in various states of severe sickness. This was a place for the very ill, who either could not afford the private doctors, or who had been bled dry by them. We were the last port of call. Once when I asked a diabetic peasant, in my special diabetic clinic, one of only two in the country, if he could afford to buy insulin, he raised his right hand in exasperated disbelief and replied in his Qashqāi accent "if I had any money would I come to see a doctor like you?" Over the next year that relationship was to gradually change as trust on the 'doctor-like-me' grew and the 'you' slowly metamorphosed into the 'us'.

Sa'di was also the first place in Shiraz to raise the slogan *marg bar shah* (death to the Shah), which later morphed into the more evocative one of *begoo, marg bar shah*! (Say it! Death to the Shah) inviting you into the bosom of the Revolution. Rostam Qalandari voiced this first. He was a thin, rather diminutive, medical student from Māzandarān in his third year. The name Rostam, aptly described his courage, though not his physique. Rostam (or Rustam), the mythical hero of Shāhnāmeh - book of kings - by one of Iran's greatest poets, Abul-Qāsem Ferdowsi - had feet that were said to sink into stone as he walked. There he stood, our Rostam, on top of one of the pillars flanking Sa'di's main gate, exposed, defiant, shouting at the armed troops outside. Day after day, and into the night. You could shout whatever you wanted, and the troops just watched patiently, resignedly. But let out *begoo, marg bar Shah* and they would just go wild and attack with tear-gas or worse. I had a special relationship with Rostam who at the time was deeply committed to Khomeini's vision of an Islamic Revolution. We trod the tightrope of mutual respect and bidirectional wariness. He would criticise me, even mock me, for my 'western concepts of freedom', but never, not once, did he censor me. In that he was unique among the Islamists at the time. We drew much

CHAPTER 18

closer after the Revolution as his vision drew closer to mine, while never abandoning his deep faith.

Another iconic figure, a regular on the wide steps leading up to Sa'di's main entrance, was my old friend from Bristol, Rahman. The steps led up from the courtyard fronting the length of the building to the permanently open front door of the flat-roofed hospital, paint white, now dirty, spreading left and right for 100 metres or so. The doors at the top of the stairs led to the wards on either side, surgical to the left, medical to the right. Facing the steps was the large iron gate to the garden with guard rooms on either side. If you stood on the top steps you could look over the wall or gate into Zand Avenue. On demonstration days, Rahman would be standing there on the top of those stairs, erect with his silver hair, impeccably groomed, and his impecably ironed blue shirt, statuesque, conspicuous, shouting *begoo, marg bar Shah!* in his distinctive sonorous voice that flew over the gate. He stood so erect we gave him the nickname 'Colonel'. We had been almost inseparable since he had returned to Shiraz. Rahman was one of the many friends who dropped into our veranda whenever they felt like it and raided the fridge for beer, wine and more. It was their home-from-home. We held an open house, as was quite common in Iran, though not among the inhabitants of the Namāzi compound who had mainly trained in the US. Friends would come, sit, drink and chat on the veranda, looking out on the beautiful Namāzi *Bāq* whether or not J or I were present.

The first large street demonstration in Shiraz actually began from the University dormitories up on the hills in the northern part of town in the autumn of 1977. The last Shiraz art festival had closed with a whimper. The Fadāi' and Mojahedin had been systematically hunted down and their entire leadership and many of their most skilled cadres killed or captured. The ten days of poetry reading had ignited the fire of revolt. For days there had been protests in most universities across the country that had begun in the autumn of 1977 and reached its peak in the winter with bloody clashes in Tehran and San'ati Āryāmehr (college of technology now Sana'ti Sharif). Over the years the focal point of the student movement had been Tehran, Isfahan and Tabriz with Shiraz usually lagging behind.

Our demonstration was a disorganised affair, unplanned and without clear slogans. Mostly students with a handful of academics. We marched south, downhill from the main campus, deliberately built on a hillside, safely segregating students from the city and its people. As we approached Felkeh[1] Namāzi to turn left into Zand Avenue our route was blocked by armed soldiers. I can still see the tip of the G3 submachine gun touching the chest of Yusef who was out in front, the first sign of the courage and recklessness that was to cost him his life.[2] The demonstration was dispersed outside the Engineering College, as we rounded from the Felkeh Namāzi into Zand. During that week there were further clashes between the army and students, some waving red flags, with many arrests and some wounded. A police car was set alight. There were even clashes with some town people. In Shiraz, as in Tehran, the University had been in the forefront of the protests. It was only after the publication of the letter insulting Khomeini in the daily Ettelā'āt in January of 1978 that the 40-day cycle of street demonstrations began. During the previous eight months, the universities had spearheaded the opposition to the Shah.

One day early in the spring of 1978 the army started to lob tear gas over Sa'di Hospital's wall. It must have been Rostam and his *begoo, marg bar Shah* that pushed them over the brink. At first, we tried washing the sting off with water, but that just spread the irritation. Someone told me to use a surgical mask soaked in vinegar. We raided the operating theatre for gauze masks and then the canteen kitchen. They had huge vats of *torshi* -pickled onions, aubergine and garlic -indispensable to an Iranian dish. The vinegar reeked of garlic, but it was moderately effective against tear gas. Rostam wrapped his hands in towels, snatched from the wards, and lobbed back the unexploded tear gas canisters shouting rhythmically *poole nafte māye, yeki digeh bendāz* (throw us another, its our own oil money) through loudspeakers which had been wired into the hospital sound system. Others soon followed. We used up all the kitchen's supply of *torshi* that day, and maybe the clean towels.

Running around, excited, shouting, tears pouring down, the pungent

CHAPTER 18

garlicky-vinegary *torshi* creeping up my nose, I was also worried of what all this was doing to the patients lying in their beds a few metres behind us with only a wall separating. The tear gas wafting in through the open window alongside the shouting and noise really upset the patients who were mainly from surrounding tribes and villages. They had little understanding of the Revolution. They sat or lay on their beds, uncomprehending and terrified. The Revolution, right up to the last weeks, was a predominantly urban affair and most of the villagers that I saw had no notion of what it was all about, which made the slogans against the Shah and the army's counter-attacks even more incomprehensible. For them the Shah represented land reform and the Education Corp - *Sepahe Danesh*. Not long before the monarchy fell, a caravan of revolutionaries from Yāsuj, the capital of Lur-speaking Boir-Ahmadi tribes, driving down to Shiraz for a demonstration was pelted by stones in almost every village they drove through east of the town of Ardekān. Pro-Shah feelings persisted even after the Revolution. A year after the Shah had fallen a villager outside the town of Niriz told me "If we get a chance we would string up every mullah from the trees over there" he said pointing to copse of trees. Students who after the Revolution went to the villages as part of the Jahāde Sāzandegi (jihad for construction, Khomeini's bid to win the peasants over) told me of hostile encounters particularly round Firuzābād, the heartland of the Qashqāi, but also in other parts of Fars province. As summer turned to autumn the peasants avoided the hospital, and even coming to town. Towards the end, my own clinic, usually full to bursting point, was all but empty.

It was dusk, autumn of that same year. The tear gassing had gone on all afternoon. They were using a new gas – they said a nerve gas. Whatever it was, unlike the usual CS gas which irritated the eyes and the lungs, this one caused intense nausea. The vinegar-*torshi* mask proved utterly useless. The canisters were also hotter and more difficult to throw back. Then one day all of a sudden the soldiers burst open the iron hospital gates and rushed us, in full military gear, submachine guns in hand. Gas masks. Invisible eyes. Non-humans without eyes. Terrifying. They pushed into the guard room at the side of the main gate. Khosrow Nasr, the Dean, happened to be on the Sa'di steps with the hospital chief Dr Mottaqiān when the attack began and had run into the guard room with a few students. He was of massive girth, weighing 120 kg or so. One of the students hid behind his large bottom as the masked men armed with G3 submachine guns burst in, confronting Khosrow, an immobile mound of dignity, protecting a terrified student behind his barricade of fat, bone and muscle.[3]

But the troops turned round ignoring Khosrow or the quivering matchstick he was shielding, mounted the steps and entered the hospital, something they were never to do again. They were clearly after someone. Perhaps Rahman, the Colonel, who had stood there erect and conspicuous. Or Fereidoon, a surgical resident with a thick black Stalin moustache, who had also been very prominent that day, shouting *begoo, marg bar shah*! and throwing back the hot canisters. They turned right into the medical ward. Fereidoon had ran in before them and hid behind the nurses desk. Failing to find him, and not being particularly choosy, the soldiers used their guns to beat up a hapless student standing nearby who had been busy taking a medical history from a patient. Life in a hospital goes on even under gas attacks. We later had to deal with the effect of tear gas and this other chemical on the patients in the two wards facing the front of the hospital.

That summer of 1978 a group of soldiers in civilian clothes, but still wearing their army boots, stormed the Ettefāqāt (emergency room) and savagely beat up Mozafariān, a surgical resident. For a long time, the bloody red coat of the resident was hung outside the Ettefāqāt for everyone to see. It was in one of these raids into the Sa'di courtyard later in the year that one soldier surrendered his US manufactured G3 submachine gun and wanted to surrender himself as well when Āzādeh, the pathologist, dissuaded him. It would have been a certain court-martial and the firing squad. The weapon, for which we had no use, became a major security problem. It was eventually handed over to a mosque. This was my first glimpse of the wavering of the conscript army. That same surgical resident, Ali Mozafariān, now a fully qualified surgeon, was arrested by the Islamic regime in 1990 and executed the following year accused of 'immorality, homosexual acts and spying for America'. He was a fervent Sunni having converted from Shi'a and despite opposition from the Shi'a clergy, created the first Sunni mosque in Shiraz. He was active in trying to create an understanding between the various sects in Islam.

Another snapshot. We had gathered for a demonstration in Namāzi for the first time. Namāzi was the paying hospital and catered for those with money to spend or had state insurance. The management was totally unsympathetic to the Revolution. Anything we stuck on the walls or notice board would be torn down immediately. We decided to break the atmosphere. A large group of students, nurses and junior doctors with one or two attending specialist doctors gathered outside the main entrance of the hospital which was a circular area with a central flower bed and surrounded by flowers. To get to the main gate leading to Felkeh Namāzi and out into Zand Avenue we had to march along a tree-lined path for about two to three hundred metres. A row of armed soldiers were blocking the gate with lorries filled with soldiers lined up on the other side of the Felkeh. A lieutenant, I think he was called Mohammadi, started to shout obscenities at us through a loudspeaker, using gutter language, unsparing to mother, sister and such. It was clear that he meant to stop us with whatever it took. Prudently we decided to limit ourselves to circling the front entrance of the hospital a few times shouting slogans for the benefit of the patients and staff.

This was the children's first demonstration, and they subsequently organised their own march round the compound shouting slogans, or rather the girls did. The 'Namāzi gang' had split in two with the girls playing at being revolutionary and the boys SAVAK agents. Once or twice the SAVAKI team captured one of the girls and tortured her to get a 'confession'. Actual, pain-provoking torture. Maryam told me years later how she trained herself not to show weakness through crying or crying out. We, the parents, were too involved to notice; revolutions occupy all available space. Later in November, during General Azhāhri's military government, nurses would ascend the roof of the 8-storey nurses home situated inside the Namāzi *bāq* and shout *allāh akbar* (god is great) with us and the girls echoing back from down below in the *bāq* proper. Rising skywards and carried several streets away by its beauty was the powerful voice of Nasrin, a voice which I still hear when we visit them in Connecticut. Once when the girls too were on the roof, shots were fired from the street. Nargess and Ameneh were quickly shunted under a water tank by Ameneh's older brother Ali-Mohammad, giggling all the way – it was all so unreal so movie-like. Nargess was eight and Maryam eleven. The bullets were real. The Revolution was no longer a game.

In the gaps between the war against the SAVAKI gang, the girls would beg or pinch Naneh Ali's juicy mulberries.

[1] Roundabouts are called *felkeh* (actually *falakeh*) in the wonderfully musical Shirazi pronunciation.

[2] Yusef Yusefi was arrested in Isfahan on the way to Shiraz in June 1981. His body black and blue with signs of beating was handed to his family a few days later. He had died under torture. He was a close friend.

[3] Sadly my cousin and friend Khosrow Nasr died in January 2020.

Chapter 19

Death to gomunist

One late summer or early autumn morning, the Medical School was invaded by the clerical groupies. About 20 – 30 young men entered the University, shouting *allāh akbar, Khomeini rahbar* (god is great, Khomeini is leader). They tore down pictures of the Shah and his wife, and any Fadāi' leaflets they could find. A few of them climbed the walls of the school and scrawled on it in a childish hand in blue. Two are engraved in my memory.

marg bar gumunist (death to gomunist – they meant communist)
    Then beneath it: gumu = god, and nist = not there, therefore gumunist = there is no god.

They ended by shouting *death to gomunists* all round the Medical School courtyard. It was the start of a continuous unrelenting onslaught on the left that was only to end in their massacre in 1981 and again in 1987.
    At the time communist activity was beginning to surface mainly in the University with some Fadāi' leaflets and other left groups appearing on the walls and some Marxist literature being sold in plain white cover. Many had been translated into Farsi years ago by the Tudeh party and the New Left and

had been circulating among the student movement abroad and clandestinely within Iran. They now became required reading for any new recruit to the Marxist Left.

This was the first salvo in the battle for the University between the Shirazi mullahs and a left that was beginning to grow in strength in the University. The campuses were to become one of the chief arenas in the battle between the secular democratic forces, predominantly but not exclusively led by the left, and the Islamists under the leadership of the clergy. Straddling the two, and leaning at times towards one or the other, was the Peoples Mojahedin Organisation of Iran (PMOI) – Mojahedin for short [1]- whose ideology was a curious mixture of the radical Shi'a Islamist teaching of Ali Shari'ati and Maoism, and who over the first two years after the Revolution grew into the largest political force in opposition to Khomeini. But now the leaders of all these groups were still either in prison or abroad.

Shiraz proper was dominated by the mullahs with their power base in the city and the Bazaar, the most militant of whom were centred round the *Masjed Ātashihā* (also known as *Qobād*) led by clerics in the Dastqeib family. The secular and left-leaning forces had their power base in the University. The conflict between the two was deep and fundamental to the modern history of Iran. As time went on it became more difficult for the left to put anything up on the walls. At first they would come from the city and tear up the Fadāi' leaflets. After the *Āshura* demonstrations (see Chapter 28) the balance of power shifted across the country and intolerance towards the left became absolute. Any left-leaning leaflet, indeed any leaflet without *'in the name of Allah the compassionate, the merciful'* at the top would be torn down immediately by the *hezbollāh* – self-appointed 'party of god' - within the medical school. Their own daily wall newspaper appeared in the canteen. When the left tried to put up its version it lasted at best a couple of hours.

Soon after that first demonstration the Left tried to organize its own march. It began in the Engineering College near Felkeh Nāmazi and next door to the pasteurized milk factory where a strike a few days before had led to the expulsion of one or two workers. It was a solidarity protest to encourage workers to continue their resistance. After the speeches addressing workers in the milk factory a group of about two and a half thousand marched up the hill, chanting a little self-consciously to beneath its summit, where the University Library stood, half finished, a dejected monument to the failed dreams of the King of Kings. Funds had run out as petro-dollars were squandered on other prestige projects or slipped into deep pockets. The route meant marching up a deserted avenue with a handful of bystanders to beneath the isolated half-finished monarchic relic perched on top of a barren hill. There in the shadow of the student dormitories, voices mysteriously emanated from a tent, previously erected to protect the identity of the speakers, like steam rising from damp canvas, to a crowd made up of students, schoolboys and a number of incongruously well-dressed individuals. On the periphery about 200 Islamists shouted *allāh akbar* and ridiculed us. The empty rhetoric from the tent, repetitive, boring, read from pre-prepared texts, was not that different from what the mullahs offered in their speeches, but without the crowd-excitatory oratorical skills that all mullahs learn. *Shi'a* clergy hone their skills in manipulating emotions in the annual ritual of *rowzeh khooni* mourning the martyrdom of Imam Hossein, he fourth imam in the Shi'a pantheon,[2] as well as the Friday sermon pulpit. In Shiraz the left did not try to mount an independent march again although in Tehran, with its much larger left, the Fadāi' were able to get over 100,000 to march behind their flags.

The attack by the clerical groupies on the University that day was an early salvo in the larger battle that was brewing between the traditional sections of society with their cultural roots in pre-capitalist relations and their natural links to the clergy and the bazaar merchants on the one hand, and the modern middle class who were the children of the new capitalist relations introduced into Iran by the Shah and his father, so to speak from above, on the other. Capitalism in Iran, like many similar countries was a vertical invader. The battle was to grow in intensity in the post-revolutionary years and remains unresolved as I write. It is the enduring confrontation between modernity and tradition that was first exposed in the Constitutional Revolution of 1906. Sometimes it takes on the mantle of class war, at others it takes place purely at the cultural level. It is being fought even now in the streets of Iran, in the resistance to the compulsory *hejab* (covering of women) in art, literature and music. And in factories where Khomeini preached: it is revolutionary to cry, the other view that eulogises the beauty of colour, treasures the human voice, freedom to choose one's dress, the right to one's body, the liberating feel of laughter, the right to be free. It is also about the right to organise, to have trade unions, to be in control of one's life, and above all, for the right to decide the political, social and economic direction of the country. In one, the word of God as interpreted through his earthly intermediaries, rules. In the other, that of men and women, as filtered through their choice of representatives.

That same battle was in a curious way echoed in my family, but with a twist that I think clearly illustrates the blurred lines within the Iranian psyche of this duality of tradition- versus modernity. The side of my family which espoused the trappings of 'modernity', western clothes, music, parties, cinema, skiing, mixed swimming, sending their children abroad for education, and also the part that gave rise to the few socialists and communists were the sons and daughters of Sheikh Fazlollāh Nuri who had taken the side of the autocratic Shah on the slogan of *mashrue'h* (following the *sharia*), or the descendants of Haj Aqā Mohsen, the feudal mullah, who had supported him and married into his family. For example, Tudeh Party chairman Kianuri was the Sheikh's grandson and a number of Fadāi' leaders were grandchildren of Haj Aqā Mohsen. Meanwhile my maternal grandfather's side, the Āshtiānis, had been uniformly pro-constitutionalists in 1906 and sided with those who had been influenced by western notions of democracy and law. Yet when involved with politics now, the Āshtiānis approved of Khomeini's vision of society and sided with the present regime. This could be pure coincidence, or the revolt of the next generation against their elders. But it so beautifully illustrates the skin-deep nature of modernism in modern Iran, illustrated with exceptional skill by Asqar Farhādi's film, About Elly (*dar bareh elli, 2009*). Even the communist left showed their attachment to tradition in their views on the role of the sexes, on their ideas of fun, on 'trivial' music (*mobtazal*, meaning popular song), on sexual mores, and even their cult of martyrdom. I once overheard a young communist in the Literature College admonishing a female comrade for a conduct that 'was unbecoming for a communist'. She

CHAPTER 19

had laughed aloud.

Earlier that year I had suggested that we try and co-ordinate the movement within the University. Mani, Bahrām and myself contacted two others and together we set up a secret cell. There was Morteza– a pathology resident, and Āzādeh a pathologist. We did not invite 'The Colonel' as he was too conspicuous. The somewhat naïve idea was to create a central core of activists with successive layers of people surrounding it. One of our first actions was to organise a public meeting at the University. We gathered a few faculty members, residents and students in a room in Namāzi. Bahrām came up with some suggestion that was vehemently opposed, and he left in a huff. We decided to hold a public meeting in Sa'di. Morteza had told us that he is in touch with some radical Islamic students with leanings towards the Mojahedin. They could invite a speaker from the city. Azādeh, our handsome wrestling champion, was to speak on behalf of the University.

The big courtyard outside the library was overfull with a large number of students and town people. This was to be the first public meeting at the Medical School. Slogans of *marg bar gomunist,* written in blue in that childish scrawl, winked at us as I listened below with the crowd. A blue-eyed student from the Engineering College, his angelic almost beardless face incongruously fronting a fanatic's brain and who was to cross my path again and again, wrenched the microphone from Azādeh and blurted out a torrent of violent abuse at the left. Azādeh forcibly took the mike back and made a very conciliatory speech, which at the time I felt was too obsequious towards the clergy. Then Movahhed, a young mullah took the microphone and spent the entire 30 minutes of his talk savaging the left, who he portrayed as the main enemy. 'We will smash the face of the communists with our fist' he screamed, getting the name right. The Shah, the regime, revolutionary demands, not even America which had masterminded this University, none of these got a mention. That was the second round of an organised attack on the left.

Mani and I felt totally betrayed. Here we were giving a platform to the mullahs to attack us in our own house. It was also my first doubt about

Morteza and his connection. We had not planned to have a mullah on the platform and when asked how this had come about, he his reply was evasive. This was my first foray into revolutionary politics. I had arrived late and was learning. Slowly learning. There were to be many lessons. It was perhaps my naïve innocence that endeared me equally to the non-political academics on one side and the Islamist students on the other. We were good teachers and clearly had no connection to the regime. As I once overheard Faqihi,[6] one of the leaders of the *hezbollāh*, admonish our Rahman 'if you want a good leftist, look at Dr M', meaning me.

[1] See Appendix 2.

[2] Throughout the Muslim month of *Muharram,* mosques, *Hoseiniehs* and many well to do families organise nightly mourning sessions where an invited cleric will describe in gory detail the martyrdom of Imam Hossein, and most of his family on the banks of Euphrates in 680 AD. Reputations are made, and rewarded, by provoking wailing tears.

[3] Faqihi gave his name to Sa'di hospital after his assassination by the Mojahedin in 1981.

Chapter 20

The academics join in

Sitting on my veranda in late one morning in July of 1978, just returned from my research laboratory, I was in peace. The veranda of Villa Seven, one of the older villas built in the 50's, opened up to the huge Namāzi *bāq* (garden) where many of the faculty were renting villas or apartments. The *bāq* glowed emerald under the intense summer sun. It was a cool silent bubble in a turbulent sea. Bahrām walked up with Rahman's silver hair towering above him and shattered the metaphor. There is going to be a meeting of academic staff from across Iran in Tehran this week, he said. Do you want to come? They are going to discuss the role of the faculty in universities.

Universities had played a vital part in the opposition to the Shah through all those dark years. The death of three students, shot by armed guards on Tehran University campus without any provocation[1] was one of the first protests a few months after the CIA-engineered coup that restored the Shah in 1953. Since then, 16 Azar (December 7) was commemorated as Student Day. One of the first to protest were Shiraz students who in May 1961 protested at the meeting of Central Treaty Organisation (CENTO) military pact, of which Iran was a key member, being staged at their university. That same year on the anniversary of 16 Azar, the first mention of revolution and armed resistance also came from the universities,[2] well before any of the armed guerrilla movements had formed. Throughout the following years universities supplied leaders and members to the opposition movement.

All over Asia, Africa and Latin America, universities were pivotal to the democratic and revolutionary struggles. Rapid and uneven introduction of capitalist relations gave to the universities in these countries a unique role. The newly educated became the voice of the displaced. Student revolts overthrew Syngman Rhee in Korea, fomented opposition in Cairo, Algiers, Caracas, Buenos Aires and Havana and battled troops on the streets of Istanbul. It was to counter the radicalism in Tehran University, especially in the Engineering College, that the Shah had created a new model Industrial University which bore his title – the *San'ati Aryamehr University* (now *Sana'ti Sharif*). It attracted some of the best engineering graduates inside and outside the country. The Shah, confident of a model which had been successfully tried in Shiraz, appointed the Chancellor, but allowed the staff to self-organise the internal running of the University. Why would future leaders and technocrats being trained to run the country by a predominantly western trained faculty take an interest in politics, he thought. The ruling elite had not read their history. The academic staff and students created an increasingly close working relationship that extended to the politics of freedom and independence from foreign domination.

The current wave of open unrest in the universities had begun a year previously in June 1977 when students used the occasion of the entry exams to Tehran University to protest at the death of Ali Shari'ati. Predictably SAVAK was blamed even though Shari'ati died in a London hospital of a heart ailment. There were further demonstrations in August. Then came the ten days of poetry reading in the Goethe institute that was attended by tens of thousands of people. *San'ati* University decided to organise a follow-up. When police prevented people from attending the poetry readings in November, thousands of people inside the *San'ati* auditorium went on a sit-in strike, the first sit-in of the Revolution. On the other side of the world that same day the Shah was attending a banquet dinner in the White House with thousands of demonstrators outside the lawn calling for his death. *San'ati* rang with the same slogan. Over there, the distinguished guests of the US president shed involuntary tears as the wind blew tear gas their way. Here thugs beat up writers and protesters with wooden batons. There were over 30 arrests. Eighteen months later the Shah was to shed real tears on the steps of the plane to permanent exile.

In January 1978, Jimmy Carter made a return visit to Iran and demonstrations spread to many universities. Since then events had moved fast. The streets of Qom, Tabriz, Yazd, Isfahan and many other cities had been repeatedly stained blood red. With the arrival of the Iranian New Year on the spring equinox, the universities had again erupted and by early May most were closed down. In the University of Babol, 22 were arrested. In Ahwaz, the guards and police fired on students killing one and wounding 24, suffering many casualties themselves. In Shiraz, demonstrations in the Teachers' Training College were joined by red-flag waving students from the Agricultural School. Police cars were set on fire and 28 students were arrested and many wounded. The next day the Office of Student Affairs was destroyed by a bomb and the University was closed. There were also clashes between students and thugs from the town. The medical school in Kermanshah, and universities in Tehran (the National - *Melli*) and Tabriz were shut after protests. All through June and July bloody and violent clashes in various campuses continued. The new Prime Minister Amuzegar, appointed by the Shah to replace Hoveida,[3] his longest serving prime minister] with orders to open up the political atmosphere a little, withdrew the campus guards and made the universities responsible for their own security and suggested moving the most militant campus – *San'ati* – from Tehran to Isfahan. The Shah again had underestimated the change in power relations. The entire *San'ati* academic staff went on strike and sent out notices across the country that they would be recruiting students themselves for the next academic year. When the government stopped their salary, the strikers created a bank account and asked for donations from the public. They went on to recruit 700 students for next year's entry. It was the beginning of a dual power taking shape in the country, and that too started in the universities. Faculty staff were now entering the battle, a little belatedly and with the usual reticence of people who had something tangible to lose. Against that background Bahrām and Rahman walked up to our veranda in Villa 7.

"Who else is going from Shiraz?" I asked Bahrām. "Some academics from engineering, literature and perhaps agriculture", Bahrām replied. I was the only one from the School of Medicine. This was still early days and one had to be careful in whom one confided. We persuaded Mani to come too, he was always ready for action. I was quite apprehensive. I had no idea what to expect. We flew to Tehran. It was 25 July 1978, thirteen months after that large demonstration in Tehran University against Shari'ati's death.

In the event, about 100-120 people gathered in the auditorium of *San'ati* on Shāhreza Avenue (now Āzādi). In the interest of security, we were not to use real names but were asked to hold up a piece of paper with any assumed name or number of our choosing. I cannot recall mine. It was all very amateurish. If SAVAK wanted to find out who we were it would not have been that difficult. The chairman asked each university to send a representative to speak. There were speakers from most of the main colleges in Tehran. Speakers from the provinces there were from Tabriz, Isfahan, as well as ourselves from Shiraz. There may have been others. The first speaker was from Tehran University who introduced it as the "father of all universities", founded by the Shah's father Reza Shah, and gave a brief history of repression within the University, the role of chancellors appointed directly by the Palace, the attacks by the army in 1953, the shooting dead of three students, and the permanent presence of SAVAK and its agents on campus. A speaker from Tehran's Melli University called it the "mother of all universities". Bahrām and another colleague from Shiraz prodded me to stand up and represent Shiraz. I had no time to think. I agreed, jotted down a few words, raised my paper with its pseudonym and went up to the podium. There I said something along the lines of "if Tehran is the father and that other is the mother then there is no doubt that Shiraz is the bastard child" and went on to briefly describe the role of Shiraz University in the overall US plans for Iran.

The meeting ended up by deciding to set up a National Association of Academics - *Sāzmān Melli Dāneshgāhiān* – the SMD. The Shiraz contingent suggested that I represent the University with Mani volunteered as my deputy. About thirty representatives, mostly from the capital, formed the inaugural committee which went on to elect a Provisional Executive Committee to which I was elected as a member. We were to write a charter (*manshur*) for the SMD and a constitution. That night we worked till late. We arranged to meet in a week to write its charter, drafted by Nāsser Pākdāman from Tehran University, our elected chair. It was a brief declaration for democratically run universities, independent of the state and of imperialist influence.

We were creating what we thought was a radical syndicate, a truly democratic and independent academic institution. What we only half saw was that academic freedom could only exist in a democratic and free society. The SMD quickly adapted to the reality of a rapidly evolving revolutionary spiral. It plunged into revolutionary politics targeting the overthrow of the autocratic regime. The political imperatives of an overthrow of the Shah side-lined the democratic demands of the *manshur*. But without a specific political framework, the loose SMD structure was to disintegrate the moment that goal was achieved. The various forces inside it went their own way.

Yet in its short lifespan, the SMD was to play an important role in the overthrow of the monarchy, one that is almost totally ignored by historians. And it brought me into brief contact with some interesting players in the arena. There was Farzād Bigleri from *San'ati University*, an astute organiser, who was later executed by the Islamic regime as a Fadāi'. His enthusiasm was truly infectious. Abbās Abbāspour, in the Provisional Executive Committee, later became Minister of Power in the Islamic Republic and died in the bomb explosion in the headquarters of the Islamic Republic Party (IRP) in 1981 alongside seventy-two leaders of the new regime. Hair well groomed, always well shaven, in his impeccable clean white shirt and ironed trousers, that as the Iranians saying goes 'could cut a melon', Abbāspour looked nothing like the Islamists I had known up to that time. His subsequent role as one of the founders of the Islamic Republic Party[4] took me by surprise. Around us people were whispering in corners, giving each other signs, nods and winks, manoeuvring. National Front and its religious offshoot, Nehzat Azadi led by Mehdi Bāzargān (the first post-revolutionary prime minister), Tudeh,

Confederation of Iranian Students, Khomeinists, perhaps some Radical Left, a microcosm of the loose alliance out there on the streets debating endlessly the nature of SMD, who can join, who can vote, who can represent whom. I was a novice among old hands.

Back in Shiraz my role over the next months was to get signatories for the charter (*manshur*) from among faculty members. Knocking on office doors, trying to find them alone, it was not easy. Naturally I approached people who I felt might be sympathetic. The Medical Faculty was still largely unaware of what was happening in their country that last monarchical summer. I will never forget the angry retort I got from Borhānmanesh, a hepatologist, a few months earlier during a visit to Yale medical school, on route to an endocrinology conference in Miami, Florida in the USA. I was trying to organise my sabbatical that was coming up in a year's time at Yale. When I pointed out to him that things were on the move back home - we had already had the 40-day street demonstrations – he replied angrily that it was all a show organised by the English, the standard bogey of the Iranian middle class. Borhānmanesh was later to lead a plot to replace me as representative of the SMD, just before the SMD died a natural death. In the end I signed up 32 members from a faculty of about 250. I was told later that my approaching them for a signature had totally taken them by surprise – they had thought of me a little eccentric young man, weirdly cycling to work, using peculiar teaching methods, extrovert, innocent, remote from politics, odd. Not at all how an academic was expected to behave, and certainly not someone they identified with politics. The sabbatical at Yale never happened.

The official inaugural meeting of SMD took place on October 4, coinciding with the first days of opening of schools across the country. Earlier in the summer, Black Friday had signalled the inexorable slide of the regime to all but the blind. We now had official delegates from about 150 universities and colleges. I had been elected to represent the Medical and Dental School with Mani my deputy in a meeting of those who had signed the *manshur*, shyly chaired by my neighbour and paediatrician Qarib. Over 1,200 had signed the Charter across Iran. It was less of a risk to oppose the Shah now.

The whole atmosphere of the inaugural meeting was relaxed. Gone was the cloak and dagger stuff. We were there as ourselves. As we were discussing the credentials of each candidate, there was a commotion when the name of Hassan Āyat came up. He represented the Madreseh Āli Qom (Qom High School). But that is not a proper higher educational institution, some complained. In the end his credentials were approved. He must be someone important, I thought. Āyat, with his face scarred by smallpox, held himself with that particular pomposity of someone who is close to power. I found out how close when after the Revolution I saw his name as a founding member of the Islamic Republic Party (IRP) and editor of its newspaper Jomhuryeh Eslami. The four Pahlavi University delegates[5] persuaded me to stand for office. An Executive Committee of nine was elected, by secret ballot and included me, Abbāspour from *San'ati*, Khoshkhoo also from *San'ati*, Fat'hi from Engineering College, Hassan Qafurifar from Mashhad, and Nāsser Pākdāman, who was officially re-elected to the chair and two others who I cannot recall. In all five members were from the various universities in Tehran and four from other cities. Qafurifar later replaced Abbāspour as Minister of Power when the latter was killed in the explosion in the IRP Headquarters. Āyat received only 2 votes from the 150 or so delegates, presumably his own and his sponsor's. The newly-elected Executive Committee, as a sop to the Islamists, asked Āyat to write the constitution of the SMD. Three years later he was assassinated at home in front of his children, probably by the Mojahedin in August 1981. The constitution was never written as events moved far too rapidly. A month later the SMD moved centre stage at the national level.

[1] In some accounts this has been ascribed to a protest at vice-president Richard Nixon's visit to Iran. However, Nixon arrived in Iran two days later and there was no student protest on the day armed commandos entered Tehran University and shot the three students as they were peacefully leaving the University grounds. See memoirs of Massoud Hejāzi – *ruydādha va dāvariha* - Tehran 1997 (in Farsi).

[2] See Homa Nāteq, Ārash monthly no 104, March 2010 p 106-115 (in Farsi).

[3] Hoveida was executed after the Revolution.

[4] The Islamic Republic Party was created by Khomeini to lead the Islamist half of the Revolution and had at its head his right-hand man Ayatollah Beheshti, the most powerful man in Iran beside Khomeini. He too died in the explosion that racked the IRP headquarters building in June 1981 and killed 74 of its members.

[5] Delegates and their deputies from engineering, literature, agriculture and medicine colleges.

21

Chapter 21

Hafteh hambaste and the final sprint

It was a Thursday in October. The evolving Shirazi autumn was playing through its russet rhapsody, winding down the summer, slow as ever, majestic in its patient tread. Earlier in the month, Khomeini had flown to Paris and reporters from every corner were flocking to interview the old man under the apple tree. Not since Cyprus' Archbishop Makarios had a cleric occupied the centre stage of world politics. Revolution had entered everyday living as if the entire country had been at it since the beginning of time. The country was in a vortex oblivious to the beauty of autumn. Strikes in the huge Isfahan steel complex, the railways, car and tractor factories, customs, port facilities, the judiciary and some banks echoed and conversed with the skirmishes on tarmac, disorienting the regime. The Shah had opened the new session of *Majles* by admitting there had been mistakes. It was to be his last autumn.

Universities too were in turmoil. In Tabriz 8,000 students from the Āzarābādegān University had demonstrated, the Shiraz academic body had written an open letter protesting at the martial law and demanding prosecution of those involved in the street killings, and for freedom for political prisoners. That week there had been major demonstrations in many universities. In Tehran they were joined by thousands of high school students.

Slogans were more radical and included release of political prisoners and demand for a popular democratic republic – showing the influence of the left in universities. Mass meetings were held daily at *Sana'ti, Melli* and other universities. The white-cover books, blank on the outside red on the inside, were openly being sold. For the first time in 35 years Marxist literature was being sold publicly.

It is against this background that the meeting of all the delegates of the *Sāzmāne Melli Dāneshgāhiān* (SMD) took place in Sana'ti that Thursday. Although I was part of a nine-man executive committee, because of distance the five academics in Tehran had been effectively running the association – issuing leaflets, setting up meetings and coordinating with the student body. At least once a month I had flown to Tehran on a Friday to sit on the Committee. We had a few joint meetings with Hassan Āyat's team who were meant to write the constitution - never to be written as events overtook us. But this meeting was to be of the entire representative body across Iran.

In the months since July, almost all institutions of higher education had set up their branches of SMD and elected or appointed delegates. About 80 people gathered on that Thursday, not a woman among them that I can recall. The universities were clearly in turmoil, the old order was crumbling, and the academic body needed to have its own revolutionary agenda. We spent the entire afternoon into the evening deliberating. Idea after idea was tabled, some totally far-fetched and beyond the scope of a group of academics who at the time were clearly in a minority within their own universities and colleges, a mere one in eight in my Medical School. Someone suggested creating a national newspaper, another a coordinated strike of all the universities, a third was for mass demonstrations outside the ministry, or even a sit in – this last rejected at the time was to be taken up later with important consequences.

The sun sank and we were totally exhausted. The smoke-filled room felt more oppressive through our frustration. Anyone having worked in a room filled with tired, frustrated and angry men will recognize that peculiar smell. Pent-up emotions have their own pheromones, no doubt of survival value to the hunter-gatherer. It all seemed futile, and we seemed to be getting nowhere. Here we were, believing ourselves the elected representatives of the 'revolutionary intelligentsia', unable to come up with anything concrete, with any answer that could justify our role among the increasingly revolutionary masses. Many of us did not relish setting off for home late in the night when the military were so unpredictable.

Then a hand went up. It was almost nine o'clock and already dark. A young man stood up and introduced himself as representing Babolsar College – one of the newer universities in Māzandarān Province. He was wearing a grey shirt open at the neck – the sort that became so fashionable among the non-Tudeh left after the Revolution. Why don't we declare a week of solidarity, *hambastegi*, with the revolutionary people of Iran and announce it nationally in the newspapers, he said. The sigh of relief was audible. The smell visibly shrunk back into its pores. Hand after hand went up to support this suggestion, yes, that was within our limited means, the arguments went. The psychology of large meetings is the same the world over. Everyone wants to have their say and add their usually uncooked thoughts. As the entire mass exhaust themselves in suggestions and counter suggestions they become increasingly heavy and sluggish. The pace of the debate grinds down. Some grope around like a slug, others buzz frantically like a trapped fly on a window, desperate to escape. And there comes a moment when any semi-credible thought explodes into general acclaim. Our man from Babolsar had provided that. The lid was off the boiling kettle. Exhausted, we unanimously agreed to the suggestion. The sticky mass suddenly perked up, feeling as light as a feather. I wish I could recall his name.

The Executive Committee – in reality a five-man Tehran body – was appointed to draft something and get it into the papers. The rest of us went home, soaked and enveloped in happy endorphins. The universities of Iran declared their solidarity with the revolutionary people of Iran. This was to be the week of national *hambastegi*, October 28 – November 3. The start date was chosen to avoid the Shah's birthday two days before but to coincide with the anniversary of his 'White Revolution'. Over the next seven days the newspapers were full of factories, offices and institutions declaring their *hambastegi* with the revolutionary people of Iran – and going on strike. Although we had seen mass strikes by blue- and white-collar workers earlier in October, the seeds of a general strike were laid that week. The term *hambastegi* caught on like a fire in a wheat field. It captured the popular zeitgeist. It gave everyone the feeling that they belonged to an entity larger than themselves. In particular, the white-collar workers followed the call of the universities. Government as well as industry came to a standstill. By the end of October there was a general strike. The rhythmic street slogans put it the Iranian way:

Shah bejoz khod koshi, rāhe degar nadārad (the Shah has no choice but commit suicide)

Tehran University and the streets around it became the nerve centre of revolutionary activity that it was not to lose even after the Revolution when it became a battle ground between the radical forces in the country and the *hezbollāh*. Khomeini shrewdly hijacked Tehran University and made it the venue of Friday prayers – and appointed the most popular cleric, ayatollah Taleqāni, an ex-prisoner of the Shah, as its first Friday prayer cleric. But not until the blood-soaked Cultural Revolution was that arena cleared of radical revolutionaries. Tehran University, and to a lesser extent all the others, became the battleground for the soul of the Revolution. But of that later.

In a small but decisive way the idea of declaring solidarity with the Revolution had caught the imagination of the nation. That week became a turning point. From then onwards strikes dominated the revolutionary stage. And their demands became increasingly political - from less than half in October to almost unanimous by the end of November.[1] The Revolution moved from the streets, where a stalemate reigned, to the factories and offices. Although street demonstrations and shootings continued, it was the general strike that ultimately broke the back of the regime. In a rentier state relying on oil rather than taxation to run its affairs, the closure of public services and petrol pumps hurts the state much more deeply than strikes in the manufacturing sector, a point the current opposition in Iran has yet to learn. That week, the army occupied the Abadan oil refinery – the same refinery Bāzargān had taken from the British on Mosaddeq's orders a quarter of a century before. It was symbolic of the beginning of the end. There is no doubt in my mind that the general strike ensured the ultimate collapse of the Shah.[2] The streets challenged the political legitimacy of the regime while the general strike destroyed its economic legitimacy. They essentially buried a regime which was already half dead.

The fact that I was there to witness the end was fortuitous. I had a scientific paper accepted at an endocrine conference in India and J and I were both excited to visit that country for the first time. Like most middle class Iranians, we had always faced West and this was a unique opportunity to turn the other way. Then the SMD meeting came up and after some heart searching, we both decided that we could not desert our posts at such a crucial time. I cancelled my ticket and lost the conference fee. The following week the airports were closed and remained more or less closed to international flights until the fall of the regime. I would have been marooned, an observer from afar to some of the most exciting months of my life.

[1] See Assef Bayāt. *Workers and Revolution in Iran*. Z Books, 1987.

[2] A number of other commentators have made a similar point. See Abrahamian E, *Iran Between Two Revolutions*, Halliday F, *Iran: Dictatorship and Development,* Hero D, *Iran under the Ayatollahs*, 1988

Chapter 22

Go martyr yourself!

Back in Shiraz we organized a series of meetings, but faced a sceptical student body, both Islamic and left. Even though the SMD had lit the match that led to the end of the regime, then and even now, their role was unappreciated. Ali Shariatmadāri, an academic from Isfahan,[1] was invited to speak on one of the first meetings held in the College of Literature on behalf of SMD. In a meandering speech on the role of intellectuals he went on to define freedom in Islam. Despite his conciliatory speech, he was mercilessly heckled and verbally mauled by the students. During question time Mrs Alizādeh, an academic who later represented the *hezbollāh*[2] in the second University *Shora* (council) stood up. 'Mr Shariatmadāri' she began sarcastically, "you said that if the professors were late in joining [the Revolution] so had the Prophet's companion, Horr.[3] But then Horr went on to be martyred. When are you having your martyrdom?" The entire hall burst out laughing. It was not easy to sell the revolutionary credentials of a faculty which had been seen as agents of the monarchy for a quarter of a century. Two years later, Shariatmadāri would make Mrs Alizādeh proud when he emerged as a prominent member of the 'Cultural Revolution' that viciously closed the universities and summarily purged the faculty, me included.

CHAPTER 22

In the margins of Shariatmadāri's talk there was a young man wearing a brown leather jacket who had been scurrying around us in Sa'di. He showed himself interested in the Revolution but what were his links to the University? He was neither student, employee nor faculty. He looked suspicious. Azādeh, the one man with muscles among us, took him aside and threatened to beat him up if he didn't leave. Later I heard that he was shot dead in the demonstrations in Mollā Sadrā Street sometime in December. Was he a SAVAK agent? Who knows.

For our own introductory meeting in the Medical School, we chose the large hall, which then called Tālār Ashraf after the Shah's twin sister and renamed by us Tālār Mosaddeq (Mossadeq Hall). It was to be a question-and-answer session. I took the chair flanked by Ronaqi, a professor in the College of Agriculture who after the Revolution, with another faculty member, went on to draft the blueprint for reorganizing Tehran's disastrous traffic. One after another students stood up to attack the academic staff for being agents of the Shah, of imperialism, of corruption, of hedonism - of all that was hated. Hands went up and verbal stones continued to rain down on us on the platform. How dare we jump on the revolutionary bandwagon at this late stage? My inability to adequately respond to confrontations, my deep innate shyness, had handicapped me all my life, including interviews. I did my best to defend the role that radical faculty members can assume in the Revolution both inside and outside the University. It was a feeble effort, not helped by my co-chairs' cringingly apologetic interjections. It was not to be the last time I failed miserably in arguing a conviction when under pressure. The pelting continued, with occasional breaks such as when a female student gave a very clear and eloquent defence of the left. A young man in a white shirt with blue eyes stood up after her, the same blue-eyed angel face who had wrenched the microphone from Azādeh on our first public meeting earlier in the year. Having impaled the left and promising a return to 'true Islam' he delivered a devastating attack on the usurpers, meaning us, who are trying to surf a victorious revolutionary tide and corrupting it from the inside. "You are absolutely right. We are always behind and are still behind, and yes, we have been a tool in the hands of the Shah", my co-chair began in a pleading voice, "but we are ready to learn and so please accept us in your ranks..." He was not allowed to finish.

From the back of the hall Mostafa, stood up. Light skinned, brown hair and light brown eyes, this tall balding man could have passed as a European visiting professor. He was a close relative to Khomeini's wife, Batool, and had been active in the Confederation of Iranian Students abroad. He walked up to the front, in a slow deliberate pace, as if he was formulating the argument in his head. It was one of the most beautifully constructed and delivered speeches I have heard. He began quietly expounding the role of classes and the place of intellectuals in formulating trajectories that I later discovered in Gramsci. He recounted the role of Iranian academics in opposition to the Shah, despotism and foreign domination over the last one hundred years, floated through the key role of the Confederation in keeping up opposition to the Shah and mobilizing international opinion against his regime and reminded the audience how many of the faculty here and elsewhere had been active in it. He went on to list the academic staff who had lost their lives, or languished in the Shah's prisons. In a quite voice, but with carefully structured sentences, with words that shot out like arrows from Mongol horsemen, he rounded on the attackers. What were they, and many of the new leaders on the streets today, doing when the road was being paved for them, in blood and pain? Far from being newcomers to the field, he was talking of the veterans of the struggle. Pioneers. In ten minutes, he had changed the entire tone of the hall. It was a masterly show of control, and the ability of words and language to form views. The SMD had little trouble with the student body after that and the meetings it went on to organise were brimming with the young.

Thereafter, despite misgivings and antagonisms, some *hezbollāhi* students helped us stick up our placards. The lines had not yet been fully drawn. But as the weeks went by the balance of power in the city and the country finally turned against the secular half. The mosque had finally saddled the Revolution. It became more and more difficult to put up SMD leaflets, or distribute them, since with the exception of one delegate, Kāzem Sadr, the others refused to put 'in the name of Allah' on the top. The SMD became somewhat marginal in Shiraz, but not in Tehran. But the Medical School kept its central role in Shiraz. One day the angel-face with blue eyes cornered me in the corridor of Sa'di and warned me that the road I was following was perilous. We will take over this country in the end and establish true Islam. We will smash the likes of you. So, change your ways before it is too late. He was a Sunni. I saw death in his eyes and I shivered momentarily inside. Then forgot. I wonder what came of him – Sunnis did not do well in Shi'a Iran.

On the last day of the week of *hambastegi* there was huge gathering on the Tehran University campus attended by thousands of high-school students. The army shot dead a number of high school boys in a running battle in front of the main gate of the University. For the first time television cameras broadcast the killing live to the nation. The massacre of its children was watched by the entire population and the country erupted. It was another turning point. The next day the Shah removed Prime Minister Sharif Emami, who had followed Amuzgār, and the new military government declared martial law. The universities were closed en masse. The week of *hambastegi* had ended in the blood of its school kids shed by the gates of the mother of universities, the pride of Reza Shah, and almost the entire country had said no to his ailing weak-willed son.

[1] Shariatmaāri had originally taught in Shiraz but at the time had transferred to the University of Isfahan. After the revolution he became minister of higher education for a time before joining the Higher Cultural Committee that oversaw the purge of universities of Leftists and others – an ironic twist.

[2] Literally 'party of God' – the self-proclaimed name for supporters of Khomeini to be distinguished from the Hezbollah Party in Lebanon. After the Revolution the secular opposition used it pejoratively.

[3] One of Mohammad's early followers, a freed slave, who was later killed in battle.

23

Chapter 23

The fat man

The invitation came from the University. It was in protest at the military attacks on Sa'di, and in particular, at the entry of troops into the wards and the tear gassing of patients.[1] The day before, the world had seen the massacre of schoolboys in front of Tehran University on television. Here in Shiraz, someone or some group must have made the decision to demonstrate from the Medical School. But like everything that happened in those days, events have their own life. Just as our plan for a meeting metamorphosed into an anti-communist tirade without any obvious stimulus, the invitation by the Medical School to lead a demonstration into town became transmutated into something quite different. A mass movement has its own life, its own momentum. It is a living organism totally different, detached, from the individuals that make it up.

Shiraz is a city of roundabouts – *falakeh*, pronounced *felkeh*. The easy-going Shirazis clearly had little room for the autocratic red-green signals. The Medical School and next to it the Sa'di hospital were situated on Zand avenue, the city's main artery. Turn right from the medical school main gate and at the end of the avenue was a *falakeh* leading to the main gate of the Namāzi hospital and orchard (*bāq*), our home. Turn left and you come within

CHAPTER 23

a few hundred metres to Falakeh Setād where the offices of the municipal council and provincial government were situated. Beyond the Falakeh, walk down Zand Avenue along its left pavement and on the way to the main shopping centre you pass the British Consul whose chalked-white walls were not stained by urine, unlike the embassy in Tehran, and a bookshop selling both Farsi and English language books. Across the road you saw the SAVAK's headquarters and a cinema which once a week used to show films in their original language. Halfway down Zand, the busy shopping street, Dariush [now Towhid] turns off south at a cross-roads known locally as *Kal-e Moshir*. Walk further along Zand and you will see the old fort (Arg Karimkhani) – at the time a municipal jail. This was to witness the last, and most bloody, drama of the Revolution.

On that the same side as SAVAK and the cinema, and before you came to Dariush, was Mr Belādi's tiny bookshop. You walked into his poorly lit shop and books lined the walls up to the ceiling on either side of a narrow central corridor leading into an even darker recess and to stairs going up to where Belādi himself, by then a thin old man with a moustache, often retreated to read. The entire intellectual life of Shiraz owed itself to Belādi, a baker's son, who introduced hundreds of young boys and girls to poetry, literature, and more. Even today old Shirāzis talk fondly of the old man, who was their conduit to thinking and reason, to knowledge and awareness. The blood of Belādi ran through the intellectual life of Shiraz nourishing two or three generations. A legend.

On the island at the centre of the Falakeh Setād, a stone throw from Sa'di, stood the statue of the Shah – looking imperiously down Zand, his back turned away from the Medical School, and Namazi hospital. It was a tempting target. Already in many towns his statues had been torn down. It was rumoured that the Isfahanis had sent Shiraz a female bra as a typically Isfahani way of telling us we are chicken. The night before a number of us decided we will pull down the statue. It was so tantalizingly close and had turned its back to us.

It was a beautiful clear autumn morning in the month of Aban (November 5, 1978). The medics gathered inside the Medical School grounds. The Cinema

Rex affair had occurred in August and further discredited the monarchical state. A fire had started in a cinema in Abadan and over 600 people had burnt to death, unable to get out of the locked fire exit doors. At the time everyone blamed the regime. Some of us had our doubts, as the Islamists hated the cinema as a cause of corruption and had already burnt the only cinema in Qom. Our suspicion was later confirmed. The enormity of the tragedy of Cinema Rex drew a much wider circle of people into the revolutionary orbit. Since then, we had witnessed Black Friday and then almost daily events somewhere in the country, culminating in the general strike of the *hafteh hambastegi* the previous week. The presence of riot troops on the hospital wards was the final straw for our Medical School.

At the head of our demonstration was a line of senior doctors mostly from the Department of Medicine. Among them was the Dean, Khosrow Nasr, in his white coat, all 120 kilograms of him. Behind them was most of the medical staff, all dressed in their white coats and many nurses, all in uniform, behind them the technicians in the Blood Transfusion Centre, also in white laboratory coats, led by J. This is the origin of the myth of the 'fat doctor'; you will still find taxi drivers in Shiraz telling this story to whoever wants to listen: "We did not know what was happening but when we saw that fat doctor in front, and all the others in their white coats. We thought he must know something. So, we followed him. And this is the mess they led us into."

This was to be a Medical School demonstration to march the few hundred metres to Falakeh Setād and stop in front the municipality offices. And secretly some of us hoped to tear that eye-sore statue down. The Medical School was going to show the *Isfahanis*. Once we got out of the main gate there were hundreds of people waiting outside. Soon tens of thousands had massed behind the uniformed staff. From that front row we could see people as far back along Zand Avenue towards Namāzi until it melted into the trees of the Namāzi Compound. We were met by a row of troops, gas masked and G3 machine guns on the ready.

Blocking our way into the Falakeh was a *sargord* (lieutenant). He was rather dark skinned and was wearing sunglasses that did not hide his eyes. I went up to him with a couple of students and doctors. Please go back, he said

CHAPTER 23

shyly, politely. It was not an order and his tone surprised me. He looked distinctly unhappy. "I have orders to stop you" he said in a quite voice. Did it quiver with emotion? The eyes visible behind the sunglasses were pleading. I thought I saw a film of water. He was clearly in a quandary. "I do not want to do it", his body language, sympathetic, spoke. I have always wondered what happened to him afterwards. Which faction did he ultimately join? Was he part of the army that attacked Kurdistan in 1979? Did he go to the Iran-Iraq war? Is he still alive? If he is where are his sympathies? Does he regret the Revolution as many do now?

But retreat was a physical impossibility. The row of soldiers with machine guns pointing at the blue sky above their left shoulder, the *sargord* not very effectively hiding behind his dark glasses, the white coats facing them, and that fat man about to enter local history were like brick walls trying to hold back an overflowing dam. The sheer mass in front and behind took away any need for a decision. One or two hours passed. There was a standoff at the entrance of the *Falakeh*. The bronze Shah still looked across Zand on his frozen horse, his back to us, taunting, tempting, so close.

Then suddenly tanks appeared from the other side of the roundabout. Tanks were something we had not seen before on the streets. Rumours began to spread – there has been a coup. Some were even suggesting that the Shah had been removed. Very soon it became clear that the Shah had removed the Prime Minister Sharif Emāmi, who with his clerical family background had been his hope of dampening down the revolutionary tide. Chief of General Staff, General Azhāhri, was appointed and he had declared martial law in all the major towns, including Tehran, Qom, Tabriz, Isfahan and Shiraz. The tanks moved forward and shooed us through the medical school gates. The massive crowd melted into the side streets. We withdrew into the courtyard and closed the metal gates.

There were about a couple of hundred or so persons gathered around the steps to the medical school. About half were from the town. Almost all were young – there were a few academics left – mostly from the other colleges. Virtually all were male. The white-coated professors in the front row too had melted away. There was an atmosphere of apprehension. We had entered a new phase. Martial law had been declared and the Shah had clearly given up on trying to mollify the crowd and had returned to the whip. The crowd inside the medical school grounds looked lost and it was unclear what to do. People started to discuss in groups. Someone, I cannot remember who, got up on the steps and addressed the crowd.

Let's elect a leader, he said in a loud voice; I suggest... and he named me. There were murmurs and shouts of approval. Someone said we can't call him by that name it has echoes of the Shah. Someone else shouted out a name that had echoes of happiness (*Shad*). More approval. I walked to the front, my innate shyness and my sense of responsibility face to face in a duel and tried to lead a discussion as to what to do. This was my first taste of leadership. I was a novice, and quickly showed it. Hand after hand went up. We should march into town. We should make a sit-in (*tahasson*) here. We should get help from the clergy. We should ask the tribal school for help. Most were repetitive. There was the usual rhetorical denunciation of the Shah and the military.

Time went by – perhaps half an hour went on like this and there were a least 10 to 15 hands up asking for time to speak. People were beginning to drift away. The momentum was being lost. Bahar, a US trained pathologist in an elegant dark blue checkered shirt, whispered in my ear that if I continue in this vein the group will evaporate. Why don't I call for people to elect representatives to make the decision on their behalf? I put this to a vote and got a unanimous yes. Five or six men came up as representatives. They were clearly self-selected. But then I too had been chosen by acclamation. I was their leader, I had to follow them;[2] "are you happy for this lot to represent you?" I asked the crowd. No one dissented.

Someone whispered that one young man is a SAVAK spy. Who knows? I threw him out. Within a few minutes the representatives agreed that we will take refuge overnight in the University. I called on those present to go home and bring back food and blankets. We will meet up in an hour – it was getting late and dusk was approaching. We had protested all day. The group, which had already become sparser, dispersed. About ten or fifteen of us were left on the stairs which led up to the large lecture theatre, the Mosaddeq Hall to us, where we planned to spend the night. I was just thinking of how I was going to get news home asking for a blanket when the iron gates of the Medical School courtyard burst open. About twenty paratroopers in full riot gear and wielding machine guns burst in. Everyone around me fled up the stairs into the School. For some reason that I cannot explain I decided to hold my ground and see what happened. Maybe the leadership issue had gone to my head. It was an instant decision and I squatted down on my haunches, still clothed in a white coat. Two columns of armed ninjas ran towards me and then parted and ran up the stairs on either side of me. It was as if they had not seen me although they could not have missed the solitary white coat in a squat. I got up after the last one had run into the School and started wandering about, somewhat dazed and a little amazed at my audacity. Maybe it was the white coat effect, I thought. A few minutes later, it was almost dark now, I saw a soldier emerge from behind a bush dragging a frightened young man and pulling him out towards the gate, repeatedly cuffing him hard behind the ears. "Leave him alone" I shouted at the soldier "I am a doctor and a professor". To my amazement, he did, and walked away sheepishly. The boy ran back into Sa'di hospital. This was my second encounter that day with an army that had lost its nerve.

[1] See Chapter 18, Sa'di Hospital under attack above

[2] Quoting Alexandre Ledru-Rolin one of the radical leaders in the Paris Revolution of 1848.

Chapter 24

The iron gate

As I write these lines, images of youth being chased in the streets of Tehran with baton wielding men in riot gear are being regularly broadcast on the internet.[1] It is like a hallucinatory dream played again after over thirty years. A blind loop of the nay-sayers battering their bare flesh against the battlements of state. The regime is very different, but the boys and girls seem to have been frozen in time. Admittedly, more heads are covered today, and the colours lean towards the sombre – black, brown and dark blue. And there are more women in the street battles – in those days women were there in their thousands on street demonstrations, but fighting the army was a much more male affair. Yet images of smashed up dormitories, the targeting of the universities and the undimmed passion of the young for freedom seem to have been frozen over an Iranian plateau for over 30 years.

Foraying out through the iron gates, goading the military, masked like aliens behind their gas masks and shields. Some are throwing stones. Tyres are burning in the street. Then the counter-attack, tear gas canisters, and a quick retreat behind University walls. The iron gates are quickly shut behind the students. There is a metal barrier separating the students and the might of the state, but also a more profound barrier. To attack a university is to attack sacred ground – not unlike an attack on a mosque. The Shah's troops took some time before crossing that red line. It took the Islamic regime's Basij militia no time at all. That is the ultimate difference between a conscript army and an ideological force that is the Basij and Revolutionary Guards. I was to learn that, face to face, a couple of years later. But tonight, the images are transposed thirty years forward. Einstein's space-time really did travel in a loop coming almost full circle.

It was another early evening. The town was in darkness. We were told that the electricity workers were on strike every evening. Even then it seemed to me that with martial law in force the blackout must have had military clearance. A group of us had gathered outside the medical school gate shouting slogans – *'begoo marg bar Shah!'* A tyre was found from god-knows where and was burning in the middle of Zand Avenue. There were no garages nearby, and we were in a very clean, middle class, part of town. No shops, no rubbish dump. Just a tree-lined wide avenue whose central flower bed had been kept watered and pruned even as tear gas and stones flew. Opposite there was the tribal school, Madreseh Ashāyery, among the Shah's efforts to placate the powerful tribes in Fars, with a long history of opposition to central government. The various tribes scattered among virtually all the provinces of the country, and many of non-Fars ethnicity[2] had played a significant role in modern Iranian politics since the Constitutional Revolution of 1906. The last tribal revolt against the Shah in Fars province had been brutally put down by his army. Some of the leaders had been bribed, other cowed by massive use of force, including bombing by jets, and the last remaining rebel, Bahman Qashqai', was lured on a false amnesty and executed, as I have already described.

Since then, the Shah made several efforts to find a final solution to the tribal threat. One arm of this policy was to settle the nomadic Qashqai' and other tribes. The other was to create an educated elite that would be more sympathetic to the Shah's project for Iran. The tribal school was built on this premise, to provide high school education for that elite. It employed some of the best teachers in Shiraz and was considered one of its finest schools.

It was from the roof of this school that the sons of the elite Qashqai', using *falākhuns* (slings) which they swung round their heads flinging stones with deadly accuracy several hundred metres away on the heads of the hooded armed soldiers below on Zand Avenue. Very Biblical.

So it was that early evening, we, shouting slogans from the street, and tribal students swinging their *falākhuns* from their roof. Showering the street with slogans and deadly stones. It was David and Goliath re-enacted on concrete. The blackout had just started and the only light on the street was that of the burning tyre letting off its acrid fumes that wafted over the walls into Sa'di. There were times that we forgot we were looking after hundreds of very sick people, many from the surrounding villages, and not always sympathetic to the Revolution. Or even understanding what was going on. This was a particularly urban revolution, with that particular urban disregard of the rural backwaters.

Suddenly a troop of soldiers, machine guns in hand, attacked us. I was with a small crowd of mostly students and junior doctors shouting slogans outside the medical school walls. We ran as fast as we could through the open gate. I saw someone, a bearded fifth-year student named Faqihi, closing the iron gates behind us. I looked round and only a handful had managed to flee into the sanctuary. "Many of the *bacheha*, are still outside. Open the gate and let them in" I shouted to him in panic, referring to the 'children', a friendly way of talking about students and young doctors. "Let them become martyrs" he replied in a calm voice, as if he was talking about a patient "it is good for the Revolution".[3] I pushed him aside, opened the gate and let in about a dozen terrified students and doctors, some of whom had been badly beaten.

That was my first face-to-face glimpse into the Islamist mind. It was that evening that I understood the rumours circulating that the Islamists themselves had locked the exit doors to Cinema Rex in Abadan that had burned down, immolating over 600 people back in August.[4] The Khomeini camp blamed the Shah, although none of us saw what advantage it could have had for the monarch. At one sweep the Islamists had smeared the Shah and given martyrs to the Revolution, martyrs that were in any case expendable as they were sinfully watching a movie. And earlier in the Revolution they had

CHAPTER 24

already burnt down the sole cinema in the 'holy city of Qom' and were later to burn down cinemas in many towns including Shiraz. Faqihi was quite happy to expend his friends and classmates. To kill sinners and score for the Islamic Revolution was an act of genius that only they could invent. And friends? Well if they are 'pure' they will become martyrs and fly to heaven without having to wait for the day of judgment. That too was 'good for the Revolution'; theirs, not ours. We already had two revolutions and one was to devour the other.

Three and a half years later, in the summer of 1981 Faqihi, now a surgical resident in the newly established Islamic Republic and an important figure in the University, took the Revolutionary Guards to the operating theatre to arrest a Mojahedin sympathiser wounded in the chest in a street battle. The boy was anaesthetised on the operating table when they whisked him away. I was taken to see this boy, he could have been no more than 17, in the infirmary of the Third Army detention centre, where all political prisoners were brought for interrogation by the *Pāsdārān* (Revolutionary Guards). He had a chest drain. He had lost a lot of blood and his wound was infected. Even through his fever and intense pain he managed a smile. His chest tube was draining a dirty blood-stained fluid and the site where the drain was inserted into his right chest was red, inflamed and obviously very painful. He winced when I adjusted his drain but immediately reverted to a smile. I prescribed an antibiotic and paracetamol, the strongest pain killer they had. He smiled back and thanked me, a fellow prisoner, and murmured something about telling his family that he is well. He was executed a few days later with the drain presumably in place. I don't know his name.

A month later a suicide bomber from the Mojahedin blew herself up, killing Faqihi. Sa'di hospital is to this day named Faqihi Hospital.

[1] Summer 2010.

[2] During the Safavid dynasty (1501-1732), themselves Turks, many Turkish speaking tribes, were settled around the borders of the country as a defence against foreign invasion. The main tribes in Fars are the Turkish speaking Qashqāi', the Lur-speaking Boir-Ahmadi and some smaller Arabic-

speaking tribes.

[3] *begozār shahid shan. baraye enqelab khoobeh.*
[4] See footnote 5, chapter *17, Revolutionary tide.*

25

Chapter 25

Rainbows over chaos

It was a beautiful mid November morning. The sky over Shiraz was its usual iridescent blue. Life went on. I was doing rounds in the field hospital (Bimārestāne Sahrāi'). My resident was one of those incompetent but overconfident nightmares. Scrawny with a black beard, Habib Mostafavi was a Khomeini devotee who went on to become head of the Department of Medicine in Isfahan University. As luck would have it my intern too was particularly bad, not just because he didn't know anything, and lacked rudimentary clinical skills, but also because he lied. He lied with his eyes open looking straight into mine. Any information he produced, I had to double check. It was my misfortune that almost all the religious students that directly worked with me that year were next to useless. While there were many very devout students who were outstanding, in my experience bad students were more likely to be religious than secular. There was a material basis for this – the language of tuition at Pahlavi was English, which middle class secular students were more likely to be acquainted with. Many went to schools with good English teaching. Some had spent some years abroad with their parents. Others would have American friends or relatives. Those coming from traditional backgrounds were severely disadvantaged. Be that as it may, I had a very difficult time that autumn on the wards.

I too was handicapped. I was still suffering from my narrow medical education in the UK. Most of the conditions we saw in Iran were new to me. Three years of laboratory research in Bristol had eroded my clinical skills still further. I had had to re-educate myself, and in the case of infectious diseases, almost from scratch. Tuberculosis, Typhoid and other infectious diseases, with cirrhosis of the liver, filled up two thirds of the beds. There was a sprinkling of Malaria and Brucellosis, the same disease known colloquially as Malta fever, which had nearly taken my father away for good, and instead took him away to Belgium for a year. To my surprise, we also saw many cases of Chronic Bronchitis and Emphysema (Chronic Obstructive Pulmonary Disease - COPD) that I had been taught was the 'English disease'. I felt at home there. Most Iranians smoked and had been smoking at least since the 16th Century and Safavid times. No doubt the smoke-filled rooms of peasant houses, where the open fire was lit in the middle of the living quarters contributed. And then there was Tetanus and Anthrax. Memories of the excruciatingly painful muscle spasms of patients with Tetanus brought on by the slightest sound or movement, so easily preventable by vaccination, the gross swelling of limbs and face near the site of entry of Anthrax spores or of snake bite with its combination of massive swelling and intense inflammation are indelibly imprinted in my inner archive of images.

At night the lights went out at 9 o'clock. We were told it was due to the electricity workers going on strike, but I found that difficult to believe as it began earlier on in the year, way before the general strike. I suspect the regime preferred the blackout as it pushed people into their homes and made it easier to control the streets at night. Was the curfew in Shiraz just an empty threat? I was never stopped on a trip to the wards during the hours of curfew. The one time we met the military commander General Esfandiāri after the arrest of Mohammad Javād Bāhonar, a guest of the Agricultural College, he was surprisingly accommodating. Maybe he was a secret sympathiser.

One night, when I was on emergency call, a girl was brought from a village near Mamasani, the Boir Ahmadi tribal area. She had just given birth. As was traditional practice they had tried to stop the post partum haemorrhage with cow dung. She was burning with fever. The womb had become infected and we immediately started antibiotics. Half an hour later one of the emergency room interns ran up to me as I was doing my late night round sorting out potential problems that may arise overnight. That was my custom when on call. It helped assure an uninterrupted night, but also drew you closer to the junior staff. He had felt some crepitations, as if she had bubbles under the skin of her groin. The girl had gas gangrene.

When we asked for a blood count, the normally yellow-brown fluid from the blood sample, the serum part once the red cells had been spun down, was deep red. Transparent, like wine. The toxins from the Clostridium[1] were liquefying her red blood cells and liquefied blood cells were of no use for carrying oxygen. Her blood was disappearing within her blood vessels. She was effectively bleeding without a drop of blood being shed. The only way to save her was to remove the toxin by cutting out her womb immediately, but we had to get permission as she was delirious. We had to act fast, and I begged the gynaecological resident on call to just go ahead and do it and we will deal with the permission later. To my surprise he agreed but as she was being wheeled to the operating theatre she died. Perhaps that was all for the best because without a womb she would be discarded by her in-laws and would be returned to her family in disgrace. She was perhaps 17.

'They threw us out' Nezām had said. We were sitting together over a cup of *chai* on our veranda. Nezām, about 22 and already beginning to go bald, was Mani's younger brother and like him had been active in the US with the Confederation of Iranian students. But he belonged to a totally different faction. He was a Maoist. It was not uncommon for brothers to choose different organisations. After the Revolution Bahrām took us to a large country house with a huge garden in Estahbānāt for a day's outing. It was a beautiful old house with a flat roof that was like a veranda, belonging to a land-owning family. While my daughters, Maryam and Nargess, waded in the fast flowing ice-cold, crystal clear water carried in a subterranean *qanāt* all the way from the hills, our host, a handsome young man, told us while sipping illicit *araq* on the roof that each of his five brothers belonged to a different oppositional organisation spanning the Left and the Mojahedin.

More commonly an elder, or charismatic family member, drew many of his or her relatives to the same organisation. Many of the organisations that mushroomed after the Revolution appeared at first sight, and before they expanded into the population, like a mini family gathering. Maybe Mani was not charismatic enough. Nezām and his group, the Ettehādieh Communist-hā (Communist Union) had arrived straight from the US to go to Tabas where a recent earthquake had devastated this small town on the edge of the central Kavir desert.[2] That was the time when some people miraculously saw Khomeini's face in the moon. When, a few days later, the locals found Nezām's colleagues bending up and down, going through the motions of prayer inside their tents they chased them away over the hill. They were praying with their shoes on. The Student left arriving from abroad had met real life in Iran and had little idea how it worked. Another day, sitting in Mani's room Nezām told me a story that explained why. Back in Michigan Nezām had developed a badly infected foot. The group refused to let him go to hospital. Peasants in Iran have no access to hospitals, he was told. When pus began to pour from the ankle Mani eventually persuaded his brother to go to hospital. Next day the comrades 'raided' the ward, stole him and took him back to their shared apartment. The foot took its Michigan-peasant origin seriously and miraculously survived. I was to meet such weird justifications on a more personal level.

Immediately after the Black September[3] massacre in Jaleh Square, Tehran oil refinery workers went on strike, alongside the Bank Melli employees after the National Bank had leaked news of massive transfer of money abroad by key personages in the regime. Years later I met one of those who had leaked the news. He became a friend and clearly had sympathies with the Jebhe Melli (National Front). Two weeks later workers from the Abadan oil refinery, Ahwāz and the Gachsārān and Āqājāri oil fields, joined the strike. The earthquake in Tabas and the mass immolation in Cinema Rex had helped unnerve the regime. The strikers created a strike committee and everywhere sympathy for them was immense. Our tiny underground group decided to

CHAPTER 25

collect for the strike fund. It was almost entirely left to me, as I had a lot of goodwill among the faculty at the Medical School some of whom had signed the SMD charter. Others saw me as that slightly eccentric, but essentially benign young man who spoke English with a strange accent. In a few days I had collected 40 thousand tomans, around 7,000 dollars at the exchange rate of the time. It was not easy and time and again I had to assure the donors that I had a secure channel to the strikers. In that world in flux, you took things on trust. You looked for reassurance from a look, a twinkle, a smile that does not hide deceit. You just trusted your instincts.

But I had no channels to the strikers. I had faked the assurance, and my smile only came over as genuine because I was convinced that I would find a way. I turned to Said, a Left-leaning student who had studied in the US. He belonged to that broad range of anti-Russian left – Maoists of various hues. After the Revolution they gave birth to at least five tiny, three middling-sized, and one large nationwide Maoist, and one truly mass-popular Kurdish organisation, *Kumeleh* (see Appendix 2). He knew someone, he said, who was in touch with the strike committee. I trusted his eyes. And his confident smile. Could he bring back some written receipt? I needed to insure my previous smiles retrospectively. There was something dishonest in that chain of smiles. Later that week I called on Said. The money had gone through he said beneath the same assured eyes, but for 'obvious' reasons they could not give written confirmation. Then an uncomfortable smile flitted across his eyes, and I felt betrayed. The chain of smiles was an artifice. My second betrayal of trust. I was never to trust on trust alone again.

In mid October, oil workers went on strike again, joining workers from steel, railways, mines, customs, tractor and car plants, most major factories, offices, judiciary, and finally newspapers. This was to lead to a total standstill of the economy by the end of the month in the 'week of solidarity' that only ended with the end of the regime. But oil was the lifeline of the country and troops attacked the strikers and arrested over 70. Our tiny group of academics went to work collecting again. In the three weeks after the previous collection the public mood had been transformed. I had absolutely no difficulty in collecting 200,000 tomans in a few days – this time as open representative of the SMD. That was a large sum of money. And this time I gave it to Sādeqi, a paediatrician with whom I had developed a close working relationship through the SMD, who in turn passed it on to the strikers' representative in front of ayatollah Dastqeib. I felt a little uneasy again as I did not trust the mullahs, but at least the worker's representatives were there and received the money directly.

She too was perhaps 17, beautiful with large blue eyes, recently married. From a tribe around Mamasani wearing her pink, orange and red tribal dress. A combination of colours that appear terrible in abstract but so beautiful in real life. The natural colour sense, untainted by fashion, which I have seen in tribal communities in Burma, India and Iran is explosive in the way clashing colours are made to harmonise. Artists like Van Gogh, Gaugin, Kandinsky, Kirchner, Delauney, van Donegan and others have also liberated colour from the constraints of 'taste'. But the *Qashqāi'* carpet, the one the girl especially made for her dowry, with all the love and care and colour and hope of the young girl entangled in its fabric, is perfection in its emotional abandon.

She sat, sad, anxious, bewildered, bypassed by the ward traffic. Under our very noses her toes and later her fingers were going black and gangrenous over a period of a few days. We could not make a definitive diagnosis, and although we thought she had some kind of vasculitis, inflammation of blood vessels, often part of a more generalised inflammatory condition, she did not respond to the only treatment we had, steroids. Her newlywed husband was constantly at her side. They seemed so in love, but as the weeks went by and she went on to lose her toes and one or two fingers, his ardour visibly cooled. In the end she was left with no visitors. I can still see her blue eyes pleading with us. She was a Qashqai' or Boir Ahmadi and could not communicate in Farsi. She was discharged home to die, rejected for her imperfections.

And so life went on. I even continued to do my research and ran the research laboratory in the basement of Namāzi. But then one day, right at the end when the University was on autopilot, I saw a man replacing a broken window. There was no one to tell him to repair the window. He just did. Real life went

CHAPTER 25

on, arched like a rainbow, above the deaths and chaos of that other life on the streets. I too had witnessed blossoms die before flowering and the death of trust. Another step in growing up. I had one foot in academia and one in revolution. One foot at the bedside and one on the streets. I was 36.

[1] *Clostridium welshii* is the organism causing gas gangrene. It causes gas which can be felt like bubbles under the skin and also a toxin that brakes up red blood cells.

[2] The Tabas earthquake occurred on September 16, 1977 one week after Black Friday. Many took the death of thousands of innocent men, women and children as an omen for victory in the mysterious ways that, in times of social turmoil, things take on symbolic meaning. Years later the Burmese people blamed the deaths of hundreds of thousands of peasants in floods to the killing of monks at the hands of the military junta, none of whom were even remotely touched by the aqueous wrath.

[3] Black Friday, and the massacre in Jaleh square, September 8, 1978. See Chapter 17, *Revolutionary Tide*.

Chapter 26

Masjed Habib

The sky over Shiraz had that luminosity that defines that city of poets. The clear morning light penetrated the skin making it transparent. It was *Eid Qadir*, a special date for the Shi'a when the Prophet Mohammad is supposed to have raised his cousin and son-in-law Ali on his shoulders on the oasis of Qadir al-Khumm on his return to Medina and proclaimed, "whoever has me as his patron (*mowlā*) has Ali as his patron". Here lies the fundamental difference with Sunni Islam and the reason for its first great schism. To commemorate the day the Shah released 210 prisoners. The University had invited the town people to gather in Habib Mosque, Masjed Habib. As usual it was unclear to me who had initiated the invitation. Later, ayatollah Malek Hosseini, a prominent cleric from Yāsuj claimed to have put out the original invitation, jointly with Mostafā Ayatollahi from the University and his brother Ali from the radical Masjed Ātashihā (Qobad), where the young Islamist revolutionaries around hojjatoleslam Abol-Hassan Dastqeib were active. It was thus a joint invitation – an early realisation of Khomeini's dream – unity of the university and the mosque.

I thought that Mohsen was in some way involved as he had close links with the young revolutionaries around the Ātashihā mosque and held regular

CHAPTER 26

teaching sessions in a *Hosseineh*. I had once attended one of these very early one morning. They all sat, eight to ten semi bearded young men, while Mohsen talked to them. What the topic was I cannot recall, but whatever it was they sat spellbound. Mohsen spun words into magical images. His talks were as colourful and as fantastic as Chagal's paintings and sometimes almost as naïve. Philosophical and psychological themes seemed to float out of the narrative into vivid, colourful and sometimes comical imagery. He would later hold similar tutorials in prison, enthralling the imprisoned students, and the thieves and drug dealers equally.

We left together in one car trying to get to the mosque before 9 am. In addition to J and me there was Asqar, Rahmān, the Colonel and Towhidi, a shy, diminutive resident in medicine, a man with a gentleness that is such a lovely gift in a doctor but rarely leaves a mark. A gentleness that allowed him to melt out of your memory. We had breakfasted on delicious *āshe sabzi*[1] together in a shop and felt warm and contented. The air too was calm. Halfway to the mosque Asqar, sitting in the front, turned back to J: "what a beautiful day to die" he said and smiled, unaware of how close to death he would come that morning. We were not so old as to think we would die young.

We arrived at the mosque just before nine. We were the last to make it before the access roads to the mosque were closed by the security forces. J had to leave us, took her shoes off and was whisked upstairs to join the other women on the second floor. The men congregated downstairs. The four of us did not go in but stood outside the west wall of the *Masjed*. Habib was a tiny unassuming mosque situated just south of the Felekeh Valiahd (crown-prince) – renamed Valiasr (the occulted 12th Imam) after the Revolution. It was a rather drab four-square building surrounded on three sides by narrow lanes. To its north there was a large field and beyond that a petrol station. On that day the field was planted with what looked like potatoes but could have been anything. My botany was rudimentary. Years ago, I was given a consolation O-level when I failed my A-level Botany having handed in an almost blank sheet of paper. I can still see the sad blue-grey eyes of the teacher, surmounting his crumbled brown suit shaking his balding head in disbelief when he gave his favourite student the news that to him epitomised utter failure. "Why?" was all he could articulate. I had no answer. I still don't understand why I failed to be inspired when he cut with his tiny pocket knife though the seeds, held firmly between his chubby pinkish fingers and ridged fingernails with their small reservoir of black dirt like a crown on the nail bed, to show me the cotyledons. He so loved those plants yet failed miserably to transmit that love. Maybe it was the brown-covered musty smelling textbook that fed boredom to the 16-year-old me. I wish I had listened to that love and allowed that passion to soak into my brain.

We saw three or four mini tanks at the far end of the field, near the petrol station, and a group of armed soldiers nearby but paid little attention. Seeing tanks and armed troops had become commonplace and no longer aroused fears. And for some reason we felt particularly invulnerable that day – maybe that was another effect of the translucent light. The three of us were chatting facing the alley alongside the west wing of the mosque with our backs to the wall. Towhidi stood shyly apart. A wider paved road, one that could take cars, led off westwards straight in front of us. We had parked our car further up on that road which was now blocked off by troops. Across the lane, on the corner of the road and the alley, I noticed a man looking over to us. He had a camera round his neck and was noting down something in a notebook. He was remarkably tall, broad shouldered, dressed in a grey suit, and what I remember about him is his thick black eyebrows and thickish lips curved in what I can only describe as a sneer. If one had been casting for a film, he would have been hired as the villain. He looked like the caricature of a SAVAK agent. He looked unfriendly. Then our eyes met, and something melted inside.

Rahmān – The Colonel – looked conspicuous as always. Standing erect with his beautifully combed silver hair among a sea of black, and his trademark immaculately ironed blue shirt, he stood out as he did in every demonstration. I suggested to Asqar and The Colonel that we should step back a row, which we promptly did. I was now facing the wall of the mosque with my back to the alley, chatting. The loudspeaker which minutes earlier had been putting out a reading of the Quran was now broadcasting a speech by Khomeini commemorating the freeing of ayatollahs Tāleqani and Montazeri from the

CHAPTER 26

Shah's prison. The 'colonel' was talking in that special way of his, what in Iran we call *ketabi* – as if he was reading from a prepared text projecting it to an audience a few metres away. It is difficult to explain it in English. He would round his vowels and would put a slightly nasal touch to the words, arching the roof of his mouth for the āāhs. It was the way you read your essays at school or gave an oration to the troops. People don't normally talk like that. They eat the end of the words and change the 'a' or 'o' into an 'oo'. Nān (bread) becomes noon. But not for our colonel. It was the combination of immaculate exterior and immaculate speech that gave Rahman the nickname 'colonel'. He was always conspicuous in a crowd, and we all worried about him.

I vaguely saw a young mullah at the entrance of the mosque in a heated discussion with a real colonel and then a scuffle. Suddenly I heard a rattling sound behind us. My experience of gunshots had until then been from films where they sounded like what I thought guns should sound like – loud bangs with a swishing sound. What we heard was more like firecrackers. Later in life I heard others telling me of a similar experience. People started running. "Don't run away!", I heard myself shout, "they are only firing in the air". Then I looked down and saw a man lying on the ground. For a fraction I could not make out why he had fallen. It seemed an odd reaction to firecrackers. But then I saw a red liquid oozing from his back. Was he dead? I don't know and I didn't stop to find out. Was I scared? That too I don't recollect. The whole image is so blurred. A rapid sequence of images coalesce into a single image of chaos. Did I have any emotions? Under fire, emotions evaporate. Or maybe the fast sequence of emotions gel into a brown cloud. Or is it that I have suppressed them?

Seconds later I heard a roar coming from my right and looking up saw two small tanks moving towards us at speed, churning dust from the field. A soldier holding a G3 automatic rifle, his lower half submerged in the turret, was staring down on us. He lifted his gun. I ran. He fired. It was aimed at Asqar who had crouched behind a parked car. He saw the man aiming and ducked instinctively, he later said. The bullet flew past his face, hit the brick wall behind him and ricocheted off. A piece of red brick hit his chin grazing the skin superficially. The tanks squash flat one of Towhidi's shoes which had come off in his flight and he limped to Sa'di, one foot shoeless. Others saw firing from the air, but I did not see any helicopters. In the unpredictable way life evolves, our life was saved by the man from SAVAK, while others had died standing where we had stood. It was my closest encounter with death until three years later, well after the Revolution was won and lost.

I run as fast as I can down the alley and rounded the corner alongside the last of the men. The tanks roll past us. There I see a number of men running in the other direction from the east side. They look scared. Only then I remember that J is stuck upstairs – shoeless. I try to get back round the side to the entrance which opens up onto the field. Soldiers bar my way – "you can't go there" one says looking as shocked and frightened as I must look to him. "Where are you going"? "I want to get my wife", I implore. "Don't worry they have all got out safe" and refuses to let me through. I rush round and try the other side but am blocked again. I can see smoke arising out of the mosque, it looks like they had thrown tear gas. The upper windows are smashed.

There she was with her black chador, her feet in shoes, distraught, bewildered. A helicopter had sprayed the upper storey windows and bits of glass had showered over the women, who in panic had fled. But no one was shot. They flew downstairs and ran shoeless. I saw my own fear in her eyes. "You forgot me, you left me up there", she said half in anger and half in relief. Self-contained as ever, she had slid her clogs under her arms when entering and was one of the few women with shoes. It was true. I had forgotten her. In the excitement of the moment, I had actually forgotten J for a fraction of time. But long enough to feel bad about it even now. Asqar too lost a shoe in his flight and limped one-shoed to Sa'di hospital. It was not yet noon.

They told us that Mohsen, who had been inside the mosque, and Rahman-the-Colonel had paraded one of the dead in the back of a pickup truck round the city. Years later Mohsen's wife Jaleh told me that this was untrue. There was always a lot of fanciful tales around any government killing. Rumours

CHAPTER 26

rapidly spread that up to 40 had died. There were tales of bodies cast down a well close to *Masjed Habib*. It is impossible to know how many died that day – but there were undoubtedly many. Journalistic accuracy tends to get blurred and subsumed in revolutionary excitement. At least seven were brought to Sa'di hospital.[2] A story going around was that a colonel, Ataolah Qāsemi, had gone to the mosque to break up the meeting and had insulted imam Ali. Then either he or one of his soldiers had hit the mullah Malek Hosseini with an umbrella. That was perhaps the scuffle I had half-observed earlier, but it is difficult to imagine the colonel holding an umbrella, and even less a soldier. The hand that held the umbrella must have poked out of different clothes. Later Hosseini ordered the death of colonel Qasemi as a 'non-believer' because of his insult to Imam Ali.[3] I don't know if this order was ever carried out.

Someone in the Medical School suggested that we needed to get news to the outside world. I volunteered to go to Tehran and get the news to the BBC reporter in Iran. The Persian service of the BBC was listened to widely and Khomeini, who was in Paris at the time, would often use this and other foreign media when he wanted to pass on a message – like calls for a national demonstration. It was easier than cassette tapes which were his favoured method of communication before his move to Neauphle-le-Chateau. I could not phone the BBC man before I got to Tehran in case his phone was bugged. They might stop me at the airport.

I took the Iran Air flight to Tehran via Isfahan early in the afternoon. At the airport I met a colleague Khodadoost, an ophthalmic surgeon. Tall, slim, standing upright, he would have been a picture of success if he hadn't looked so morose. We chatted, as two colleagues do, over the usual trivial problems of work, now given colour by the revolutionary backdrop. I asked him how his work as the most famous ophthalmologist in Iran was affected by the Revolution. Khodādoost, like many in Pahlavi University, had trained in the USA. He was a first class surgeon had a huge private practice among Arabs coming from the Gulf States for corneal grafts and other eye operations. Shiraz, with its gardens and ready alcohol was also a holiday destination for Gulf Arabs. "I am still making a million tomans a months"[4] he said.

The conversation had somehow meandered to finances. That was 100 times my salary. Arabs were still apparently flying across to go under his knife. It was joked that the Iran Air direct flight between Shiraz and Dubai was set up mainly to cater for Khodādoosts's practice. I felt neither envy, nor resentment but a kind of perverse contempt. That was how some of us on the left felt about wealth. In the ideological cocoon I and my colleagues lived, Khodādoost was a class enemy. I noted how unhappy he looked despite his wealth. But maybe he was just unhappy to see me. We had so little in common – living so close and seemingly in two different worlds. And there were so many different cocoons in those days, each in almost total ignorance of the other.

As soon as I arrived in Tehran, I rang up Andrew Whitley, the resident BBC reporter. How I got his number I do not recall but someone in Shiraz, perhaps a fellow academic, gave it to me. I identified myself, no surname, but said I was a faculty member of Pahlavi University and had news of a massacre. We agreed to meet in a restaurant somewhere in North Tehran in the late afternoon. I got there an hour earlier to scout the area. The café was in a concrete high-rise building surrounded by a large grey concrete forecourt. I can still see that courtyard, expanded into a massive concrete wilderness through the filter of time, just as my grandfather's courtyard has ballooned in my memory into a vast space. Memory expands and contracts space as well as time and does so in an arbitrary fashion. The picture I remember is overcast grey. There were no shadows and no colour. Just grey granite. The walls had been painted grey. It was eerily empty, and the greyness seemed accentuated by the lowering sky. I was a long way from the warm blue sky of Shiraz. I felt alone and very vulnerable.

I walked across and peeped into the café. It too was empty except for one couple, perhaps a pair of lovers, deep into each other in a secluded corner. Love floats above revolutions, unconcerned. My fear was filtered through films I had seen. My father's generation had their imagination imprinted by the stories told in childhood by a nanny or servant. Mine mainly floated in a sea of movie imagery. I am not sure which creates the greater distortion. I wondered why he had chosen such a remote empty spot. There was no going

CHAPTER 26

back. I had committed myself and felt that I could not do otherwise. I had told Whitley that I would be holding a magazine – the sort of thing you see on a film. It did feel a bit like a bad B-movie. I sat down at a corner table and ordered a coffee.

All my life I had an intense fear of going to a restaurant alone. I would walk up and down in front of a restaurant, sometimes for an hour or more, trying to pluck up courage to go in. Even if I had not eaten all day, I rarely managed to cross that threshold. Once or twice when I managed it, and it would always be a self-service so that I didn't have to call over the waiter, but still it felt like the entire restaurant was watching me eat. Eyes, eyes, more eyes, poring, mocking, looking, just looking. With sweat pouring down my face and soaking my shirt, I would gulp down whatever I had on my plate, not looking up. Not daring to look at all those hundreds of eyes I knew were staring at me, and through me. Today I got some courage from my mission but begged him to be quick. Was I sweating?

I immediately recognised him by his very English way of walking – slightly stooped – wearing a crumpled jacket. He too recognised me. It was not that difficult as there was not much visual competition. It was strange meeting a foreigner. Most had left or were cocooned in their ex-pat bubbles safe from the dirt of the Revolution, distanced from what they did not understand. But then my parents too were in a cocoon. North Tehran was akin to another world, not unlike what it is like today. I showed him my university ID card, which he scrutinised with great care, and we spent the next 10 minutes establishing who I was. Unsure that I had convinced him – he looked very sceptical throughout our conversation - I recounted what I had seen and also what I had heard, including the 40 dead and the dumping in the well and the shooting helicopter. Then I walked away and went to my mother's as there was no flight back that night. Next day I was told that the BBC had broadcast a detailed report on the Masjed Habib massacre on its Persian service, including apparently the well and the helicopter. Three days later Malek Hosseini was arrested but was released later that month when the tribes of Boir Ahmad threatened to march on Shiraz. Later the same month, there was to be another massacre in *Masjed No* (new mosque) – which I did not witness.

I did not hear the broadcast. This was an example of the way the BBC and other foreign services helped spread the message of the Revolution. Khomeini, who was initially suspicious of the foreign media, massively warmed to them after arriving in Paris in October 1978. The BBC became particularly important between November 1978 and January 1979 when a national press strike meant they were the only source of news. That same year on November 5 some revolutionary forces (the Mojahedin according to one account) attacked the British embassy and destroyed its communications equipment.

Next day, from the comfort of North Tehran, I flew back to our rented villa in that oasis of green tranquillity, Bāq Namāzi, which the translation of 'garden' or 'orchard' does not do it justice. The plane (sycamore) trees were still shedding their leaves. It took the trees a long time to part with their leaves in Shiraz, even though they had yellowed long ago, an annual love affair enacted in the city of love. Autumn was a slow long-drawn-out process in Shiraz. The Revolution, impervious to the rhythms of nature, was rapidly speeding up. We were too involved to sense the incongruity. The irony of the contrast between life in Bāq Namāzi and the world outside eluded me.

[1] Āsh is a form of thick soup made of vegetables – thick enough to be a total meal, often taken with flat bread as breakfast. Shiraz is famous for its *āsh sabzi*.

[2] I have taken the figure seven from a reminiscence of another eyewitness, Dr Mostafā Moin, at that time a paediatrics resident and a friend. He went on to become Chancellor to the University and our paths crossed again two years later (this time on opposite sides of the divide), and later Minister of Science in the Islamic Republic.

[3] This story was confirmed by ayatollah Malek Hosseini, who went on to represent the *velayate faqih* (supreme leader) in the province of Yāsuj in the Islamic Republic.

[4] A Toman is ten Rials. At the official exchange rate of the time that was about 7 Tomans to the dollar. After the Revolution Khodadoost went on to

CHAPTER 26

build his own eye hospital, still functioning, in Shiraz.

Chapter 27

Reflections

There are moments that hover over your life like your shadow. They are often trivial but haunt your thoughts, often without an exit. What do they represent? What do they say about your fears or your hang-ups? One is the image of the young boy unravelling a rag doll lovingly wound up by Ensy to see how it was made only to discover a wooden cross and a pile of rags but no doll. The feeling of ungrateful guilt is with me today, 17 years after her death.

In another we were driving down the valley of Dashte Arjan with Ensi and Ezzi in the new year *Eid* holidays. We witnessed all three seasons flit past us in the course of twenty minutes. Leafless oak bushes dotted the patchy snow at the top, which gradually developed fresh fragile emerald green leaves. Within a few kilometres the emerald turned through shades of viridian to olive-green with dashes of brown leaves sitting proud with their serrated edge on branches. At the bottom Dashte Kāzeroun with lush green proper tree-sized oaks in full summer outfit. Now here was the forest I had been promised by everyone in town – almost. We were sliding downhill through the seasons when Ezzy, sitting beside me, turned and said "you have no ambition" meaning I did not want to make money. "I do, but not the ambition

CHAPTER 27

you have in mind" I replied sheepishly, and then a torrent of anger rose to my throat, which I swallowed. He remained unconvinced till the end. Ensy had brought her chador and prayed beneath the oak tree. The photograph is still among the remains of the life we had to leave behind in haste five years later.

The Revolution did affect some routines. Our regular Friday picnics ceased. Before that, come rain, snow or shine, we would pack the children in the white Peugeot and take off with a packed lunch. Usually Asqar and Faramarz with their families would come too. Asqar's wife Fay was American and like most of the American wives never really felt comfortable in Iran but blossomed on the picnics. Of his children Dariush, Kamran and Mitra, only the middle one slotted in age-wise between Maryam and Nargess. Nushin, married to Faramarz my school mate, came from a landowning family from Mashhad and maintained a barely perceptible detachment in her relationships. Both their children Sohrab and Roya were younger.

When we first arrived in Shiraz we were told there is a forest just south of Shiraz. We spent an entire Friday that autumn searching for this forest, driving off the main road onto tiny dirt roads towards hills on the horizon with a greenish hew on their grey-brown curves. Perhaps the forest was on the other side? There it was, the forest of Shiraz, a sparse covering of hills with oak bushes, none more than two metres, and most less. They never grew to full height, partly because they were regularly used as fuel by the nomadic *Qashqāi'* passing from their winter to summer pastures through it every year, twice a year. In the first two years of our marriage J and I had worked in Burton-upon-Trent where Maryam, "Our Maryam" as the natives would call her, was born. We went in search of Sherwood Forest where one of my childhood heroes had allegedly roamed. Robin Hood would today die of sunburn, or skin melanoma, in what remains of Sherwood Forest, with the coverage given by the few remaining trees. There was no shade in Dashte Arjan either. The word *jangal* (forest) covers both the Amazon and our bushy-hills. Within a few months of our stay the dotted greenish-brown hills metamorphosed into a lush forest in my eyes. Colour is so subjective. So subversive.

We had discovered Dashte Arjan, a valley through which the main road would wind downwards towards Kāzeroun. The mountains on either side were covered by the oak-bush-forest digging down between rocks and strewn with stones splintered by wintery ice. The native lions and tigers had long ago been hunted to extinction. We would spread our picnic on the foothills of the mountain at the beginning of the Dasht where the road turns right into the valley to begin its descent to Kāzeroun, and beyond to inhospitable Borāzjān where the SAVAK holed up many of its political prisoners. They too would have travelled through our forest and valley. You could almost feel the silence into which the children's laughter cut. Nargess and Kamran, with Sohrab, the junior boy in tow, devised a game of making a *hameh cheez* (literally 'everything') sandwich from every edible thing on the picnic spread and spent the rest of the afternoon finding somewhere in the rocky slopes to hide it - or eat it. Both the older boys, Dariush and Kamran, had inherited Fay's pale complexion. Kamran had Asqar's cheek and imaginative acrobatics, Dariush was an intensely shy teenager with a strong inner core that I was to discover. Sohrab had eyes that even at that age seemed to tinkle with humour and yet project the physics professor he would become. The two girls, Mitra and Roya, were young enough to be toys for us and the older kids. When there was snow, we would take out a huge inner tube from a lorry to toboggan down. That is until Asqar and Maryam jumped the snow at speed and hit the stony earth with a thud and a flip. Asqar's bloody face put an end to that adventure. Some weekends we would explore other areas. It was fun.

On a river east of Shiraz, we found a section that was swimable – Bande Bahman (Bahman Dam). It was there that Nargess lost the stylish plastic sandals she so loved, and where Faramarz had to extract a large splinter J had got stuck under her toenails, with the children watching wide-eyed. Once we went to Bande Amir – a dam on the river Kor erected in the tenth century on orders of Azed ad-Dowleh Deylami[1] one of the few Farsi speaking dynasties that ruled Iran after the Arab invasion. All around was a vast beautiful tree-covered area, shady, poetic in a Shirazi way. Until the mosquitoes attacked. We lit fires around us, but they dive-bombed us through the gap between the smoke, as they had done in the Po valley, on our journey homewards. The

CHAPTER 27

Revolution put an abrupt end to these excursions, but the tree-lined *Bande Amir* dam was a recurring dream that came to me in my cell and still recurs in my dreams, an oasis of green, peace and beauty surrounded by barren blue-brown hillscape and desert. The dream censor had snipped out the dive bombers.

Life was green in Bāq Namāzi. The veranda on Villa 7 opened up to a vista of green. It was a home to a wide range of friends, doctors, artists, singers, piano and ballet teachers, television producers. After dusk they would come, go to the fridge and take out a bottle of beer or open a *Pakdis* bottle of red wine and sit chatting on the veranda which looked out on the green of the *bāq* with no other villa visible. Our house was always open, and friends came and went. Sometimes I would be working inside, and they would come and help themselves to the mortadella-like *kālbās*, pickled cucumbers *(khiārshur)*, bread, or anything else in the fridge. It was very informal. But as the Revolution wore on, the mix of people gradually changed.

Foroud Esmail Beigi, Faramarz's brother, was the artistic magnet to our friends. He had directed Jean Genet's *The Maids* and J had played the maid, perilously navigating the two sloping planks he had suspended across the stage. J had agreed to the role as no other woman would wear the black tights he had insisted on for the character. When Foroud went back to the US other members of his group, such as the television artistic director, the ballet teacher or the six-foot giant of a man who had studied opera in the US and could drain a bottle of white wine in one swig, also stopped coming. Rahman-the-Colonel, his girlfriend, Bahrām, Ahmad and his wife Tāhereh, Āzādeh and a number of other medical people became the new regulars. Those visits have become hazy with time. Perhaps I was too preoccupied elsewhere, or perhaps I later suppressed the images for security's sake. Or it could just simply be old age.

And the children? They were mostly invisible to us. The *bāq* swallowed them, only disgorging them at mealtimes. In the summer when it was too hot to picnic in the midget 'forest' or by the river, they would spend their day in the pool - alternately swimming or dive bombing the two beautiful nurses sunbathing in their pink bikinis. The girls would both marry surgeons, the younger from the University Faculty. A decade later the older met uncle Sassan in a new year party in the USA fell in love and married, two more fish in the small pond of middle-class Iran. The veranda with its view of pomegranate and persimmon trees, pale green leaves with orange-red blobs like Christmas decorations, made a perfect stage for plays and magic shows for which the children sold tickets and where the last word was nearly always by Nargess.[2] But as the Revolution began to creep into the *bāq* and encompass the children they too changed the pattern of their friendship with the line-ups reflecting the revolutionary sympathies of their parents. The girls drew closer to the Mahluji children Ameneh and Zahra.

The last play they did was enacted under the shade of a plane tree. It was a comedy satire on the fast-fading monarch, called *Shah va Mardom* – the Shah and the People - funny and surprisingly sharp in its observations. Maryam and Zahra had written the script, adapted from a play they learnt in their drama classes, and fought over who should play the main roles. Maryam and Ameneh, Mohsen's younger daughter who had inherited his sarcastic wit, monopolised the lead roles. Nargess, excluded, sulked but ultimately joined in. They were hilarious as only kids untainted by adult inhibitions could be, although not all the parents warmed to their barbed bites at the Shah. Over the following weeks they vanished into the green of the *bāq*, intermittently visible to the grown-ups, joining in the roof-top sloganing sessions, spectators drawn inexorably into the drama around them. There was less and less time to worry about looks. Teenage angst went the way of the clothes. The teenage years simply flew over the head of Maryam and Nargess. They woke up adults.

Yet in those days of perpetual movement, love was simultaneously in the foreground and background, flitting so quickly from one to the other that the two merged into one. The love for J gave me a cloud of protection, like a spell, and let me walk. Yet we felt much less need to express that love in its more physical forms. Did I tell her I loved her? Did we make love? We must have

CHAPTER 27

done but it seems so incongruous to the picture I am building in my mind of those days. I guess part of the way we viewed the world and our place in it was through pupils suffused with love. Love was somehow intertwined with all the new emotions that were whirling around us. The excitement of the battle – a battle that lasted until that day in June 1981.

[1] The dynasty, otherwise known as Āl Buyeh (932 – 1055 CE) were Shi'a and originated in Māzandarān and for a time ruled most of modern-day Iran and even captured Baghdad, subduing Al-Mostakfi Be'llah the Abbāsid caliph.

[2] Nargess recalled the words 30 years later: *bachehā biyāeen az in shirinihāye khoshmazzeh bekhorid* (children come and eat from these tasty cookies) what they meant she cannot recall. Memory retains and discards strange bits.

Chapter 28

Āshurā-Tāsuā': University and the Mosque

It was ninth day of the lunar month of Moharram in the Muslim calendar. The next two days overflow with emotions for Shi'a Muslims. All over the Shi'a world they openly mourn the death of Emam (Imam) Hossein, the ultimate martyr in Shi'adom. The entire cult of martyrdom, so central to Shi'a belief, revolves round the death of Hossein and 72 close followers in the desert of Karbela. Hossein was a grandson of Mohammad and the younger son of his cousin Ali, and to the Shi'a, his legitimate heir. Two days every year they relive his martyrdom, and that of the male members of his family and close associates at the hand of the *Khalifeh* (Caliph), Yazid.

Following the death of Ali's eldest son Hassan, who having renounced his claim to the Caliphate, was nonetheless poisoned on orders of the founder of the Ummayed Caliph Mo'āvieh,[1] Ali's second son, Hossein, refused to accept the legitimacy of the new Caliph Yazid, Mo'āvieh's son, and responded to the invitation of the people of Kufeh, a town in today's central Iraq, had invited Hossein to come over from his exile in Hejaz, on the Arabian Peninsula, to take his legitimate position as *Khalifeh* (caliph). Hossein marched with his family at the head of an army to take up the mantel. When the Ummayed Caliph, Yazid's army blocked the route on the dry dusty desert of Karbela on the banks of the Euphrates, Hossein's army melted away leaving 72 close relatives and followers. Encircled and deprived of water they went to battle on the ninth day of the Moharram, *Tāsuā'*. On the tenth day, *Āshurā*, first his half-brother Abolfazl- al-Abbās, and then sons Ali-Akbar and Ali Asqar were killed before Hossein himself was slain by Shemr who commanded the Caliphs' army, and his family made prisoner. The severed heads of Hossein and the others were paraded in Damascus along with his captive wives and sister. In Shi'a mythology his sister Zeinab is said to have made a defiant speech in front of Yazid and his court denouncing tyranny and corruption. The entire tale is told and retold in bleeding detail every year. In my grandmother's house, as in many a devout home, I heard and reheard the story and the wailing of the women in the *rowzeh khooni* ceremony every Thursday evening. There a mullah – *rowzeh khoon* – would recite the story of Karbela to an audience. The more wailing tears he could wring, the more his remittance and the greater the likelihood of re-invitation. Hossein and his brother Abolfazl are folk symbols of heroism against tyranny and have acted through the ages as role models for countless rebellions in Iranian history. The defiance of Zeinab has been a model for Iranian women, whenever they stood up against oppression. These are tales deep in Iranian folklore and central to Iranian Shi'a rebellions against foreign intruders and usurpers through the ages.[2]

It is thus that every year huge processions are organised throughout the first ten days of the month of Moharram reaching a frenzied crescendo on day nine (*Tāsuā'*) and ten (*Āshurā*). Each neighbourhood would mobilise its entire male population who would march beating themselves in rhythm to chants on the chest with their hands, on the back with metal chains and sometimes on the scalp with knives with blood flowing freely. There would be flags and banners commemorating the martyrs and the *panj tan*, the five most important persons in the Shi'a pantheon, Mohammad, his daughter Fātemeh, his son-in law Ali, and grandsons Hassan and Hossein, in the form of an outstretched hand. Each neighbourhood would vie with another for the best *dasteh* (group) and would compete for the greatest expression of collective grief. There would be plays depicting the story and young boys would be led on horse or camel representing Ali Akbar and Hossein's other children. There would also be representation of Hossein and his slayer dressed in executioner red, this last a cursed role.

It was on this model that the demonstrations throughout the Revolution were organised. That is what the Islamists were good at. It is no coincidence that the street mass demonstration was the natural way of expressing revolutionary sentiment in Iran, then as now. It was also the way they were able to gradually remove all non-Islamist slogans, and change the chanting from its secular-revolutionary, militant and rhythmic form with left or democratic slogans to the tearful tunes and formats of the traditional Muslim laments, now given new words. In the two days of *Tāsuā-Āshurā* demonstrations that year we saw the final implementation of that transformation. So early slogans such as 'worker, peasant, student, unite, unite!' and *'begoo! marg bar shah!'* (say it! death to the Shah!) were replaced by a wailing sing song that was the same as the chants and laments normally recited in the *Āshurā* marches but with new words which initially still reflected the demand for democracy and had some echoes of militancy:

Zire bāre setam nemokonam zendegi
 Jān fadā mikonam dar rahe āzādegi
 Marg bar in shah,
 Marg bar in shah
 Marg bar in shah,
 Marg bar in shah[3]

The beginning sung as a lament, but last stanza shouted out in militant precision – a hybrid on the way to the wailing lament. But these gradually metamorphosed and degenerated into pure sing-song weepy lament, more and more focused on Khomeini's leadership and the Islamic character of the Revolution:

Khomeini ay emam!, Khomeini ay emam.

Any dissenting slogan was, where possible, immediately repressed. This was particularly easier in the provinces such as Isfahan and Shiraz, while in Tehran the Left-Secular forces were in such numbers that they could retain

CHAPTER 28

their slogans, to the end. We also saw here the beginning of the argument that we should all speak with one voice and sort out our differences later. From Paris, Khomeini kept repeating the call for *vahdate kalameh*, a united voice against the Shah.

The night before December 10, we had a meeting in our house. Asqar was there with Rahman the colonel and Hooshdaran to whom the rest of us looked up for political analysis. He had spent some years in the Shah's prisons, and we held him in the same awe we held all former political prisoners. The army had announced that they were withdrawing into their barracks for four days. All airports were to be closed to air traffic. That itself was strange. Why would they close the airports and cut off links with the outside world if they are not contemplating a coup? Finishing off what they left unfinished on Black Friday? The country had been plunged into the mass general strike a month previously. Maybe tomorrow everything was going to be overturned. Early that morning I had gone to the Āteshihā mosque with Mohsen and there sitting around the room were the young men who were going to be the main organisers of the great march that was to replace the traditional *Tasua* march of mourning. A bearded youth, already balding, was given the task of organising bread, dates and water along the route of tomorrow's marchers. That night we went to bed extremely apprehensive.

I left home at seven for Sa'di hospital. I put on a black shirt. As I kissed J it felt as if it was our last. A farewell kiss. A wave of tension and tenderness passed our lips as they touched and parted. No words were exchanged but she understood. The look in her eyes was warm, full of a deep, deep love. Yet there was none of the sadness one would expect in a last look. Just understanding. And love. We were both doing what we had to do. The inevitable. That was a look I was to see again and again in the coming years. I kissed Maryam and Nargess with a new passion and walked over to Sa'di where the University contingent was gathering. Did the children feel the tension? Both were old enough to empathise but too young to know death. For one moment, the thought of not seeing them grow up sank like a knife into me. But the 'I' quickly melted into the 'we' or even into that timelessness that surfaces in moments of history. You become part of a stream of history, part of the inevitable. There is no 'I' in a revolution. Only necessity.

I had agreed to act as steward. I put on my steward's armband. Majid, one of our best residents and a close friend was there and I asked him to keep an eye on me in case I was shot. We prepared our banner: 'University is the Bastion of Freedom'. Rostam Qalandari, the same Rostam who had been the first to shout, 'say it; death to the Shah!' in Shiraz turned to me. "What kind of a slogan is this", he sneered. 'This freedom you talk about is western. We should be talking of the unity of the University and the Mosque". "You are mistaken Rostam", I replied shyly. "Freedom of speech, and of thought, is the central plank of learning". He was unconvinced and we had a long, heated argument. We had clearly drifted apart over the last few months. A year later Rostam sidled up to me. "Seyyed,[4] you were right on that day", he whispered aloud. He was a free spirit, and he remained a Muslim, but had quickly learnt to reject what was done in its name. Rostam died young, of a heart complaint, I learnt in exile. He was one of the most courageous men I have ever met. I miss him even now. The boy, with his short-cut hair accentuating his Mazandarāni head, remains as vivid as any memory can.

The University group was not very large, perhaps 1,000 people, and we made our way to a large square near the Shah-Cherāq shrine where the rest of the town had gathered. On route, there were many people watching from the pavements. 'enqelāb, enqelāb, tamāshāgar nadāreh' (no bystanders in Revolution) we shouted and attracted a few thousand more to the ranks. But many preferred to watch from the side-lines. The fear of a coup, of a massacre, was palpable. A group behind us started shouting the old Fadāi' slogan: Unity, Struggle, Victory! Their banner was immediately pulled down and torn to shreds – tear down the slogans of discord – someone had shouted. That was the first time I witnessed the systematic attempt to silence any other voice other than that coming from the Mosque.

The crowd grew by the minute as we waited in the winter sun for two hours or more. I later discovered that the delay was because of a dispute between the two main ayatollahs, Dastqeib and Mahallāti, as to whose car should be in front. The petty dispute reminded me of that between the clerical leaders of the Constitutional Revolution of 1906. In the end something was sorted out and the procession moved north to Falakeh Mosaddeq, then to Falkah Valiahd (now Valiasr) and then turned west into Zand Avenue. The University lines had swollen to uncontrollable levels. At first, we, the stewards, had been keeping an eye on the balconies looking out for snipers, but as the march became more and more chaotic, we forgot the danger and vainly tried to keep some order in our ranks. Without success. As the march grew the sheer size acted as a magnet drawing in bystanders. In any case, I had long lost contact with Majid who was meant to keep an eye on me. There were tens of thousands of people in front of us. Behind us, as far as the eye could see, was a magnificent mass of people, the women and men grouped together, separately. The slogans had become much more organised than before – mainly concentrating on the "evil triangle of America, Russia and Israel".

We marched west down Zand Avenue approaching Kale Moshir. Half a kilometre or so ahead of us the Shah was looking down on us from his pedestal on Falakeh Setād, provocatively, challengingly. We felt invincible. I felt an enormous thrill that we were going to pull his statue down at last. It had been a sore – and it was literally next door to the Medical School. With the passage of time, it is difficult to understand the almost irrational passion that the pulling down of a statute created. It was almost like the destruction of an idol. In my inflamed imagination it was like spitting in the face of the regime, like pulling him down from the throne. It was more than humiliating the regime – it was like sacrilege. As a child I remember silently swearing at God and then feeling an intense fear of retribution, but then swearing once more just the same, uncontrollably, an autonomous me. Then more intense trepidation. I did so feel like showing my contempt for this earthly god that day. We were confident that we would prevail, but it was not to be.

This became quite clear as the demonstration reached the Kale Moshir junction. Dariush was the main shopping street of Shiraz and it ran southwards from Zand. If instead of turning left as the march organisers were urging us to do, you marched ahead, past the white walls of the British Council on your right, you would come to that odious statue, sitting smugly on its horse looking over our heads. But the road ahead was cordoned off by stewards from the Bazaar. We were asked to turn left. The feeling among us at the University and the huge crowd that had gathered behind us was of intense rage. We felt utterly betrayed and many among us decided to defy the stewards and march ahead. An angry exchange followed between the people at the head of our column, the stewards and the leading mullahs. We were told the army had barricaded themselves on the roof of the municipality building on Falakeh Setād and were prepared to shoot anyone who tried to tear down the statue. In the end they, in negotiation with a handful of army officers who were also blocking our way, agreed to try to persuade us to forgo the statue. In return, the army agreed that the next day – Āshurā – we could march past the Fourth Army Barracks. The radical negotiators from the University reluctantly agreed and passed the message down the line. This was a foretaste of what I would witness over the following years – the readiness of the clerical leadership to compromise in order to curb radicalism.

The next day on Āshurā the University column was bigger and better organised. The fear of a coup had receded, and it was safe to openly express dissent. Even the most timid realised that the army was not going to oppose the march. All across Iran the army had withdrawn to the barracks except for some token presence. The streets were left to the Revolution. It was another beautiful, and surprisingly warm, December day. The chants at the beginning was *"bekoori cheshme shah, zemestoon ham bāhāreh"* (let the Shah go blind, winter has become spring).

We carried the same banner proclaiming the University as the bastion of freedom right at the front of the Medical School column. I was in the front row with Ebrahim, a neurologist and a number of junior doctors and students. The march was exceptionally long as we retraced yesterday's route but now proceeded to the Fourth Army barracks. By the time we reached there, the University ranks had swollen to 50 or 60 thousand. The main slogan alluded to the attack on Tehran and other universities: *javanhāye dāneshgāh be khāk o khoon oftādand*, 'university youth have hit the dust in blood'.

It became immediately clear that extensive preparations had been made to curb our radical enthusiasm. All along the last part of the route to the army barracks, a distance of two or more kilometres, semi-bearded men lined up with some of our Islamist students, holding hands in a chain. They extolled us to chant *artesh barādare māst* (the army is our brother). There were to be no slogans against the Shah. Any attempt to do so was immediately silenced. This was a total departure to what had gone on before. The only slogans allowed were those praising Emam Khomeini who, if my memory serves me right, was given the title Emam for the first time the previous day, with its implications that he represents the occulted 12th Emam – Mehdi - on earth.

As we approached the walls of the 4th Army barracks, the cordon around us became more dense and the exhortations to avoid any slogans against king or army more strident. There were perhaps 40 to 50 thousand people who had preceded us, and they had all obeyed the commands of the stewards. As the Medical School front line reached the wall, we could see hundreds of troops lined up behind the fence with one sergeant standing outside the first gate next to an officer, with his hands resting on his holster. We began the chant of *begoo, marg bar shah!* (say it: death to the Shah!) which was immediately taken up by the people marching behind us. There was a frantic rush by the bearded minders to shut us up. I saw a lieutenant inside the barracks glaring at us. A few seconds later the sergeant reached for his revolver, but the officer standing next to him immediately restrained him. A few minutes later, when our front line had passed the main gate, I heard a shot. No one was hurt, we found out later.

The chants of *begoo marg bar shah!* became louder and louder, as was the chant:

toop tānk mossalsal digar asar nadārad,
shah bejoz khodkoshi, rāhe degar nadārad

Guns, tanks, machine guns, of no use now,
Shah has no option but suicide.[5]

Thousands of people had joined the University column, most not even belonging to the University. They told me later that it was an hour after we passed before the stewards were able to stop the anti-Shah slogans. Once again, I saw how a slogan or policy that describes what people really want will catch on with little effort and that it is difficult to suppress. A concept that speaks to the heart of people.

That day it is estimated that between 300 and 400 thousand people marched. The slogans were more organised, the bystanders less, the control by the Islamists much better, despite the brief loss of authority. But on that *Āshurā* we also saw the chasm widening between the secular opposition, epitomised by the University and those organised by the Mosque that was to culminate two years later in the 'Cultural Revolution'. That night J and I walked through the city. It was entirely in the hands of the people. An extraordinary feeling of exhilaration overcame us. It was as if for the first time we belonged to this city. We walked for hours in this trance. There I saw the balding youth I had met in Ātashihā mosque leading a band of men with candles in a S*ham-e qariboon, a* ceremony symbolizing the desolate state of the survivors of *Karbela*. Most of those boys I had seen in that mosque early that morning were to become Pāsdārān (Revolutionary Guards) commanders.

Forty days later, on the 40th anniversary of the martyrdom of Hossein (*Arba'in*), almost the entire population of Shiraz and its surrounding area was on the street in the largest demonstration seen in that city to date. The University academics were allowed only one banner. It was again to be 'University is a Bastion of Freedom'. That was when the blue-eyed student warned me of the dangers that lay in wait for me if I persisted on the line I was pursuing.

There were no bystanders on that day. It was peaceful. It was huge. I peeled off outside Sa'di Hospital and watched just the women marchers passed by, occupying the entire breadth of Zand Avenue, taking over two hours to march past. The slogans were about Khomeini and the brother army. They were sung without much enthusiasm. A stalemate hung over the air. All non-Islamist slogans were purged. Khomeini had become an *Emam*. The slogans became laments, the militant rhythms being replaced by the whining lament of mourners. It was as if the whole nation was invited to mourn. The army stayed in its barracks.

CHAPTER 28

On or about *Āshurā* the character of the Revolution changed.[6]

Martial law was effectively over. The revolutionaries had the streets but government eluded them. Over the next weeks there would be sporadic marches here and there, but it was like shouting in an empty hall, not unlike our children's march around Namāzi compound. You just heard your own echo. There was no tangible enemy to fight. In Shiraz the entire two years of street battles was turning into an anti-climax. The young revolutionaries from the Masjed Ātashihā effectively controlled the city. But government seemed unassailable. Street tactics had reached a dead-end. It was a general strike that put the last nail in the coffin of the Shah's regime. A general strike that had been universalised by another timely slogan – *hafteh hambastegi* – the week of solidarity a month earlier.

[1] The Ummayeds were the first dynasty of hereditary caliphs (661-750 CE) with their capital in Damascus.

[2] E.g. the *Sarbedaran* (literally 'those with head in the noose') who rebelled against the Mongols ruling Iran in the mid 14th C. The Union of Iranian Communists adopted the name in their Amol uprising in 1981.

[3] I will not live under the yolk of oppression, I will give my life on the road to freedom, death to this Shah,…

[4] A direct descendent of Mohammad. When the safavid dynasty made Shi'sm many Sunni Iranians were offered the 'privilege' of being related to the prophet in return to taking up the Shi'a religion.Hence the plethora of *seyyeds* in Iran.

[5] This slogan was modified to fit the demonstrations of May-June 2009.

[6] On or about 1910 human character changed: Virginia Woolf,

Chapter 29

The Sa'di village plot

The killings took place that evening. We had just taken two Vice-Chancellors hostage: my first, and last, hostage taking. What started as an amateurish attempt to put pressure on the regime to release two mullahs ended by us thwarting a clumsy plot to divert the revolutionary energy into murderous inter-religious conflict. It began as a quasi-Quixotic side show which could have petered out in a farce. Events and the creative thinking of colleagues turned it into a tragic drama. It was Wednesday, December 13, 1978.

Times were tense. Revolutionary momentum had been building up and would soon reach the crescendo that led to the final uprising that overthrew the monarchy. The military government of general Azhāri had been in power for nearly six weeks but had been unable to quell the tide. Night after night, once the curtain of curfew shrouded the cities, people would climb on their roofs and shout *allāh-o akbar* (God is great). And to underline the spiral nature of historical experience, as I write these lines[1] the people of Tehran, Shiraz, Isfahan and many others are repeating that strategy, this time with the Islamic regime in their sights. Unable to stop this unique form of protest, Azhāri went on state television and blamed the chanting on recorded tapes being played from rooftops. Thereafter, with their unique wit, street marchers

CHAPTER 29

added a new rhyming slogan to their repertoire:

azhāri-e bichāreh,
  olāqe chār setāreh,
  bāz ham migi navāreh,
  nāvar keh pā nadāreh

Loosely translated it went like this: you poor Azhāri; you four-star-ass; still saying it's a tape; do tapes have feet? Azhāri was a four star general. During the second half of November and early December, factories and offices that had returned to work after marshal law had been introduced, returned the call of the SMD for a week of solidarity and went back on strike. The national strike was to continue until the end. Most damaging was the strike of oil workers. Oil production fell from 5.7 million barrels per day in October to 1.8 mbd. Queues for petrol would extend from Moshir Fātemi (now Enqelāb) to *Falakeh Namāzi* a distance of 2 kilometres. People would leave their cans in rows of 1000 and 1500 and walk away, supervised by fifty or so young men. There was trust. There was also a revolution to complete. Those were particularly bloody months. The death throes of the Shah were sprayed with showers of bullets and blood.

On December 2 demonstrations in several cities had lasted for three days and newspapers reported over 700 killed. The death toll in Qazvin alone was over 130, some crushed under tanks. In Mashhad, 200 university students and others gathering outside a prominent cleric's home were massacred. With the tendency of revolutions to exaggerate their costs the figures for all three are almost certainly an overestimate. A week later hundreds of thousands gathered in the vast Tehran huge graveyard – Beheshte Zahrā – to commemorate the 40th day of the youthful martyrs of Tehran University on the day Azhāri had taken office and declared martial law. And now, the rooftops rang out with Azhāri's 'tape machines', chanting and shouting and rocking the cities beneath the stars, blanketing the sky now that bayonets of light had stopped stabbing it. We too did our share, including the children, from the top and bottom of the eight-storey building which was the nurses' dormitory in Namāzi compound. And three days previously we had walked the massive *Tāsuā'* and *Āshurā* marches, when the people took over the city, and the mullahs finally monopolized the Revolution.

There were a large number of academics there in Sa'di Hospital that night. The previous day a prominent young cleric from Tehran had come to talk at the Agricultural College. Mohammad Javād Bāhonar, who later briefly became prime minister in the new regime before being blown up by a bomb,[2] dressed in the traditional clerical brown cloak (*abā*) and white turban, had been stopped at the Qor'an gate on his way to the College and turned back. He had returned to Shiraz, changed into civvies and slipped through the roadblock unrecognized and gave his speech. In one of those peculiar coincidences, I happened to be a fellow passenger on the plane on route to an SMD executive meeting in Tehran that day. The plane had taxied out and was about to take off when it unexpectedly stopped on the runway. A car pulled up and a man who looked like a caricature of a SAVAK agent climbed on board. It is no fault of mine that SAVAK apparently recruits its agents on the same principles as Hollywood – big, burly, thick eye-browed, moustachioed, and morose. The man walked up and down the aisle two or three times scanning every face with a theatrical frown. He stopped in front of two clerics sitting side by side a few rows in front of me on the other aisle. After a minute or two they quietly left the plane with him. On arrival in Tehran I immediately phoned one of the faculty of Bāhonar's arrest. It was a guess on my part – I had never seen him in life or page. I flew back later that evening or early next morning.

The following day a number of academics, went to see the military governor of Shiraz to protest at his arrest and demand his release. Bāhonar had been invited by the Faculty of Agriculture and was therefore a guest of the University. The Dean of the Medical School, Nasr, and his deputy Asqar were there along with many of the senior faculty. The general, Esfandiāri, had been very polite, but evasive, and refused to make any promises. That night in protest at the continuing arrest of Bāhonar and his colleague the faculty staged a sit-in at Sa'di Hospital. There were perhaps 25 of us, all male, covering most of the colleges. Some had brought blankets. I planned to sit

CHAPTER 29

out the night. A few colleagues had earlier gone to the university offices and taken the two vice chancellors Dr Qavāmi and Dr Qorbān hostage. It was a strange sight seeing Qavāmi who came from a prominent and ancient Shirazi family,[3] tall and dignified and a little lost as to the role he was forced to play, politely following his captors. Qorbān was the son of Dr Zabihollāh Qorbān, founder and the first Dean of the Medical School, and taught at the College of Agriculture.

They were sitting around in the conference room on the second floor of Sa'di Hospital, while I was having a smoke on the hospital stairs, when someone ran over from the Emergency Room. A family had brought a boy in his early teens with a gunshot wound in his leg. Asqar and another doctor ran back. There had been shooting and killing in *Qarieh Sa'di* (Sa'di Village), the family told them between wails. Sa'di Village close tp the Qor'an Gate within the city limits. It housed a large Bāhāi' community who are considered apostates by the Shi'a. We decided to send a hospital ambulance to investigate. Fereidoon, a surgical resident at the time, immediately volunteered to go. Short and stocky, with a thick Stalin moustache, his whole physique shouted his left sympathies. The image people project is a reflection of their ideology, tunnelling deep into hidden corners. We all wear uniforms that define not just our class position, but our place in the ideological lattice of the time. Muslim girls wearing headscarves and boys with a stubble, the thick moustache of the Left, the tweed jacket of the Oxford Don, leather patch on the elbow, or later the ear stud and mohawk hair, and today the carefully coiffured wavy strand of hair coloured blond or more, defiantly poking out of the compulsory female headscarf on Tehran's streets. All statements of self-identity.

Fereidoon and I were instinctively drawn to each other, partly because of his beliefs, but also because he was both funny and reckless. It was Fereidoon who had been chased into Sa'di hospital wards by armed soldiers earlier during one of the raids. It was Fereidoon who had showed me how to use vinegar from the pickle jars he took from the canteen, soaked onto surgical gauze, to protect against tear gas. And it was he who had first recognised the new gas canisters they were throwing at us which caused intense nausea, rather than burning your eyes and lungs. Now he grabbed a white coat and jumped into the front seat of the ambulance. Rahman, *'the colonel',* joined him. Scratch away the sense of humour, and the airs and they were two halves of the same apple. The hospital gates closed behind them, and we sat on the front stairs waiting.

It was dark when the ambulance came back through the main gate of Sa'di Hospital. They had been gone but an hour, but the elasticity of anxious-time had stretched it to breaking point. The light filtered feebly on to the stairs from the entrance hall of the hospital. Outside there was total darkness as was the norm in those December nights. You had a glimpse of the Shirazi casual attitude to life when you saw families still spread out on their picnic, complete with samāvar and pots of āsh (thickish soup) and polo (rice) minutes before the curfew was due to start, calmly eating and drinking. But when the ambulance drove through the gates of Sa'di Hospital, the curfew had already been in force for some time. The streets were deserted except for the military vehicles, the lorries filled with armed conscripts sitting out the night in discomfort, boredom playing tricks with time, perhaps dreaming of their village, or someone they love or just food.

Fereidoon jumped out first with his usual agility followed by the colonel who would not permit a mere massacre to ruffle his composure. Fereidoon spoke in his deep voice in a breathless allegro appassionato. The army had surrounded the village and stopped anyone entering but the two, leaning on their white coats, had talked their way in. The army commander who had cordoned off the village claimed ignorance of the events but said that they had heard machine gun shots and had sealed off the area. He had a vague story that the Bāhāi's had shot a Muslim group as they gathered for prayers in the courtyard of their home. The ambulance carried four bodies. One, a non-commissioned officer (*ostovar* which is a warrant officer) in full uniform, with a single fatal bullet wound, who we later learnt was a Bahai' called Seffatollāh Fahandaj. They had found him on the flat roof of an adjoining house overlooking the courtyard where our ambulance crew had picked up the other dead. Sa'di Village housed a large community of Bāhāi's.

Fahandaj belonged to a well known Bāhāi' family while the three others were reputedly Muslim, a woman and two men, performing some kind of religious ceremony in the courtyard. They had all more than one bullet wound. Their clothes were of people of modest means. She was wearing a grey pullover which even through the dirt and the congealed blood showed its age. The thread on the elbows was so thin it would not have lasted her a week. It is strange how blood darkens so much. Perhaps she thought she would wear it for the last time for that evening's ceremony before discarding it. Or mending it. There would be time for neither. The men were middle aged, all dressed neatly for the ceremony, but clearly not affluent. These were typical lower middle class Shirazis. Our two doctors and the ambulance driver had entered the courtyard and found a number of dead bodies scattered about the yard of which they carried three out. They also found the officer on the roof, collapsed on his G3 submachine gun, shot dead. At first sight it looked like he had fired into the courtyard and then committed suicide. They hauled him down with his US-made G3. They also brought back handfuls of spent cartridges.

We took the dead to the mortuary and the weapon to the Department of Medicine office where a number of faculty members had now gathered. On seeing the weapon Āzādeh, a pathologist and a former wrestling champion became very agitated. "If they find the machine gun, they will screw us" he muttered anxiously. The naked fear in his eyes clashed incongruously with his muscular physique and his thick Sufi moustache calmly drooping over and obscuring his lips. Asqar helped him hide the gun in a cupboard and shoved the bullets into the ice compartment of the refrigerator in the office. Our esteemed hostages had meanwhile been moved to one of the intern's rooms to get some sleep. During the ensuing confusion my cousin Bijan Sheibani, a professor of agriculture, who as a friend of Qavāmi and Qorbān had volunteered to guard them, set both free, ending our amateurish exercise at hostage taking.

We went down to the hospital mortuary. Āzādeh, using his skills as a pathologist, came to the conclusion that the shot that killed Fahandaj had an entry and exit wound that made it unlikely that he had shot himself. It was likely that he too had been killed by someone, perhaps after he had shot the group below. Their wounds were compatible with having been shot from the roof. We had to know more.

At dawn, with the curfew over, the ambulance driver went back to the village, this time taking Asqar and a lawyer whose name I cannot recall. He was well known in Shiraz, and from talking to him and hearing his history I got the impression that he had Tudeh sympathies. My guess was confirmed after the Revolution. The courtyard was covered with patches of blood which Asqar meticulously photographed. The remaining bodies had been removed. The two of them also went on the roof and saw the single pool of blood where Fahandaj's body had been found. By 6 am they had returned with a report that corroborated Āzādeh's forensic conclusions. He had interviewed a number of witnesses and discovered that there had been a gathering of Muslims in the house returning from a religious demonstration, it being the mourning month of *Muharram*, who had been performing a ceremony in the courtyard when they were shot. From the blood marks it was estimated that between 10 and 15 persons were killed, including the warrant officer.

Meanwhile, news came of Muslim gangs rampaging through Sa'di Village and burning Bāhāi' homes. Over the early hours the story gradually emerged. Apparently Fahandaj, who had been somewhat unbalanced, had been instructed by someone in the military or gendarmerie to shoot the Muslims who, he was told, were plotting an attack on Bāhāi's. He was then killed, by a single shot that was made to look like suicide. The aim was to start an anti-Bāhāi' pogrom. Āzādeh, Asqar and Fereidoon immediately set about recording their findings on cassette tape while the lawyer took the ambulance to town to alert the religious leaders of our findings. Within the hour Abdol Hossein Dastqeib, the nephew of ayatollah Dastqeib, and Hojjatoleslām Mesbāhi, another junior cleric, came to Sa'di Hospital. After listening to our findings and the plot hatched by SAVAK to distract and divert the revolutionary energy, they went to quell violence and stop the burning. Later that morning we heard that a similar episode had taken place in Evaz, a Sunni-dominated town in the midst of the overwhelmingly Shi'a Fars Province with the aim of inciting Shi'a-Sunni riots. By the time the sun was up SAVAK's plot had been foiled and my colleagues had been instrumental in uncovering it.

CHAPTER 29

There is a sad ending to this tale. After the Revolution, Colonel Azematollāh Fahandaj, an uncle to the dead warrant officer, was sentenced to death by the revolutionary court and executed on December 7, 1980 almost a year to the day of the massacre which he was accused of masterminding. No real evidence was given, and according to witnesses he had not even been in the vicinity of the killings that night.

Later that morning we went out into the street and engaged the soldiers outside Sa'di Hospital who at first accused us of lying and then refused to believe that the military had been involved in the massacre. That is, until we carried the body of Fahandaj in full uniform outside the gates and laid it out in the middle of Zand Avenue in front of the troops outside. There was a commotion, and the soldiers were visibly shaken by the discovery that one of them had fired indiscriminately into a religious gathering. We returned the body to the mortuary. Asqar's photographs were meanwhile taken by Morteza, who earlier that year had been part of our secret cell, developed and the prints exhibited in the College of Literature where they were all pilfered and disappeared along with the negative film, which also mysteriously disappeared.

There they lay, lined up untidily on the stony floor of the hospital morgue, with Fahandaj the Bāhāi' placed a little distance apart on the right, as if he might contaminate the Muslims even in death. And this is how the citizens of Shiraz saw them after the gates of Sa'di Hospital were opened to the people and they filed passed the three, with looks of pity, or sadness, some with tears. And then they would file past Fahanjad, still in his soiled and bloody uniform, and spit on his body. I would like to think that the spittle was directed more at the army than a religious minority. But who can see into an individual's heart? Between us we estimated 50,000 filed past the corpses and most had shown their revulsion by the only way they could. From that day Sa'di Hospital became the peoples' hospital.

Next day was the funeral for the Muslims that were shot in Sa'di Village. Since the mass demonstrations of *Tāsuā' and Āshurā*, when the army seemed to have conceded the streets to the people, even the life-loving Shirazis had lost their fear. The crowd almost encompassed the entire population. Even

J's mother, mummy Foruq, visiting us from Tehran, insisted on marching. There she was, tiny, round, angry, determined, slowly walking up Dariush street with her peculiar rolling gait. We found ourselves stacked up among thousands of people in Shiraz's main shopping street, covering its entire width and stretching back to I know not where. The cortège was about 200 metres ahead of us, just before Dariush joined Zand Avenue, known as Kale Moshir, led by some prominent mullahs. Asqar was in that first row and behind him a row of mullahs including Dastqeib. They had obtained permission for the funeral procession from the military governor and when a group of soldiers dismounted from their lorry a few hundred metres ahead they did not think much of it. Asqar did not feel threatened even when the soldiers knelt down and took on firing positions. He had turned his back when a sudden burst of gunfire sent panic rippling through the front rows. Everyone ran and threw themselves on the ground as the firing continued. Asqar found himself with three mullahs on top of him. He felt secure!

It was mid-morning and the street-wide column was immobile when we felt, well before we actually saw, the panic ahead and people running back. "They are shooting!" people shouted. A stampede followed. There are many shopping alleys and passages coming off Dariush and the crowd started rushing into these. Mummy Foruq fell into the waterless ditch (*joob*) that runs along most streets, dry but full of discarded trash. I lost contact with J who in the commotion lost her watch, not a cheap one. The funeral was ending in a farce – mingling with the tragedy of one person shot dead and many wounded.

How the bodies were buried I did not inquire. One of the peculiarities of revolutions is that you deal with the problems ahead rather than what went on before. We were not recording for posterity – we were out there to change a regime. The same day as the Sa'di massacre, student demonstrators in South Tehran were fired at with live bullets. It was a bloody revolution. Less than a month later the Shah fled the country.

[1] August 2009 – in the aftermath of the fraudulent re-election of Mahmood Ahmadinejad to the presidency many cities erupted in mass street protest

that were suppressed in blood with thousands arrested and tortured. The skies of Tehran, Shiraz and Isfahan resound nightly with the same cries of *allāh-o akbar* and death to the dictator.

[2] After the Revolution Bāhonar joined the Revolutionary Council (*Shorāye Enqelāb*). As minister of Culture and Islamic Guidance he was involved in the Islamic Cultural Revolution which purged the universities of the left and secular forces. He became chairman of the Islamic Republic Party after Ayatollah Beheshti was assassinated in the bomb that exploded in the Majles, and then prime minister when Rejāi' was elected president after the dismissal of the first president, Bani Sadr. Bani-Sadr fled to Paris. Bahonar was blown up in his office by the Mojahedin alongside Rejāi' after less than two months in the job.

[3] The Qavāmis are descendents of Qavām al-Din Hassan, minister in the 14th century *Āl-e Mozaffar* (Mozaffarid dynasty). In Reza Shah's reign Qavām al-Molk, head of the Khamsein tribe, was made governor of Fars province.

30

Chapter 30

Unreality of reality

Those months passed across our lives like a storm cloud. We had to look to the sky. Except for J, the rest of the family has simply faded from my memory. Almost everything I write about the children is from *their* memories. All I remember is their open-air play *shah va mardom* (Shah and the people). Little more. They were there, safe within the walls of Namāzi. How did they get to school? Was there a school? Who took them? All those images have been erased. Perhaps never existed. Unasked questions or is it suppressed memory? Social upheavals lift you up as on a magic carpet. Mountains are mere bumps below like those projected on screen with boy Sabu looking down on in awe while being undulatingly flown on his magic carpet one night in a thousand-and-one.[1]

Did we understand where the Revolution was heading? J and I certainly had no illusions about what Khomeini wanted and what he represented. I had already seen the *death to gomunist!* and felt the fist of mullah Movahhed on my lefty teeth. Initially these concerns were a shadow somewhere close, but only a shadow. But we had seen it sideways.[2] Instinctively, perhaps as a way of justifying hope, justifying risk, we pushed the issue of our relations with the Islamists till after the conquest of the citadel of state. The Shah

CHAPTER 30

was the rampart we had to climb and conquer. Our focus. Our Orléans. Within six weeks the shadow slid across the wall, Hitchcock-like, behind the huge crowds that greeted Khomeini's arrival from France. The overwhelming dominance of the Islamist discourse was there on our screen. We sat watching a mass of heads and bodies moving as if in unison, mesmerised by this man. Even J was suddenly jubilant. We had a big argument. I felt we had lost this round. Lost badly. But the prize, a secular revolution, remained to be won. The fog would surely lift when the sun shone.

Yet popular illusion that this man could deliver not just the removal of the hated king but also fulfill their desire for freedom and independence – the central slogans of the Revolution – would take a long time to dispel.

And our parents? They withdrew into their shell, not comprehending what was happening to their lives, and to their children, who appeared even more alien. Parental love transcends incomprehension but does not lead to a change of heart.

There are times when I wonder if, by telling this story as I remember it, I am opening it up for questioning, for alternatives. As if by hindsight I am justifying my clairvoyance. 'By telling the story one loses the facts,' Alan Bennett wrote, it 'shakes them out and makes them available for interpretation and rearrangement'.[3]

Then we forgot and plunged back into completing the task at hand. Maybe the illusions would fall away fast. The contest was ongoing. The contest was to be very long.

[1] Sabu Dastagir was an Indian actor. He played in a number of Hollywood films in the 30s and 40's. The film may have been *The Thief of Bagdad*.

[2] 'Only what is seen sideways sinks deep' E.M. Forster.

[3] Alan Bennett. *Untold stories*. Faber and Faber, London 2005. I find much in common with him, not least my inability to respond promptly to a new situation. It comes from an innate shyness, a deep lack of confidence, one that you learn to cover up as you grow but always lurks there, somewhere, a handicap.

Chapter 31

Invading SAVAK

Like boulders running down a mountainside, events tumbled over one another. Three days after the Sa'di Village massacre, 100 members of the SMD took refuge in the offices of Tehran University. The sit-in was to last for 25 days and was the first in a series of events that was to catapult Tehran University into the centre stage of Revolution in Iran. On the same day, prisoners in Sanandaj burnt down the prison and 400 escaped having looted the prison armoury, while in Khomein, government and police offices were set on fire, demonstrators were shot in Mashhad, and a US adviser was killed in Ahwaz.

A group of professors and senior lecturers, all SMD members from across the country, occupied the offices of the Ministry of Science and Higher Education in Tehran's Villa Avenue, demanding the reopening of universities. On the street outside, thousands of university students gathered in support. From early morning to curfew time the streets round the ministry resounded with slogans. When school children gathered outside the US embassy to protest and then marched through Tehran shouting anti-Shah slogans, the military government closed all schools until further notice, freeing them to revolt even more. Damned if you do or don't, it seemed that the regime could

CHAPTER 31

do nothing right. On the third night a group of the professors had gone to the roof of the ministry when a sniper shot dead Kāmrān Nejātollāhi, an academic from Tehran University. Security forces then stormed the building, broke up the sit-in, arrested the protesting professors, and took them to Jamshideh military barracks. Dozens of students were gunned down during Nejātolāhi's funeral.

I missed all this as we were kept busy in Shiraz. We organized a memorial service for Nejātollāhi which was attended by over 5,000. Later, the Iran-US society building was set on fire and two men were shot during demonstrations. Over the same two days, between one and three hundred were killed in one of the worst crackdowns in Qazvin, 60 km west of Tehran. Khomeini appointed a committee of five led by Mehdi Bāzargān, who 25 years previously had taken over the oil installations on behalf of Mosaddeq, to do so again and negotiate with striking oilmen to resume production for internal consumption.

On December 30, 1978 the Shah dissolved Azhāri's military government and appointed National Front member Shāhpour Bakhtyār as Prime Minister, a last-ditch effort to mollify the Revolution. He was to be the Iranian Kerensky, a sad figure with an even more tragic ending when he and his secretary Sorush Katibeh were savagely butchered with a knife at their home in Paris by agents of the Islamic regime on 7th August 1991. The National Front promptly expelled him on his appointment by the Shah.

Nejātollāhi's death triggered more demonstrations. The largest, in Kermanshah, was 150 thousand strong and as they approached the provincial headquarters they were fired on, killing 30 and wounding 300. In Mashhad, tanks were used in the streets and in one of the bloodiest encounters several hundred died. Yet something new happened there when two tanks reportedly surrendered to the people. The regime's last death throws were getting bloodier and increasingly desperate. Such was the turmoil in the country when the SAVAK headquarters in Shiraz was occupied by people.

Occupation of the SAVAK building in Qazvin, Yazd and closer home, in Firuzābād the *Qashqāi'* 'capital', had led the way. In Shiraz, the attack on the SAVAK headquarters in was initiated by a group that a soon surfaced as the

Committee of Fars Revolutionaries (*Komite Enqelābiyoon Fārs*), made up of various Left groups.[1] Ayatollah Dastqeib is said to have initially opposed the attack, despite Firuzābād beating Shiraz to it. But he later changed his mind after thousands had already assaulted the building. As we will see, the same *Komite Enqelābiyoon Fārs* would later go on to organise the first meeting of all the Peoples' Councils that had mushroomed in Shiraz a few days after the overthrow of the regime in the Engineering College. Mani, my friend, would to stand up claiming he represented 4,000 armed guerrillas. In revolutions, comedy and tragedy, reality and fantasy, rub shoulders in a strange hypnotic dance.

As it happened, a group of us were talking to the cleric most closely involved in university affairs, Seyyed Abdol Hossein Dastqeib, in the Sehhat Library of the Medical School when someone came to tell us of the attack. J, Bahrām and I, who earlier that day were dismantling the intricacies of the dialectical transformation of quantity into quality while the revolutionary lava was melting down the SAVAK building, quickly made our way down Zand Avenue and got to the ransacked SAVAK office as night fell. It was an ordinary house, totally indistinguishable from its neighbours. Two days earlier Javān who was the head of SAVAK in Shiraz had fled the city and later the country. Maybe someone had warned him. If he knew he did not tell his deputy who resisted the assault and died alongside two SAVAK agents and two of the attackers. Whatever the reason for Javān's flight, it looked to us as if he had arranged for many of the files to be removed or destroyed. Here quantity had been actually been converted into quality, thousands of files into ash. But there was enough left for a van load to be taken away. The attackers had also ransacked the armoury but the army, which had passively observed the assault and the shootout without intervening, had confiscated most of the arms as they emerged from the building. Collusion or collapse? Was the army, or parts of it, planning a smooth handover? After the revolution we learnt that in that same month General Robert Huyser, commander of US forces in Europe and deputy head of NATO, had been sent by US President Carter to Iran to encourage the Shah to leave Iran and to either organise a coup or oversee as peaceful a handover as possible to preserve the army.[2] That day, a few

CHAPTER 31

G3 submachine guns slipped through the net and were brought to Namāzi where they were grabbed and disappeared. We came across the ashes and the few files still on the shelf. We grabbed some. It was January 11, 1979.

Crowds were roaming the courtyard, torch in hand, listening for voices from the labyrinth of secret dungeons everyone was convinced were buried deep beneath the garden. People were desperately listening for emaciated, tortured prisoners to save. One man claimed he had been a prisoner there and had seen the subterranean cells. Suddenly a man jerked my shoulder. Someone was calling from underneath, he whispered as if afraid he would be overheard. Habits die hard. I listened to the silent earth. Can't hear anything. Two men began to dig in the garden anyway, one with his bare hands. There was an empty pond, the sort you find in most Iranian courtyards, lined with blue tiles. The tiles were cracked and chipped. Another young man, who looked like he had not slept for days, went off to find an implement to dig into it.

Someone found three large sacs containing what looked like dried apricots. "It is human skin", the woman said, a mix of fear and excitement in her eyes, :"victims of torture". I shrugged. It looked like plastic. Another dug up some bones and showed them to me when he heard I was a doctor. They were not human, I assured him. He shot a suspicious look my way. I could have been a torturer out to hoodwink the revolutionary people. I decided not to argue the point. Some turned their attention to the surrounding houses.

One belonged to Mrs Namāzi which had a view onto the SAVAK courtyard. The other belonged to Dr Qorbān, the man we has taken hostage a month, and a lifetime ago. His house had a *bāq* that encircled the SAVAK building. There were murmurings. How could they have been neighbours and not known what went on there? And maybe there are labyrinthine dungeons there. Someone had obviously called for help. Standing outside the door of Mrs Namāzi's house was a tall well-fed mullah, Aqā Majdi, the Grand Ayatollah Mahallāti's corpulent son, famous for his *bon vivant* lifestyle. I know this lady and she is not a *Savaki* he repeated to anyone who came by. On his instructions they posted a note on the doors of Mrs Namāzi and Dr Qorbān's homes telling people not to assault them. Despite this the doctor's house was ransacked the following day, totally, as if a hoard of locusts had descended on a field. Nothing, not even the toilets and plumbing was spared. They then dug up some bones from the garden, definitely not human, and set the house on fire. It was totally senseless. Shiraz owed a lot to him. Dr Zabihollāh Qorbān was the architect of Shiraz Medical School, then successively the Colleges of Literature, Agriculture and Engineering, and became the University's first Chancellor, a highly respected physician and teacher. He even set up the first pasteurized milk factory in Shiraz next to the Engineering College and near Namāzi, the site of the only independent left demonstration I described earlier. He should have chosen his neighbours better. Mrs Namāzi was spared the mob. Aqā Majdi's girth was obviously not wide enough to protect Dr Qorbān.

SAVAK had created a myth of invincibility around itself with rumours that one in eight of Iranians worked for it. Ezzy, my father, told me a story that punctured that myth. On June 28, 1963, the Shah was invited to visit what was later renamed the College of Science and Technology (Dāneshgāh Elm va Sanat[3] that Ezzy had built from scratch on a piece of barren land in the eastern suburb of Nārmak in Tehran. "Is it wise to have a visit so soon after *15 Khordad* uprising?" Ezzy had warned Dr Khānlari, the Minister of Education who had originally invited him to set up the college, alluding to the June 6 (1963) nationwide uprising against the Shah's 'White Revolution' organised by the clergy and savagely put down by the Shah's security forces. But preparations had already been made and the Minister was reluctant to postpone. Major Najmābādi from SAVAK, who later headed the special guard to the King, visited the College the day before and gave a list of names to be given the day off the next day. The Shah came and spent many hours visiting all the workshops. He took a particular interest in the welding workshop and asked if he could have a go. There they were, the Shah wearing the visor, Ezzy and a single student, who looked very agitated. Perhaps the poor boy is overawed by the king's presence, my father thought. Next morning, on arriving at work everyone congratulated Ezzy on a close shave. Apparently, the student's father had been shot dead during the demonstrations earlier that month. Ezzy had misinterpreted his agitation as awe. It was a close call

CHAPTER 31

for the Shah and Ezzy. SAVAK succeeded better in the next decade by using a mixture of mediaeval torture[4] and a policy of random fishing of youth picked up in the streets and interrogated, hoping to tie them into a network by observing linking nodes, the same principle we use in epidemiology today in network research, without the torture. Science and barbarism marching to the drums of the 'Great Civilization'.

The archives had been ransacked. The *Komite Enqelābiyoon Fārs* had removed a small van-full. A week or so later I was handed my own dossier by a student. It contained a two-page report of a meeting in Sa'di Hospital when a group of us had sat down in the Department of Medicine library to talk tactics. As we were about to start, Āzādeh had pulled aside a young man wearing a brown leather jacket, and asked him to leave the room. We had met him before in the week of solidarity foraging round the speakers' platform. When he had protested, Āzādeh, just picked him up by neck of his jacket, as if he was a chicken, and threw him out. They say he is a *Savaki* (SAVAK informer), he told the meeting. There was no proof, but he had no business to be there – this was a private meeting of doctors. I read the report of that meeting in my dossier. It was written by someone told to snoop and found himself on the wrong side of the door. Mohsen Mahluji had been painted as the leader of the Communists and me as a radical Muslim. It could have only been from the pen of the leather-coated chicken. He had got the list of those in the library right. The rest was pure, but poor, fiction. Āzādeh had been right with his hunch. If the other reports were as fictitious as ours, no wonder the regime was out of touch with what was going on down below. It was signed with a pseudonym, and I passed on my file to the students who were trying to identify the agents. I was later handed about twenty dossiers to work on and tried to use who reported what to decipher the pseudonyms, another effort in turning quantity into quality, random case histories into indictment. The amateur sleuth in me only managed one name. I never found out if the others were more successful. Or what they did with the files from SAVAK. After the Revolution, many former *Savakies* were recruited to the service of the Islamic rulers. I was to find this very useful in prison. The brown-leather coated man was shot dead during a demonstration. The randomness of terror.

On January 13, the SMD called for a week of opening of the universities. Faculty and students invaded Tehran University. Over the next days, almost all the universities opened and became centres of popular assembly. Three days later the Shah left Iran in tears. The streets exploded with jubilation. I saw men crowded on an open lorry dancing. I saw women dancing – a most un-Islamic behaviour. I saw people cutting out the picture of the Shah from the 1000 toman bank notes, the highest denomination in circulation. I breathed a sigh of relief.

Ten days later, the whole nation watched its school children being shot outside the gates of Tehran University once again live on state television. The last gamble with Bakhtyār was drowned in what was seen by the country as the 'massacre of the innocents'.

[1] Article by Abbās Mansurān on www.alfabetmaxima.com (in Farsi) http://www.alfabetmaxima.com/news_list.php?table2=dastan&&news_id=49

[2] General Robert Huyser, had meetings with the Shah and oversaw his departure from Iran, and senior army commanders, such as army chief of staff General Qarehbaqi who later handed over the army to Khomeini. Earlier Huyser had met Khomeini's closest colleague Dr Beheshti and the first post-revolutionary Prime Minister Mehdi Bazargan in Paris. The exact role of Huyser in the final events that led to a change of regime remains obscure and full of contradictions.

[3] At the time it was called the Honarsārāye Āli Nārmak later changed to Dāneshkadeh (College) and later Dāneshgāh (University). Ezzy supervised the building on a 43-hectar site in North-East Tehran, recruited the staff and was its first director. The first post-Revolution prime minister, Mehdi Bāzargān removed him from the post without any explanation. See also Chapter 34, Heady Days.

[4] In addition to whipping, electric shocks, suspending, the steelyard, SAVAK with the help of CIA had developed the notorious 'Apollo' - a metal helmet-like contraption with two metal projections poking into both ears.

CHAPTER 31

You could not move your head as they whipped you with cables, and your screams would echo in the helmet. See M.S. Kia, *Entangled lives*, in press, for real life experience of torture techniques in the Shah's and later the Islamic regime's prisons.

Chapter 32

Citadel and television

This was another senseless slaughter on the day after the Revolution was stillborn. Two weeks earlier, the Shah fled and Khomeini established the Revolutionary Council and appointed Mehdi Bāzargān as interim prime minister. Yesterday burning street barricades were set up every hundred metres or so in the capital and the Homafar air force cadets, alongside Fadāi' and other armed guerrillas overran the air force barracks. That afternoon, the Shah's appointee Bakhtyār, not even in control of his own office, fled Iran, "as if the weight of Damavand mountain was taken off my shoulder" he later recalled in Paris. The old regime had shot its bolt and melted away. The army high command had declared their neutrality and army commanders had gone to pay allegiance to Khomeini.[3] Tehran fell. The Revolution was over in all but name.

Come quick. It was Mehran's breathless voice on the phone. "It is the citadel", he sounded as if he had sprinted to the phone, "they are slaughtering people in the Arg". The people of Shiraz had at first overrun and disarmed the *Kalāntari* (police station) number 3 and handed over the arms to Ayatollah Mahallāti at his mosque. They had then moved on and assaulted the 250-year old fort, the

CHAPTER 32

Arg, erected by Karim Khan Zand, founder of the short-lived Zand Dynasty (1749-79) and the only king in our history who has a near-decent reputation. And he was no king, having refused the royal title preferring to be called *Vakil al Roāya*, literally 'advocate of the people'. The Arg Karimkhāni, to give it its full name, fell into disrepair during the following Qājār dynasty but was later converted to a municipal prison in Reza Shah's reign, and remained so until that day. And the people of Shiraz wanted to conquer their Bastille. And like the latter it held no prisoners. The Shah had built a modern prison outside town and named it Ādel Ābad, 'the place of justice', newspeak Iranian style. But for obscure reasons the police had fired on the assailants. Fired to kill the very day all was lost and the central government had collapsed.

To get there I had to make a round trip as the Falakeh Arg, on Zand Avenue, and the *Arg* itself, lying a hundred metres to the north of the avenue, was a battle ground. Mehran, a distant cousin of my wife, wafer thin with massive crown of dense black hair and a very thick Stalin moustache, was waiting. We stood there near the entrance to the bazaar. Don't go too close, he warned. He was a resident in psychiatry and true to his training was cautious. An unnecessary warning as I too had become prudent having seen the sickening absurdity, the futility of unarmed civilians facing live bullets. Once more we were mere observers to a massacre. The firing continued for two hours, G3 machine gun bursts, and single shots, and they kept bringing wounded people past us. Then a group of Qashqāi' tribesmen mostly armed with rather ancient looking Brno rifles arrived, later to be joined by air force cadets. Until the arrival of the poorly armed but crack shot Qashqāi', the police had been shooting at unarmed men, picking them off one by one.

We had no useful role there, so we decided to help take some of the wounded back to the relatively new Shiraz Hospital which was a few hundred metres east on Zand avenue on Falakeh Valiahd (now Valiasr)– where I had been shot at outside Masjed Habib a few months, and a memory-leap back. As I walked up the hospital stairs, they wheeled a man in on a trolley. He was young, perhaps in his early 20's. His brain was partially spilling out of a head wound almost the size of my fist, with something that looked like steam floating away from its pinkish convoluted surface. He was still breathing when I told the young porter to take him downstairs to the mortuary. "But he is alive", the boy protested, tears in his big black eyes. Not for long, don't waste time on him. There were wounded everywhere. In the morgue that afternoon I counted 41 bodies and about 40 wounded in the emergency room. We went back to the *Arg* to find the armed men had captured the citadel, and the police escaped by lorry from the back door. It was ransacked and I picked up a bullet as a souvenir. With that, the Revolution in Shiraz was over.

The cost of the Revolution will never be known. One estimate put the dead as 10-12 thousand with a further 40 to 50 thousand wounded.[1] Shiraz had been on the whole spared from the massacres that were commonplace in other cities. Two were killed in Masjed No, about seven in Masjed Habib which I witnessed, thirteen to fifteen in the Sa'di Village massacre and one more the following day in the funeral, and a few others during street demonstration, and two when assaulting the SAVAK building. Compared to Tehran, Tabriz, Mashhad, Qazvin, or Kermanshah it was a relatively peaceful Revolution. It may have something to do with General Esfandiāri, the martial law commander of Shiraz. When I saw him once in his office to protest at the arrest of our invited speaker, Bāhonar, he did not seem to relish killing. The fact that he was not prosecuted afterwards, which may of course have alternative explanations since many of the top brass in the previous regime also escaped arrest and prison, may confirm my suspicion. So, the 40 or more shot dead on that day, was nauseatingly futile, on the day after the national uprising had been won. The added tragedy of dying, like the poet Wilfred Owen, in or after the dying days of a regime. The ghost of this tragic day was to reappear in my life as a grotesquely comic coda.

When I got back to the hospital, I was told that Mohsen Mahluji, Mani, one other academic with four *ashāyeri* (tribal) gunmen wielding Brno rifles had conquered the television station. In fact, the station was handed to them without a struggle. The town had already capitulated before the fall of the citadel. Mohsen had placed two rifle-armed Qashqāi' outside as guards and taken charge of broadcasting with the help of the staff who had stayed behind. "The television now belongs to the people" was the announcement over the airwaves and went on to ask for armed men to guard the buildings. The two poorly armed tribesmen could not have put up much resistance to a counterattack. Rumours of a coup by sections of the army loyal to the Shah had been circulating across the country over the last few days. We certainly did not feel out of the woods. Eleven armed men arrived, some Tudeh and the others from the Mojahedin. A division of tasks – Mohsen for liaison with the city, Akbar for public relations and Mani security. Mani set a password, Mehdi Rezaii, (one of the originators of the Peoples Mojahedin of Iran - PMOI) for the guards. No one was to be allowed in without the password and nothing was to be broadcast without Mohsen's approval. Later that night Mani returned and was waved in, no password asked. Furious. Such an amateurish affair.

The first broadcast of the conquered radio station was a revolutionary song by Victor Jara, the Chilean singer whose hands had been chopped off by Pinochet's henchmen in that infamous Santiago stadium in 1973. The blood froze in my veins, and I cried uncontrollably. It was followed by *lā elāha ellallāh* (there is no god but Allah) in an excruciating kitsch pop version. Later the station repeatedly broadcast *bāhārān khojasteh bād* (welcome spring), a revolutionary song by Kerāmat Dāneshiān,[2] executed by the Shah and hastily recorded by Esfandiar Monfaredzādeh to be broadcast on the anniversary of their execution. It became an anthem of the left over the next years. Both tapes, the crudely popified religious incantation and the revolutionary promise of spring, were to disappear from the airwaves soon - for different reasons.

A few hours later Hojjatoleslām Movahhed arrived representing Ayatollah Mahallāti and the new regime. Dastqeib arrived later, to represent his father, a rival to Mahallāti. The University had 'conquered' the station and we were determined to keep our hold. But the mullahs were there, polite but clearly unhappy to share. We argued a little. "Just leave us" Movahhed turned to me reassuringly "Islam will give you everything, don't worry", he smiled, the smile of victors. Was this the same mullah who had waved his fist screaming and threatened to smash it into our mouths? Then a Mr Kāshani appeared from nowhere. "*Ab tobeh ru sarash rikhtim* (we have poured the water of repentance on his head)" the mullah assured us, pointing to the man who had run the television station. Kāshani, who did not look at all wet, gave us his version of a victory smile. More like a condescending sneer. He was later officially appointed to head Shiraz Radio-Television.

The next few days were farcical. Civil authority had collapsed, and radio and television were the only means of communication. The city was without rulers. Each corner was under the control of one or other group. *Komitehs*[3] had mushroomed everywhere. Arms were openly sold on the streets, even G3 submachine guns with bullets. The TV was the centre of government for the province of Fars and beyond. But the mullahs had not yet quite got the hang of governing. We, from the Faculty, had set up a 24-hour rota, eight hours at a time, while the mullahs went to bed at night, leaving government to the duty professor on call.

On that first morning I was on call. It was early morning, a beautiful February day, Nargess's birthday, the 23rd. We were sitting with the television controller discussing which of the hundreds of messages of solidarity which had come in should be read. The telephone was ringing continuously from all parts of Fars asking for instructions, giving news, telling of troop movements, of villages being captured, of arrests. One group was stranded in the middle of nowhere and wanted us to organise a rescue vehicle. Another telling us of the threat to a group of dervishes. It was a whirlwind of confusion and excitement. Movahhed was squatting on the carpet a few feet away, apparently happy to let me get on with it. He refused the fried eggs offered us for lunch. We don't want eggs, he retorted curling up his nose towards his turban, bring us bread and cheese, the food of the poor. He ate the fried eggs anyway. With relish.

Suddenly I heard a commotion to my right and saw a uniformed officer, a *sarlashgar* (major general), arrive in full uniform. He still carried his sidearm. "Should we not disarm him?" I whispered into Movahhed's ear. He seemed surprised at the suggestion, but Āzādeh, who was there to take over from me, disarmed him anyway. As he was chatting to the mullah I was called away to another phone call from somewhere in Mamasani. A group of Qashqāi' tribesmen were planning to dismantle and take away a television aerial on top of a hill and could I send a jeep to rescue it. Frantically ringing here and there,

CHAPTER 32

I could not locate a single person in possession of a jeep or similar vehicle. The next thing I knew the general was heading towards the broadcast room. "What is he going to do?" Azadeh asked our mullah. "That was the general in charge of security in Shiraz. He is going to read a message of solidarity to the people of Iran", Movahhed replied in that calm, slightly condescending voice mullahs use to address those not wearing a clerical cloak.[4] "I have read his message and it seems good", he said with a finality that left no room for dissent. That confidence, which leaves no room for questioning, must be part of their training. "But how do you know what he says is not some kind of a code to military units to get up to something," I said. Another look of bafflement followed by grudging recognition. They managed to take the message away just in time before the general read it. He was visibly angry but kept his cool. Wait until we call Tehran for confirmation, we said. While Āzādeh went to phone he slipped away, minus his handgun. The mullahs were truly new to this job of ruling. The major general was later executed. I have no idea what happened to the aerial but there was another telephone from the 3rd Army Barracks. People are attacking, wanting to disarm it. A few minutes later someone rang. They had been able to remove the triggers from the G3 machine guns. Two years later, those same barracks became my enforced home for three months.

That evening Rezā Khajehpour, a professor at the Agricultural College, was on call. Around two am a phone call came from Jāsk. It was a soldier in the local garrison. Two US warships had been sighted off this key island on the Persian Gulf. There is no commander here, no one in charge, no officers. They have all gone. The caller was panicking. Was this a prelude to military attack? Reza started ringing around to the Third Army Headquarters, to the airport, to anywhere he could think of. Finally he managed to get through to one of the command centres in Tehran who sent out two Phantom jets to investigate and chase them away. That was the night a professor of agriculture became commander in chief of the Southern Provinces. Three days later the mullahs threw us out. They learnt the art of government fast.

[1] James A Bill, *The Eagle and the Lion,* Yale University Press, 1988, p 236.

That may be an exaggeration, if my own experience is generalisable. I was told of 40 killed in the Masjed Habib massacre, a figure the BBC later broadcast, when the actual number turned out to be nearer 7 – see chapter 26, Masjed Habib.

[2] Dāneshiān and the poet Khosrow Golesorkhi were arrested with a number of others accused of plotting to kill the Shah and executed in 1973. Both defended their Marxist beliefs in court and condemned the Shah's dictatorship. The Shah never allowed reporters into trials of political prisoners again. Dāneshiān adapted the song from a poem written on the death of Patrice Lumumba by Dr Abdollah Behzadi, a Tudeh poet.

[3] Revolutionary *Komitehs*, often centred on the local mosque or *Hosseinieh* took over the running of neighbourhoods.

[4] *aba* which Shi'a clergy wear over their shoulders. When I was a child my clerical family used to call the rest of the population *fokoli*, literally someone with a bowtie!

33

Chapter 33

Heady days

Those were exciting days. That spring the hills round the city looked greener than I remembered. Suddenly we had 'light and air' and could breathe.

Things just ran by themselves. Earlier I had seen a man come and mend a broken window; there was clearly no one to tell him. This was his revolution. He, we, owned the country. Now I saw pedestrians stopping a car that had crossed the central grass-reservation, the one so often used as picnic ground by pleasure loving Shirazis, telling them off for breaking the rules. This is our city now, they scolded him. He squirmed and apologised. Red traffic lights were obeyed. I was told of two cars colliding. Each driver apologetically blamed himself while a bystander offered to pay the costs as he was 'well off'. Apocryphal or not that was the atmosphere of the time. It was a time of trust, like the mile-long queues of cars at the petrol station looked after by a few dozen youths who would also watch over the rows of cans in their thousands, left to be filled in turn, unattended, trusting. No stealing, no cheating and if the older inhabitants moaned the youth would talk to them gently about 'our town'.

One day, walking through a deserted corridor in the Medical School just before the February uprising, I saw a cleaner, mop resting on the wall next to his bucket with its dirt-grey water, pull a white covered book[1] out of his white coat and sit down to read. Cleaners did not read in the *ancien régime*; in fact, very few people read. Books were published in editions of two to three thousand. National newspapers had a circulation of 50 thousand or so. They made their money from official advertisements, and you bought them to find out whose funeral you had to attend. And it ended its useless life usefully with the grocer or fruit seller for wrapping up fruits and nuts, a form of recycling practiced in most peripheral societies. That circulation had exploded to over half a million – a million on the day the Shah left. Since many people shared a paper, multiply the actual readership several fold. Everyone wanted to understand, to learn, to expand their horizons. That was one of the most startling outcomes of the Revolution. Life went on in autopilot even more organised than before. This was our city. And for a while everyone in the town seemed so cheerful, you would think the Shah never had any supporters.

But the white-covered Marxist books which had made their appearance on the pavement stalls the previous summer had a dark side. The Islamists saw the hand of SAVAK behind them and the intention to sow division in the ranks of the Revolution. I too wondered at times how the Shah allowed their sale. Perhaps books by Lenin on the streets of Iran would send warning messages to the Carter administration which was pressuring the Shah on human rights. That first post-Revolutionary summer I read Lenin's three-volume selected writings, published in one large volume in Farsi, from cover to cover, an interesting experience, that I never repeated with Marx or anyone else.

On the third day there was the first meeting of representatives of all the Councils (*Shora*) that had been spontaneously emerging in every factory, office and neighbourhood in Shiraz. It was held in the engineering college and was called up by the Committee of Fars Revolutionaries (CFR) who had earlier masterminded the attack on the SAVAK headquarters. Behind it was the Worker, Peasant, Student group (*Kargar, Dehqān, Dāneshjoo*), an amalgam of a number of left groups, which was probably the most active left circle in Fars province until a few months after the Revolution. The pro-Russian

CHAPTER 33

Tudeh and the pro-Chinese Ranjbaran (which split from Tudeh as Sāzmān Enqelābi Hezb-e Tudeh) parties were not permitted to attend. Mani stood up in that meeting saying he represented 4,000 on the left. Or did he say guerrillas? Mani loved to exaggerate, and in truth reality for most of us had slipped behind a red mist of optimism. Numbers lost their meaning. A German doctor once told me, quoting his father, that during the 1920's hyperinflation in the Weimar republic, when asked their age, some would reply 24 million or even billion and trillion. We had our city, we had formed our Councils (*Shoras*), which somehow had got enmeshed and entangled with our prior image of the Soviets in the Russian Revolution, and we could do what we wanted with them. Or so it seemed.

That meeting was broken up by a number of academics who had overnight catapulted to positions of power in the University. Among these were a professor at the College of Literature, Pāydārfar, my neighbour the paediatrician Dr Qarib, an engineer called Āyatollāhi, who became quite powerful in the city, and a power-hungry gynaecologist Dr Borāzjāni. In an underground newsletter which a few of us began to publish sometime later, we nicknamed the latter *shishloolband* (six-shot-gunslinger) as he went on to simultaneously occupy six posts. The Islamists were rather short of talent then. There were also those who had ingratiated themselves with the *hezbollāh* in the last year with suspicious credentials. Even the Islamists began to feel uncomfortable with the likes of Pāydārfar.. The CFR went to organise a large meeting in the College of Literature on the anniversary of the execution by the Shah of the poet and film-maker Kerāmat Dāneshiān and the Fadāi' attack on the Siāhkal police station and then faded into the sea of emerging much larger groups on the left, the Fadāi', Peykar, Rahe Kargar etc. [see appendix 2]

On the morning of February 9, two days before the final surrender of the Shah's military, Khomeini and his appointed prime minister Bāzargān, declared the Revolution over and ordered all those on strike to go back to work. For many, not just on the left but also those who identified with an Islamic vision, the Revolution was just beginning. Some obeyed the leader, even if not entirely happy with the order. Others, mainly on the left, simply ignored it and went on to stage the uprising of February 12 symbolised in the capital by the attack by the Homafaran air force cadets and armed Fadāi' guerrillas on the air force barracks that same day. The big schism had started. At one end of the spectrum were those who wanted to initiate radical social change and at the other end those who simply wanted to rule but with different sets of social conventions. And millions in between, each with their individual or collective dreams who looked up to Khomeini to colour them in like a children's colouring book and make them blossom into fruit. He was the leader who had led them this far and most saw no reason to question his judgment. But Khomeini had his own vision, saw people as sheep to be guarded by the Shi'a clergy, and as his first President Bani Sadr later said, neither had, nor needed, advisers, counsellors or spokesmen. Khomeini also had a head start.

As far as Khomeini was concerned, an Iran where the Shah was replaced by himself was an end in itself. The slogan of 'after the Shah it is the turn of America' (*Ba'd as Shah nobat-e Āmricāst*)shouted outside the Medical School on the morning of victory was never to be repeated. The task now was to transform society into an Islamic one. There was to be a cultural revolution, folding back many of the changes Iran had undergone over the last 70 years. But Khomeini needed to build his machinery of coercion first. Priorities were women, the judiciary and education. Women were an easy target. Ignoring the promises he had made in Paris, the Revolutionary Council, (*Shoraye Enqelab*) made up of close associates of Khomeini, mostly clerics, and a handful of Bāzargān's men, decreed that women could not go into government offices without covering their hair. There was a huge demonstration in North Tehran, which most on the left ignored. These were bourgeois women, 'perfumed and with fur-coates', not worthy of radical left support, we murmured. Unfortunately, as Samuel Taylor Coleridge said 'experience is a lantern on the skies which shines only the waves behind us'. Not for the first, nor for the last time, the left ignored Niemöller's warning.[1]

The red mist was blown off pretty quickly. The next day in Tehran, the Fadāi' and Mojahedin headquarters were expelled from Tehran University. In Ahwaz, thugs belonging to the local Islamic Revolutionary Komiteh[2]

CHAPTER 33

disrupted a talk by Mortezā Mohit, Marxist writer and translator. In virtually every university there were clashes between Bāzargān's minister of higher education, Shariatmadāri, who was appointing chancellors (or supervisors, *Sarparast*, as they coyly called them) from above, and the academic body who wanted to elect their own. Within days they had appointed Amir Hooshang Mehryār to the renamed Shiraz University, to take over from Dr Farhang Mehr a Zoroastrian, as *Sarparast*. There were protests everywhere and in most of the larger colleges the academic body ignored Bāzargān and went on to elect their own Council (*Shora*) by the entire faculty, staff and student body. The *Shora* then went on to choose their own *Sarparast*.

In our medical school, a three-man provisional *Shora* was elected with Asqar Rastegar representing the staff and chosen as its chairman, Mehdi Mohassel, a resident in medicine who had been a prisoner of the Shah, was elected by the interns and residents and a student whose name I cannot recall chosen by the student body. The second *Shora* of the Medical School was elected a few weeks later. In addition to Asqar and Mohassel, it included among others Dr Shahid Sales, Mrs Alizadeh (that same Alizadeh who before the revolution had harangued Shriatmadāri now minister of higher education, during the 'week of solidarity') and Ajaluyān, a third-year student who was chosen by the student body. The last two were militant Islamists, *hezbollāhis* as they were known colloquially, and showed the changing balance of power in the Medical School. But the *hezbollāh* was as yet in a minority. Ajaluyān, with his unsmiling face and sparkle-free deep-set eyes, not looking directly at you but seemingly through you into a dark unknown, eyes that years later I saw in the President Ahmadinejād, would have a big say in my life. With animal-like premonition I felt a deep fear of those eyes as we sat around a table drafting the new university curriculum.

For many of us at the Medical School, Pahlavi University (renamed Shiraz), the Shah's darling and the bastard child of the capital's Tehran and National Universities, could not continue as of old. Its entire structure had to be democratised with a greater input by those it employed and taught. It had to be independent of the state, self-governing in a real sense, free of imperialist influence, with a curriculum that reflected the needs of the people of Iran, and devoted to training the cadres of a free, democratic and independent Iran. This was what we had fought for and for the first time we saw the possibilities of moving towards those goals, utopian as it may seem with hindsight. We refused the government's order to restart classes until we knew what we were meant to teach and learn. The majority of the faculty were totally unhappy with this but had no choice. Most students and junior doctors point blank refused to go back to the old ways.

The Medical School *Shora* held large open meetings, the Assembly, in Talare Mosaddeq, now officially renamed from Ashraf Hall, and discussed the new curriculum. Names are a signpost to aims and aspirations. Separate days were devoted to different issues. How does education act as an arm of the politico-economic system? The role of Pahlavi University in realizing the Shah's 'Big Civilisation' and imperialist plans for the country. What is meant by the right to free health care and what models have been tried and tested? What is meant by independence of university and academic freedom and how do they relate to the obligations of the university to society? We researched and discussed the many educational reforms introduced by successive governments during the previous 25 years; what were their deeper aims and how had they impacted on the socio-economic state of the country. We studied various educational models used around the world and what is meant by problem-based and evidence-based medicine. We looked at models of education and health care in the West, in Cuba, in China and elsewhere. Each Assembly was devoted to a particular group of topics and attendance was voluntary.

It very soon became clear that we needed to do this kind of work in smaller units. So, the *Shora* asked the Assemblies to elect smaller groups from among themselves to discuss the issues. I was elected to the committee that discussed the medical school curriculum, headed by Ajalyuān, the third-year student elected to the second *Shora*. Each committee had representative from the others so that work could be coordinated. The blueprints were then to be amalgamated by the combined groups and once a curriculum was ready it would be put to a vote.

CHAPTER 33

Bāzargān had impacted my life twice, once by removing Ezzy as head of the Narmak Higher College (Honarsārāye Āli Nārmmak, later to be renamed as College (University) of Science and Technology) in an apparently arbitrary act. Ezzy had hewn the place from scratch out of a rock-strewn wasteland in the eastern suburbs of Tehran. Why he was removed was never made clear – Ezzy was the epitome of a good technocrat, efficient, incorruptible, totally honest, and essentially apolitical. The second impact, more in character, was by appointing Mehryār as Chancellor in Shiraz. Mehryār had been active in the National Association of Academics (SMD) as had the new head of National University in Tehran,[3] Dr Taqizadeh a pathologist. Both were long-standing National Front members and we had worked together in the anti-Shah student movement in London almost two decades ago. One day Mehryār, I and a few other National Front members, had driven to rescue Dr Taqizadeh from a beating at the hands of SAVAK agents in West London. Suddenly these two were on the other side of the barricade. There were to be many more barricade jumpings. The SMD was seen as kingmaker, appointing chancellors and ministers.[4]

Borhānmanesh, the same colleague who in Connecticut had denounced the Revolution as a creation of the British, was calling for a general assembly of the SMD and new elections. He had already got himself elected as Head of the Department of Medicine, my department, and now had his eyes on more exalted heights. He had joined the SMD as soon as he saw its potentials as a ladder to the Dean's Office. The assembly was to be held the next day. Overnight 80 to 100 new members paid their 100 tomans and signed the manifesto. The hall was packed with two thirds of the faculty of the Medical and Dental Schools attending. Mani, as current deputy representative gave a short, subdued report. We both knew that we were about to be deposed. I was not going to go quietly. I stood up and gave a point-by-point detailed account of what the SMD had organised in the Medical School – twenty two counts of achievements. They listened politely, and impatiently, waiting for me to shut up and sit down so that they could get on with the business of electing a representative and go back to their clinics or offices or whatever. You could see hate, you could see pity, and you could also see embarrassment in some eyes. When I was done, Borāzjāni, the gynaecologist who later went on to take multiple jobs, got up. "Dr S...", he began in a sarcastic, dismissive almost contemptuous tone, "has attributed everything that people had done, that the people of Shiraz had achieved, to himself, as his own. We never elected him, and he is not our representative," he ended. Several people stood up to defend me and others who, not wanting to directly attack me, introduced the argument that times had changed and required a change of leadership. There is nothing like the prospects of a grab for power that separates friends from sheep. Mani resigned. I refused. Against Borhānmanesh in a secret ballot I received 53 votes to his 60 with some abstentions. I felt good as it showed the line-up in the Faculty was not as bad as I had imagined. Borhānmanesh never got the post of *Sarparast* that he so coveted. The SMD died a natural death a few weeks later. Who pocketed the membership fees I never found out.

Looking back, the SMD was a democratic progressive organisation with aims that went beyond the trade union rights of its members. As such it could only survive in a democratic society. And even as a trade union it failed just as all similar attempts in the country failed against the onslaught of the Islamists who could not tolerate any institution, no matter how miniscule, that they did not totally control. Such was the fate of the Iranian Medical Organisation (Nezām Pezeshgi), which licensed and regulated medical practitioners, the teachers union that was broken up through expulsion of 25,000 teachers, the lawyers association, and many others. 'The university is the bastion of freedom', our banner had proclaimed; they hated it before the Revolution, they hated it after they rode to power on the back of a popular revolution, and they hate it now. The battle for the University was vital for Khomeini and went on for two years and it was contested at every step. The mullahs only managed to reign in the University by closing it down in the 'Cultural Revolution', and when that was resisted by physically purging, arresting and even executing its most active agents.

A few months later a group of us, from a wide variety of ideological backgrounds, set up a discussion on the nature and ingredients of national medicine – *tebbe melli* – using the term first put forward by the first minister of health – Dr Sāmi.[5] There were Islamists, Tudeh, Fadāi' and other left groups, and also many who did not belong to any group. But soon the outside pressures on the University and events developing in the country became more distracting. The most active persons gradually melted away into their other activities. Yet some of the deliberations and conclusions of the *tebbe melli* workshop found their way into the work of the Medical School *Shora*.

After the Cultural Revolution a year later, the Ministry of Health in Bani-Sadr's government, was tasked with the running of the medical schools nationally. The new Ministry came up with its blue-print for medical education. To our astonishment, it was almost identical to the curriculum we had produced in Shiraz Medical School minus its core – the democratic decision-making process that was so central to our entire enterprise. But even that skeleton remained on paper as many of the medical faculty members across Iran were expelled or left for either their private offices or abroad.

[1] When the Nazis came for the communists, I remained silent; I was not a communist.

When they locked up the social democrats, I remained silent; I was not a social democrat.

When they came for the trade unionists, I did not speak out; I was not a trade unionist.

When they came for the Jews, I remained silent; I wasn't a Jew.

When they came for me, there was no one left to speak out.

Pastor Friedrich Gustav Emil Martin Niemöller.

[2] The *Komiteh Enqelābe Eslāmi* took shape in most neighbourhoods in the last months of the Revolution under the auspices of the local mosque or *Hosseinieh*, and organised street demonstrations and other revolutionary actions. After the uprising they acted as the security arm of the mullahs and were gradually merged with the Revolutionary Guards Corps and the *Basij* militia once these were set up.

[3] Now Shahid Beheshti University.

[4] In addition to Shariatmadāri, Abbāspour became Minister of Power, Āyat

and Qafurifar were given important positions within the Islamic Republic Party, the latter taking on Abbāspour's post after he died in an explosion.

[5] Dr Kāzem Sāmi was the leader of *Jonbeshe Mardome Iran* (JAMA – The Movement of the Iranian People). Before that he had inaugurated the Movement of Socialist Believers in God (*Nehzate Khodāparastāne Sociālist*). He returned to private life after the resignation of Bāzargān and was murdered outside his office in 1988 in mysterious circumstances.

Chapter 34

Digging deeper

I was waiting for inspiration. I disliked intensely the regime that had emerged out of the volcano of the Revolution yet could not explain why in theoretical terms. I cast a blank vote in the referendum when Khomeini gave the country only one of two choices: Islamic Republic or Monarchy and had briskly dismissed all other choices, making the referendum meaningless. Week after week I would buy anything that was for sale in kiosks, from the literature stalls of groups on campus, from what we call a *basat* spread out on the pavement and from the one bookshop in town which stocked left literature. There were translations of most of the communist classics, some as if transcribed into pidgin Farsi word by word with a dictionary. I bought every paper put out by the political groups that had emerged out of the amorphous mass of the Revolution, those that had real presence nationally[1] and even the mini-groupings.

I found virtually all their analyses of the regime superficial and mere slogan waving. No depth. No analysis. Just a continuation of the leaflets dished out during the Revolution – bom-bi-bom literature, all pomp and little substance. Not a word from the largest group on the left, the Fadāi', on the nature of the regime, even though they were fighting it in Turkaman Sahra[2] and

Kurdistan, in factories, schools, universities, indeed anywhere there was resistance to those ordering the Revolution to pack up and go home. They reported all these conflicts in their weekly paper *Kār*, but not a word as to what that meant with regards to the nature of the Revolutionary Council that had taken charge of the country or the regime as a whole. In Fars province the Fadāi' were encouraging land seizure. I helped them print the paper issued by their local peasant organisation by passing it on to Yousef, who had access to a stencil machine. Still not a word. It was as though the dragons they were fighting here, there and everywhere somehow belonged to a fairy story with no relation to who was running the country.

The SMD continued to remain active for a time in Tehran by protesting at the censorships imposed on the radio television, at the Shah's army not being disbanded and even the Shah's Chief of Staff, Qarehbāqi being reinstated. They organised seminars and drew up guidelines on the election of university administrations. But the SMD in Shiraz was dead and a group of us set up a new organisation of the teaching staff to pursue our original goals. After heated debate it was named the Association of Progressive Professors (APP). "Isn't that too presumptuous?" a few of us dissented, "should it not be left to others to call us progressive?" We lost the vote to the much larger engineering and agricultural college contingent. It is uncanny how quickly a gathering of like minded people gels into semi-distinct blobs with a few individuals floating in between. There was a minority in the APP around the Medical School contingent who saw it as a weapon for fighting for the ideals of an independent, free and anti-imperialist university, a continuation of the ideals of the SMD manifesto, and a majority with roots in the Confederation of Iranian Students abroad (CIS) with a more political agenda. By starting its first leaflet with the words *'the supremely counter-revolutionary Revolutionary Council'* (*Shoraye enqelabe beqayat zedde enqelab*) the APP called the entire new regime to battle. It was either heroic or quixotic. It was certainly the product of a group confident of victory. The three of us protested at this too but this too was voted out. "Aren't they counter-revolutionary? Should we not call a spade by its proper name?" mocked Mostafa, the unspoken leader of the majority. It was the same Mostafa who had so effectively turned the tables

CHAPTER 34

on the Islamist students during the week of solidarity. I had to explain away that leaflet in my trial two years later.

But the fact that those straddling the middle ground between the two views gravitated to accepting the defiant language gives a picture of the balance of power in the country, at least as it was perceived within the circles we moved. In some way we were all overconfident. Early on J and I went to a parent-teacher meeting in the children's primary school, Ardavān, to meet the newly appointed head. The unsmiling new head began talking about how Islam required separating the boys from the girls from the very first year and finding gender-matched teachers for them. I just lost my head, raised my hand, and uttered a series of expletives against the new regime and at his religion. If I had done that a year or two later, I would have talked myself into a nightmare. As it is, he looked even more glum, turned away and pretended not to have heard. They went on to separate the pupils in two daily shifts morning and afternoon, switching each week. But segregation at teacher level took many years, particularly in secondary schools and especially because of shortage of female science and maths teachers. They were simply short of teachers, especially after the massive purges that followed victory.

One day Siamak, one of the residents, came up and shyly suggested that I might be interested in a couple of pamphlets. I was game to anything. A regime rising out of a massive popular revolution whose main slogan was 'independence, freedom, Islamic republic' and with widespread popular support[3] was dominated by conservative, reactionary mullahs who were curbing that freedom, forcing a return to previous social relations, preoccupied by bringing in *sharia* punishments of lashing and stoning, and determined to push women back into the home. My entire being felt the defeat of all my ideals, the waste of all those lives, and was desperate to join an opposition group who went beyond slogans. I was also looking for an explanation. What was the nature of this regime so unlike anything that had gone before? With the exception of Tudeh, which under its new general secretary Noureddin Kianuri, had backed Khomeini right from the start, most of the left was either hostile or undecided, or more accurately simply confused. The three pamphlets that Siamak surreptitiously handed to me galvanised the Iranian political scene. Overnight, a new force had entered the left and rapidly absorbed some of the best brains and dedicated militants from the other organisations. Hardly out of the womb, Rāhe Kargar became a player on the national scene.

The group had formed in the Shah's prison from of the cadres of left groups, and a handful of Mojahedin, who had escaped death in battle or the firing squad. In these pamphlets they had produced a well-argued rejection of the Tudeh reformist line without totally throwing out the legacy of the October Revolution. They discarded the third worldism of Maoists and their simplistic division of the world into three camps and criticised their own previous glorification of the gun in the guerrilla movement in Iran, which they had helped create and in which they had fought. Samson-like, a small group of cadres had effectively challenged the three pillars on which the entire edifice of the left had been resting until that point. Then in the ground-breaking pamphlet *'Fascism, nightmare or reality'* they had begun to explore how a regime with popular roots can act as caretaker for capitalist relations when neither of the two main classes in society, the bourgeoisie and the working class, could impose their direct rule. They referenced their arguments with 18th Brumaire of Louis Bonaparte (1852) where Marx talks about a ruling caste acting as an exceptional state of the capitalist class guarding capitalist relations from the onslaught of the working class at a time when neither class is strong enough to take political power. And by going back to Marx, in the process, they had broken with another fundamental rule of left politics in Iran – to exclusively use later 'official' interpretations of Marx and Engels - by going direct to the original texts. There it was, an argument totally alien to the Iranian Left, (and indeed most of the world's left) that you judge a government by its policies and not its supposed class origin.

Later, with the occupation of the US embassy and the fancy dress charade of anti-imperialist posturing, they used the same arguments to highlight how you cannot oppose imperialism by suppressing working class and other independent organisations.[4] The petite-bourgeoisie, if that was indeed the class origin of the new government, was not necessarily progressive – a mantra for both the official communists and the Maoists. Whether they were 'progressive' or not depended on their policies. I was bowled over. And in a few weeks the first issue of its paper came out with the title: The Revolution is dead! Long live the Revolution!

Why did they not succeed in their aim of becoming the main force of the revolutionary left? And why despite systematically dismantling the entire theoretical edifice of the Tudeh's suicidal policy of support for Khomeini's regime were they unable to stop a substantial section of the left following that line into the self-annihilating abyss? As usual the reasons are multiple. The language did not help. Not only because it was at times difficult – you needed a PhD in Farsi to fully grasp that first leading article, although in time this weakness was overcome. No. Their language was difficult at a more fundamental level because it put forward concepts that were alien to the almost politically illiterate left that had suddenly ballooned into a force of several hundred thousand without the necessary knowledge to go with it. The left wanted a few simple formulae – not unlike religious dogma. It is uncanny to survey the left world-wide today and see little has changed.

Then there was the immense prestige of big-brother in Moscow. As one senior Fadāi' majority[5] leader in Shiraz told me, "they must know better", emphasising the 'must' as you would a *fatwa*. Finally, and this was something I got to know better with time, political groups of the Left, like most Islamic groups, essentially read only their own literature. Suddenly faced with a complex reality and without the intellectual tools to understand it, the left drew walls around themselves and comforted themselves with a set of certainties. Behind these walls they felt more comfortable in reading things that confirmed their views – caricatured in the UK as 'Guardian readers', for example. The left-leaning modern petite-bourgeoisie who had ignited the fires of the revolution watched it taken through to victory by the boys from the poor neighbourhoods, those on the margins of the Shah's march to the 'Great Civilization', those who had used the tactics of *Āshurā Tāsuā'* marches to organised mass demonstrations, who spearheaded the attacks on cinemas and *araq* (vodka) shops but also banks and offices, and who now, riding on their motorbikes, were breaking up kiosks or street vendors (*basati*) selling left literature. Here were Fanon's Wretched of the Earth using the same slogans, that the left had thought its own, to smash up the left and any cry for democracy. No wonder the left was confused. And the particular security blanket they chose for comfort was sometimes fitted in with their already formed views, not infrequently through pure chance. Family members gelled round a charismatic relative, and then closed the door.

But the new nation-wide opposition also included young believers who would not abandon their Islamic beliefs, but who could not stomach the often risible nonsense that was being regularly broadcast in the name of Islam. Who could not understand why a regime that claimed to represent the *mostaz'afin* (literally 'the weak', the term used by Khomeini to denote the lower strata of society and avoid the unclean word of working class) was curbing freedoms; dragging its feet on land reform; apart from seizure of the properties of the Shah and his closest associates, was calling for business as usual for private industry and agribusiness and was reassuring the US and its allies. They flocked in their hundreds and thousands to the Mojahedin who, while initially looking left for allies, gradually moved away into their own cocoon as they misjudged the popular discontent and planned their own Bonapartist coup - with disastrous results.

[1] In the months after the Revolution the groups that had any real impact on oppositional politics at the national level (leaving out the Kurdish, Turkaman, Arab and Baluch – the national - organisations aside) were, in order of influence, the Mojahedin, the Fadāi' which before their split were the largest left group, Peykār (the largest among the many Maoist groups), and Rāhe Kārgar. The Tudeh party had an intellectual influence far beyond its numerical strength, operating above all through the authority of the Soviet Union and 'brother' parties. Tudeh used this authority to split the largest left organisation, the Fadāi' and steal cadres from virtually all the other groups.

[2] With the help of the Fadāi', the Turkamans living along eastern Caspian Sea, had occupied the large agribusinesses belonging to the Shah's closest allies and ran it in the form of peasant cooperatives (*Shoraye Dehqāni*) coordinated by a central headquarters - *Setāde Markazi Shorāha*. They had also created the Turkaman People's Political-Cultural Centre (*Kānune Farhangi-Siāsi Khalqe*

Turkaman). In April 1979 the new regime attacked both, killing many. Later, on the anniversary of Siāhkal, which was also close to the anniversary of the revolution, Revolutionary Guards led by Mehdi Rezāi', who later became their national commander, attacked Turkaman Sahra in a particularly brutal attack. Senior Fadāi' cadres including Tomāj, Makhtum, Vāhedi, and Jorjāni were arrested and summarily executed by the 'hanging mullah' Khalkhāli.

[3] The referendum on the Islamic republic was given a 99% vote – for once not an entirely manufactured result.

[4] During that first year Khomeini's regime bloodily attacked Kurdistan, Turkaman Sahra and the Arab movement in Khuzestan. They forcibly disbanded all the spontaneous *Shoras* (Committees) in factories, agribusiness, government offices, universities etc and killed, imprisoned or expelled its leaders; imposed a compulsory veil on women and banned them from a number of key jobs such as law, and such 'masculine' university courses as engineering; they purged the schools of 25,000 teachers and smashed their independent organisation as well as those of many professional bodies – doctors, lawyers, writers; they purged the judiciary and introduced the mediaeval law of qesās (an eye for an eye); and even rejected a lukewarm land reform proposed from within their own ranks.

[5] Following the seizure of the US embassy by the regime the Fadāi' split in two with the majority of its Central Committee joining the Tudeh party to support the regime and a minority breaking away in opposition [see appendix 2].

[6] Franz Fanon, a psychiatrist from Martinique and working in Algeria wrote Wretched of the Earth (1961). His books including Black Face White Mask (1952) were highly influential in forming the Third-Worldist anti-imperialist discourse. He died of leukaemia at a young age.

35

Chapter 35

Glimpses of the basement

So it was that a man still feeling young but approaching middle age found himself involved with attending secret cells, recruiting supporters, printing the weekly organ for the entire southern Iran, printing propaganda posters, organising theoretical training of new recruits, helping prepare exhibitions of photographs of atrocities by the *hezbollāh*. With a few friends I had already spontaneously formed a cell that distributed the national paper in the University even before I had made any formal contact with them. Later we bought our own stencil machine and would receive the stencils from Tehran and spend all night printing them, stapling and packing them for distribution in Shiraz, Mamasani, Yasuj and other towns in the south. I would then shower, shave and go to work. The energy of a fight, invigorating, intoxicating, indescribable, unrepeatable.

And there were moments of black humour. I was to teach two comrades, both working class and female. But where? The compound was out of the question as was their homes. Best to picnic out of town and out of sight of prying eyes. There was a beautiful spot under the shade of trees next to a stream and within sight of wheat fields. The tree-lined stream was in a slightly sunken dip, a little below the field of harvested wheat, the stubbles

CHAPTER 35

of which was being pecked by crows. We had used this spot before with Changiz, a veteran of the Shah's prisons, without mishap.[1] This was our second teaching session. We had spread our carpet beside the water and were busy dissecting a particularly difficult subject on the nature of the state under capitalism.

It was a hot day but the breeze under the trees kept blowing our bits of paper into somersaults. The clear water was playing rumbling music in the background, when I spotted a policeman in full uniform approaching on the path that ran along the field a little way above where we were sitting. He was tall, for an Iranian, thin and had a small moustache. The flitting of the sunlight falling on his blue uniform was like an apparition. My heart exploded. I had never been good at adjusting rapidly to unguarded moments. The man in dark blue uniform walked swaying slightly side to side, as if on a stroll. The girls quickly pushed the bits of paper under their bags and pulled their white cotton chadors[2] printed with tiny flowers over their heads. Seeing a man approaching middle age sitting with two young girls on a carpet with a flask and cups of tea, a knowing smile spread across his face. "These are my students" I answered his question with a voice that was not mine "we are studying together". What is their name, the man in the dark blue uniform asked, not looking directly at the girls? His moustache quivered, suspended over a mocking smile. I had no idea. I knew them by a pseudonym. I made up a name and Nasrin, one the two girls with a dark complexion that suggested she came from down south by the Gulf, quickly added another invention. Would he take us to the station, my heart pounded? 'I am Dr ...' I said, giving him my real name and feeling the red glow spreading upwards from my cheeks across to the sweat that had beaten it to the surface on my forehead. I pulled out my University ID card. Neither girl looked nor dressed remotely like a medical student. The dark-blue uniform was clearly not taken in by the girls but chose to accept the explanation. It may have been respect for the medical profession. Or he was cocking a snoot at the Revolutionary Guards. The municipal police, children of the *ancien régime*, had little love for the new rulers, as I later found out in prison. Smirking, the uniformed man gave me a 'dirty-old-man' look and walked off. There were no more lessons with the girls.

It was late evening, perhaps around ten. The knock on the door jolted me out of my reading. It was Shahab. "I need your help" he blurted out. His agitation made the eczematous patch on his forehead bright red. He entered but he would not sit. "I have just brought a van-load of paper for the press but the gate to the house is too low, and we cannot unload it in the alley as we can't trust the neighbours". He meant the house that was now housing a proper printer which had taken over from our amateurish basement stencil printer. "I just can't drive across town at this time of night with a van full of pristine printing paper. Do you have anywhere we can store it for a few days?" I had to think fast and remembered a friend who had a house at the end of an alley with only orchards as neighbours. We drove to the van which was parked outside a modern house with an iron gate opening into the courtyard with a metal crossbar at the top. No one had thought of measuring the headroom when they had ordered the paper.

We drove across town, rapidly conjuring up some story about carrying paper for the Medical School in case we were stopped by the Revolutionary Guards (Pāsdārs). It was a feeble story. We were driving away from the University, and what would an academic be doing hauling paper in the middle of the night in a van. But that night the Pāsdārs were otherwise engaged. The friend's son answered the door followed by his father, sleepy eyed, surprised and not a little scared. We had arrived unannounced at an hour when no one visited anyone. By the time the four of us had transferred the hundred or so packs of paper into the spare room it was midnight.

Such cavalier inattention to detail was to cost the left dearly in the disasters that would decimate it in 1981. For an organisation that had talked of the possibility of 'fascism' it was unforgivable, yet they too would suffer in the bloodbath. As for the man approaching middle age, that night death once again brushed his flanks and walked away. They were to meet again a few more times.

CHAPTER 35

[1] Changiz Ahmadi, was imprisoned by the Shah for a number of years accused of belonging to an Azari armed group (Raziliq). In prison he rejected the armed guerrilla tactics and helped create Rāhe Kargar to which I was later affiliated. He was arrested by the new regime in 1982 and severely tortured before being executed in the summer of 1983.

[2] A loose cloth which covers from head to toe leaving the face exposed.

Chapter 36

The Cultural Revolution

Khomeini, suppressed anger knotting his eyebrows, had openly regretted not erecting gallows at every crossroad earlier and went on to order this troops to invade Kurdistan by land and air, ironically on the anniversary of the coup that toppled Mosaddeq, August 19, 1979. Now, seven months later, in his new year's address he called for a fundamental revolution in universities to purge them of professors 'attached to East and West' and to turn them into a healthy environment to teach Islamic knowledge (*ulum*). Thus, he paved the way for the final battle to conquer the universities which only ended with the mass arrests and executions of 1981, over a year later.

The regime that emerged once the noise, smoke and dust of the victorious uprising had settled was composed of various factions, as it does even today after over three decades. Almost immediately the newly created Islamic Republic Party (IRP) began a systematic campaign to push back the democratic freedoms won in the Revolution, step by step. It started with the compulsory veiling of women followed by the closure of newspapers. The sequence was carefully planned. Women were easy targets and the first newspaper to be closed was Āyandegan. It began with Āyandegān's publication of a Le Monde interview with Khomeini in Paris, with Bani

Sadr translating, in which Khomeini had guaranteed freedom of speech. Khomeini's office immediately announced that 'the Imam had never read this paper and does not endorse its contents'. The next day *Āyandegān* republished the offending interview, with the rest of the paper blank. It sold a record one million copies. Meanwhile a group of *hezbollāh* working in another daily, Keyhān, forcibly took it over, with Khomeini's blessing. Four months later the Pāsdārān occupied Āyandegān office and imprisoned its editorial board accusing them of links with Israel. Ettelā'āt, another daily, quickly followed. All three papers had been close to the previous regime but had played an important role in the Revolution and their 57-day strike was a significant blow to the monarchy. They had resumed publication on Khomeini's orders. Reza Marzban's Peiqām e Emruz, a popular daily from the left, also disappeared. Even Mardom, Tudeh's paper that wholeheartedly towed the 'Imam line' vanished. The only papers left on display on the stands were insiders, what Brecht/Weil called *der Jasager* (the 'yes men').

Following the first brutal battles of Kurdistan and Turkaman Sahra the IRP felt free to slowly stifle the democratic atmosphere of the country. Neighbourhood and factory *Shorās* (Committees) had already been either purged and taken over by the *hezbollāh* or disbanded. The second war on Turkaman Sahra ended the brief flowering of Turkaman culture and autonomy and drowned their peasant *Shorās* in blood. With these moves the IRP also hoped to weaken its more liberal allies, Bazargān's government and Bani Sadr, who despite the efforts of the IRP was elected as the first president. His election showed the increasing disillusion across the country against the repressive policies of the IRP operating through the Pāsdārān and the *Komiteh* - neighbourhood Committees centred on the local mosque or *Hosseinieh*. Both the left and the liberals had to be squeezed out and eliminated. Stepwise.

There were daily attacks on kiosks selling literature. Thugs repeatedly attacked the area around Tehran University led by Zahra Khānum, a formidable woman with her chador wrapped round her waist. She became emblematic of the *chomāqdārān* – the baton-wielders – so beautifully caricatured in Manuchehr Mahjubi's satirical paper Āhangar, reborn later as *Chalanger* in the UK where he died in exile. In Shiraz the *basāti* street vendors setting out their literature, often oppositional, on the pavements of Zand Avenue were frequent targets. Most of the *basātis* were schoolchildren sympathisers of dissident political groups, left or Mojahedin. It was a hazardous business and you risked beatings and arrest. *Hezollāhis* roaming on motorbikes would identify any *basāt* and call in their gang – that was before the days of mobile phones. One day I was looking at the titles of the papers on sale in a wooden kiosk in Ferdowsi Street that had been there since my arrival to the city when suddenly, like a pack of crows descending on a bowl of rice spilled on the pavement, club wielding young men, black stubble symbolising their devoutness, appeared from all around and tore up his books and papers and savagely beat the proprietor. There he sat with blood pouring from his shaved head, bits of paper strewn around him. A sympathetic crowd quickly gathered and helped him on his feet and salvaged what they could of his wares. Someone gave him money.

With the start of the academic year at the end of September, universities re-elected their *Shorās*. Outside parts of Kurdistan and a few other sanctuaries, the one place where the IRP with its Islamic Societies could not establish their hegemony were the universities. In all the major universities they were in a minority, in many, less than one fifth voted for them. 'Universities are the bastion of freedom' our banner had read in what seemed a generation ago, - the one Rostam had ridiculed. And today they were one of the last stockades behind which the democratic aspirations of the largest revolution in Iranian history had barricaded itself. And my old critic Rostam would have been on board, on side.

We were busy with the excitement of redrafting the very nature of what it meant to be a medical school in our era, when Khomeini masterminded his most spectacular coup. In November 1979 the students following the Imam Line, as they called themselves, occupied the US embassy. Thus, he executed a move that wrong footed his enemies and gained the new regime huge kudos at home and abroad. It was a coup de theatre that was as brilliant as it was without cost. Khomeini was catapulted to the forefront of the 'anti-imperialist' struggle in people's eyes without needing to fire a shot. Inside and outside Iran the left was split, with a large section going under the flag of the Imam until four years later, having served their purpose, their turn came to face the firing squads, prison walls or to confessing to a mountain of 'sins' on television. In the universities, the split in the Fadāi', the largest group on the left, with the majority siding with the regime, removed a substantial section of the left who were organised in the Fadāi' student movement, Pishgām, to either actively side with the regime's Islamic Society (Anjoman Eslāmi) or become side-lined.

I had just returned from a trip to Asyut, Upper Egypt, on a training course organised by the WHO Mediterranean Section to improve the performance of my endocrine laboratory. My research laboratory in the basement of Namāzi, which I used for both research and clinical care, was part of an international consortium of laboratories for which the WHO provided external quality control. In Asyut I was bombarded by students passionate to learn about the Revolution in Iran. Antagonism towards Sadat and his regime was palpable, and he was an ally of the Shah. They spent hours bombarding me with questions. It was not easy to tell how they took my lack of enthusiasm for Khomeini's regime. For them he was untouchable, and I took care not to insult him directly but talked about the regime in the abstract, warning them of the severe curtailment of personal and social freedoms. Walking the tightrope of dampening their enthusiasm for the post-revolutionary regime in Iran while explaining my participation in the Revolution was not easy.

In the either-you-are-with-me-or-against me framework of thought you were either pro-Shah or pro-Khomeini. It was difficult, if not outright impossible, to imagine anyone saying no to both, just as today people find it difficult to understand that opposing the regime in Iran does not mean agreeing with US-designs on the country. 'A plague on both your houses', I argued. The students were polite and enthusiastic and listened to all I said. Yet Asyut was on its way to becoming the centre of the Islamist movement in Egypt. But that was later. You could still buy beer in the bazaar, sold openly by a vendor just as you entered the market road, his stall in the middle of the road. Maybe he knew what was coming and had placed himself strategically to have a ready flight path. A few days into my course the Shah arrived in

Egypt where he was to die. That was unwelcome news and hearing it really upset me, something my colleagues on the course could not understand. I immediately foresaw that should I ever be interrogated in the future I would have great difficulty explaining my presence in Egypt at the time the Shah arrived. I had predicted correctly.

Soon after returning home Ayatollah Beheshti, the head of the IRP and Khomeini's closest adviser, warned in a speech that the party will ask the people to rise against the 'Leftists' in the universities. An attack was clearly imminent. A few days later Rafsanjāni was talking in Tabriz University and IRP students, on the pretext that leftists had interrupted his speech, occupied the main university building. The IRP warned of the looming 'shadow of bloodshed in the universities'. Finally, in a Friday prayer sermon in April, Ali Khamenei', (The current Supreme Leader appointed by Khomeini on his deathbed in 1988, despite his rather lightweight credentials as a learned cleric) accused the universities of leading the armed resistance in Kurdistan and Turkaman Sahra and of waging war against Islam. He ordered a *jihad* against the universities. That afternoon the Revolutionary Council gave student groups in the University three days to evacuate their offices. Bani Sadr and the liberals within the Revolutionary Council were warned not to ignore the 'will of the people'.

Bani Sadr was in any case not particularly enamoured of the left which, not wanting to be seen as soft on liberals, had targeted him almost as much as they did the IRP. Mindful of being side-lined by the *hezbollāh*, Bani Sadr who before the summer holidays had initially opposed closing the universities, now asked for the dispute to be resolved through his office. But the *hezbollāh*, under the shield of the Komiteh and Pasdārān, beat him to it by attacking Tehran University even while the political groups were in the process of vacating their offices and despite the presence of thousand outside the university gates in support of the students. In the battle that followed, scores of students were shot dead and by next morning the regime had control of Tehran University. Not to be side-lined, Bani Sadr led the 'people's' occupation of Tehran University and made a speech applauding the birth of government control over it. Down south we did not hear of the deaths until one or two

CHAPTER 36

days later.

In Shiraz, most of the groups and their supporters plus hundreds of others had gathered in the College of Literature on the last day of the ultimatum to make a final stand. I was not there. If I remember correctly, I was in charge of ward beds and was doing my rounds. But J was there with Yusef, Mani's brother. She had enrolled in the English literature course that year after she was sacked as head of the Shiraz blood transfusion centre despite the fact that she had led the revolutionary movement in that Institute. Today she joined the students in defending her new home. Early in the afternoon the *hezbollāh* attacked, beating and tearing up as they went. J had driven there in the Peugeot and for the next two hours helped transport the fleeing students, most of them with cuts and bruises, some extensive, over the back wall and to Namāzi Emergency Room which was safer than Sa'di. She had to make this trip a number of times and by the time darkness fell she was exhausted.

That night the sitting room felt darker than usual. Both of us were shaken. We were watching television trying to work out what was happening across the country. An atmosphere of fear hung over us. An era had come to an end, and we knew that the road ahead was now much steeper and rockier. I was floating between feeling fear, despair and anger when the telephone rang. "It is the Pāsdārān headquarters in the Third Army barracks" the man at the other end said in a quiet, polite voice, "is that Dr ..." My heart began to race out of my chest. "Yes, speaking" trying to hide fear, which never hides. "Do you know Mr ....," and he gave a name I had never heard. "No, I don't know such a person". "But he insists he is one of your patients. He saw you with a heart condition". "But I am not a heart doctor. I specialise in endocrinology, things like goitre and diabetes" I said making sure he understood that it was a long way away from the heart. "I have so many patients I cannot remember all their names" I continued, convinced that this was a trap to get me to the barracks. He thanked me politely and I put the phone down. We looked at each other certain of a plot. Perhaps they will come for me here. Two days ago my name had appeared near the top of a list of 92 academic staff from the University who were to be expelled. Many of the names were of members of the Association of Progressive Professors. Someone, we later found out who, had leaked names, under threat.

A few minutes later the phone rang again. It was the same Pāsdār. "He wants to talk to you himself, I will put him on". The heartbeat began its race, though less recklessly. "It is me Dr …" and the disengaged voice gave a name that meant nothing to me "don't you remember. You saw me recently. It was my heart. Don't you remember?" I remembered nothing and denied remembering. "I have so many patients I cannot remember them all" I was now fully convinced that this is a ploy. I put the phone down. It rang again immediately. It was the patient with the unknown name. "But you saw me yesterday. You know. The boy with a leaking heart. You know me well don't you" he emphasised the last two words. And the penny suddenly dropped. It was Yusef. Yes, he did have a leaking aortic valve, a congenital defect. I had indeed once listened to his heart and heard the murmur. It was his fresh young voice. How stupid of me and how brilliantly persistent of him to have persuaded the Pāsdār to ring three times. "Put the brother Pāsdār on please" I said my heart now slowing down to a trot. "I do, I do remember him. I am sorry, there are so many patients and it is easy to forget. Yes, he is a good patient of mine". "Can you come over and see him he is complaining of chest pain and shortness of breath". I got the exact address. "Be careful' Rahman the Colonel who was with us that night said. "Why don't you take someone with you from the emergency room in case anything should happen to you?"

Behruz was there in the emergency room, an old friend. Immediately he put on his white coat and we drove to the barracks in the Peugeot. Outside, I asked him to stay in the car and to inform everyone if I was not out in an hour. I guess I felt that a concerted protest by students and doctors would release me. I went to the front desk and introduced myself to two bearded boys, not much more than twenty. They were expecting me, and they took me to a room in what I took to be the infirmary where Yusef was laying on a bed. I took a particularly detailed history and made a thorough examination. The Pāsdār stood politely three or four steps back. He whispered that he had been arrested along with over 400 people but had complained of chest pain to see if he can get out. It was a long shot but worth a try. "Yes" I said confident now "he needs to be admitted to hospital". I had to explain this

CHAPTER 36

again to another Pāsdār who was probably a superior. They conferred with each other, rang up somewhere and to my amazement agreed. I went out, flattened the car seat, drove it into the courtyard, lay Yusef on it with Behruz sitting beside him, and drove off, all the time expecting someone to stop us. To be safe we took him to Namāzi and admitted him overnight in case they checked. They were too busy moving the 400 prisoners to Ādel Ābād prison where they sang revolutionary songs all night long. All were released within a few days. The next time Yousef was arrested would be his last.[1]

The attack on Shiraz University cost three lives including Nasrin Rostami and another 491 casualties.[2] The human cost was heavier in the mother university, Tehran, where over 30 were killed and hundreds wounded in three days of battle. It was repeated across the nation's campuses, 12 killed in Ahwaz, six killed in Rasht, 350 injured in Mashhad on the battlefields of academia. The University, the bastion of freedom, had fought every inch of the way. Nothing particularly cultural came out of the 'Cultural Revolution' either then or since. But Khomeini had laid the first stone in his dream for the *vahdate howzeh va dāneshgāh* – oneness of seminary and university.

The next day all universities were closed and did not open for another three years. The list of 92 expellees from Shiraz went up with my name and those of Asqar, Faramarz and Khosrow on it, but because of objections at all levels they were unable to implement it for another year when, after three waves of arrests, the University was finally conquered for the *hezbollāh* – for a time.

[1] Yusef Yusefi died under torture in 1981 (see footnote 2, Chapter 18, Sa'di Hospital under attack).

[2] Kayhān newspaper.

Chapter 37

Mojahedin headquarters

Teaching went on in the Medical School. Patients continued to pour in and with them bedside teaching opportunities, now in *farsglish*, a mish-mash of Farsi and English. The pre-clinical school, year 1-4, had been closed down but clinical students did not go home. The running of our hospitals depended on externs, final year students, as much as interns and residents. We were on a morning post-take round when we came to a middle aged, somewhat balding man with a paunch in severe shock, having drunk badly distilled bootleg vodka. He had methanol poisoning which if it doesn't kill you may leave you blind. "You should let him die" said one of the devout students "drinking is a sin and he deserved to die". "Since when is alcohol a capital punishment in Islam?" I said with undisguised disgust. He chose not to pursue the discussion. The black marks were adding up. The man lived and kept his sight.

That year Ramadan began in midsummer, July 25. The sun rained scorching heat on earth. I wanted to study the effect of deprivation of food and drink during daylight hours on the body for a month and how the body could adapt to the denial over that time scale. In no time I recruited ten volunteer students and residents. It seemed everyone wanted to participate. Bāhār Bāstāni, a very bright resident who in secondary school had attended the elite Alavi

CHAPTER 37

Islamic college in Tehran, beamed when I suggested he might volunteer. "It would scientifically prove the benefits of Muslim fasting" he chirped. The research involved tests first thing in the morning and again just before the sunset meal, the *eftar*, in the first few days of Ramadan, to be repeated again on the last few days of the month. It involved weighing and blood tests looking at sodium and potassium and some hormone measurements, cortisol, prolactin growth hormone and I think insulin. Life in hospital was busy so I was only able to get six to repeat the tests at the end of the month. Bāhār looked distinctly uncomfortable when I showed him the results. There was an average 1.5 kilogram weight loss between morning and evening and little sign of an adaptive mechanism by the end of the month. The most interesting result was a fall in mean potassium levels to 3.5 which is at the lower limit of normal. I suggested to Bāhār that the reason people feel particularly listless after the *eftar* evening meal is that the sudden food intake may force the potassium down even further. I did not publish the results partly because we needed more data and partly because I was unsure of the reaction. I thought I might repeat it the following year with larger numbers and samples after *eftar*, but that was not to happen. It was to be my last year at the Medical School.

The Mojahedin had their headquarters in Ferdowsi Street. It had been registered in the name of Taqi, the same Taqi who had made the critical speech at his graduation reception. The same Taqi who would be my closest friend inside the Third Army detention centre and later in Ādel Ābād. It was mid August, mid Ramadan. A few days earlier a major demonstration by the Mojahedin in Tehran was attended by hundreds of thousands and harassed by club-wielding thugs – the *chomāqdāran*. I was in Sa'di when one of the doctors rushed in to tell us that crowds had gathered outside the Mojahedin headquarters (*Maqarre Mojahedin*) and were pelting it with stones. There were reports of wounded inside.

The two of us put on our white coats and filled a bag from the emergency room with first aid equipment and persuaded an ambulance driver to take us there. A large crowd had gathered outside the two-storey house, all men.

Facing them was a ring of young men and women arms locked in front of the door, a human chain protecting the brick building with fragile bodies against stones. They were all fasting. It was still Ramadan. Every once in a while, a stone would hit a boy or a girl who would fall. Immediately the chain would reform while they pulled the wounded back through the door into the safety of the house. They did not fight back. The crowd seeing our white coats parted, almost instinctively as the soldiers had done for me in front of Medical School in that other era when we too were building up a revolution layer by layer. The human chain unchained for us, and we entered the house. The mass of bodies closed up behind us like water in a pond behind a stick dragged through it. Inside was a different world.

Downstairs in a room behind the stairs the leaders appeared to be in permanent conference. They pointed us upstairs. In a large room, what would have been the master bedroom but was now bare of furniture young boys and girls were huddled in groups of two or three around wounded colleagues on a worn Kerman carpet that covered the centre of the room. Around the edges of the room the yellow ochre terrazzo flooring, a standard in Iranian homes, was littered with cushions, rucksacks, anoraks and other bits and pieces. This was our infirmary. There I met two other students, Sohrab and Mahmoud, both of whom were to play a large part in my life afterwards. We sat ourselves in the centre making a makeshift *Ettefāqāt* (Emergency Room) and began stitching up. There were enough people better at stitching up than me. I felt redundant. Looking around I saw that blobs and streaks of blood had made strange patterns on the dark red and blue carpet. I began to roam and chat.

Most were schoolchildren though there were a few university students, including medical students. They were the ones who had delivered first aid before we came with our surgical equipment. In stark contrast to the mob outside, girls outnumbered boys. The wounded were being brought in almost every two or three minutes. I went to the roof and saw that the mob had now completely blocked Ferdowsi street, extending back to beyond the bend on the road. The ambulance had withdrawn and could not be seen. We were clearly besieged without an escape route. The *Pāsdārān* too were out of sight.

CHAPTER 37

It was to be a conquest by the *'hezbollāh hamisheh dar sahneh'* (always-on-the-scene *hezbollāh*).[1] I spoke with one girl. She was perhaps fifteen or sixteen with big blue eyes set in a pale round face and surrounded by a light grey *maqna'eh*.[2] That innocent look gave her enthusiasm an ethereal feel. She looked like a painting of the Madonna I had seen somewhere. Or was it Joan? She was a schoolgirl from Qasr Dasht, the beautiful suburb of Shiraz where from the air the large orchards (*bāq*) created a mosaic, a patchwork of green and brown. She went down to join the human chain as did her school-friend.

Suddenly one of the older men from the command room below stairs came up and told us that the house was being set on fire. We had to evacuate immediately. I saw smoke coming up the left side of the house which was surrounded on three sides by a garden. Would we get out on time? A doctor (maybe Taqi or Sohrab?) was still stitching a young boy's eyebrows which had a particularly large gaping gash. "We will be caught upstairs with no escape" I hurried them. He cut the stitch, with the wound half undone. Smoke was coming up the stairs when, with our last patient, we ran down and into the street. The Pāsdārān had materialised, arresting anyone they could identify. Those with a wound were easy targets as the Mojahedin had chosen not to fight back. That was the time when they still professed loyalty to Khomeini despite the fact that he had publicly rebuked and disowned them. The sea of stone throwing thugs parted to allow the Pāsdārs. Taqi and I walked through with our wounded patient, protected by our white coats and went over to Sa'di to deal with the wounded that were arriving there by the dozen. Many were arrested that day including Sohrab who was released some hours later having been forced to sign a letter promising good behaviour in the future.

Those were relatively lenient days, with only the more serious opposition, in Kurdistan or Turkaman Sahra and some factory *Shorās* for example, facing the firing squad or long prison sentences. The real crackdowns were still to come. On that day I forged a very powerful emotional tie to those thousands of passionate boys and girls who, hungry and thirsty, had stood like a rock against rocks. A discipline they were to show again and again. Such energy, such love, such idealism, such courage, wasted by a leadership that increasingly saw them as expendable ammunition for a doomed and futile programme. I was to share prison with some of them including Sohrab, Taqi and Mahmud. What I will never know is how many of the young boys and girls under that roof that day lost their lives over the next two or three years.

A few days later, on the anniversary of the CIA-engineered coup that toppled Mosaddeq and returned the Shah, Khomeini made his famous speech ordering the attack on Kurdistan and regretting that he had not raised gallows on crossroads earlier and threatened to throw the 'American and non-American' left into the dustbin of death.

[1] Always-on-the-scene *hezbollāh* – the formulation used by the official mouthpieces of the regime to describe the thug-like men (and occasionally women) used to break up opposition activities.

[2] The head covering favoured by the Mojahedin which totally covered the hair and neck and was tucked into the short manteaux over a pair of jeans leaving the entire face exposed like a full moon in the early evening sky.

Chapter 38

War

The refugees poured in in their thousands. In September 1980 Saddam's army invaded Khuzestan province and occupied Abadan, and after street-by-street fighting conquered what was left of Khorramshahr, the port city on the Shatt al Arab river by the end of October, advancing north towards Dezful and Ahwaz before being stopped. While not totally unprovoked, it still took us by surprise. Immediately we heard of the attack Fereidoon and I rushed to the nearest centre and volunteered to be sent to the front. Our names appeared second and third in the book of volunteers in Shiraz, a point that came in useful later. We had volunteered partly out of a sudden surge of nationalist sentiment and partly because that would reduce any taint of being unpatriotic should the issue arise in the future.

Since the occupation of the US embassy the previous November the left had been split down the middle with a large chunk sliding closer to the regime which tolerated them as they would a dog; unclean but useful as a guard, handy in neutralising the defiant left and valuable in projecting the right image to the outside world. That was how my Aunt Tayyebeh, with a house in the middle of the partially built wilderness of north Tehran, had used her guard dog, chained during the day, and released to roam the courtyard at night. There was a rivalry among various political groups to show who was the most anti-imperialist. On the one side stood the Tudeh and the Fadāi' Majority, the latter having split after the US embassy charade which they saw as proof of Khomeini's anti-imperialism. On the other the remaining Left. The Mojahedin occupied the middle space, trying to obtain a position within the power structure while at the same time preparing for the eventual inevitable rupture. Having been openly rejected by Khomeini and labelled hypocrites, and with the Islamic Republic Party controlling virtually every organ where power resided, they increasingly sided with the president, Bani Sadr, who in turn, lacking his own political organisation, came to depend more and more on them. It was a marriage of convenience, consolidated when the Mojahedin leader Masoud Rajavi later briefly married Bani Sadr's daughter.

The next day, in the company of a number of residents and students we set up an emergency collection centre in the grounds of the Engineering College. Scores of students went out to knock on doors and collect unused medicines. By late afternoon the entire courtyard was full of huge cardboard boxes brimming with half used and often untouched packets of pills and bottles. On display on that concrete courtyard, in full colour, was the evidence of the kind of pill-pushing doctors we had been churning out and a graphic portrait of how little our patients cared for our opinion. With a couple of doctors, we started going through them, sorting them out in categories and throwing out the utterly useless. More than half were nothing more than padding, filling up the prescription forms with vitamins, tonics, tranquilisers, junk. The antibiotics and pain killers were either untouched, or at best most ended up at the bottom of the cupboard a day or two into use. We went home exhausted at well after midnight and resumed the next day. We had at least two lorry-loads of drugs that the local *Komiteh* took over.

The refugees arrived in their hundreds and were housed in empty apartment blocks, three of which were in Ordibehesht Street opposite Sa'di Hospital. At first there was total chaos. Disasters are often blessings for political organisations. Years ago, during the previous regime, flooding in the south Tehran suburb of Javādieh allowed leftist students from Tehran

University to spread their influence and create networks. Later the Tabas earthquake in 1978 became a Muslim playing field as the left was weeded out and expelled. As I write, the massive floods in north Pakistan have provided fertile ground for the Pakistani Taliban and the Shi'a-hating Lashgar-e Tayyebeh. Saddam's attack provided both sides emerging from the Iranian Revolution with a golden opportunity to win new friends and influence. Khomeini was not deluded when he called the war a gift from God (*rahmat-e elāhi*). And the Left too was trying to take a bite from the gift.

A number of female comrades went in and helped the refugees self-organise. Mistrusting at first, the refugees in all three buildings quickly accepted their suggestions and set up their elected *Shora* which supervised allocation of rooms according to need. They collected food and clothing and handed them over to the *Shoras* for distribution. They collected money and bought milk powder for the babies. It was not difficult to establish a close relationship with the inhabitants as there were very few ultra-devout among them. Many had either left leanings, or at least were not hostile. With its long history of industrial organisation and the presence of a relatively large number of foreign advisers, Abadan and the oil producing parts of Khuzestan were particularly secular and where the Islamists had made relatively less inroads. During the Mosaddeq era this was where the Tudeh party had its greatest influence and during the recent revolution the decisive oil company strike was predominantly under the leadership of the left. It was not a coincidence that the Islamists had targeted Cinema Rex in Abadan to both undermine the Shah and also deliver a blow to the secular culture so dominant there.

It did not take the local *Komiteh* long to muscle in and expel the girls, although they continued to keep contact with elements within the communities through whom they smuggled in left-literature. The Khuzestani refugees remained a thorn in the side of the regime for a long time, refusing to be integrated into the Shirazi background. They even set up their own bazaar, in rivalry with the locals. Their particular openness and energy contrasted with the laid-back fun-loving Shirazis who had continued to enjoy their picnics into the curfew hours. One of J's first experiences in Shiraz was to ask two men who were warming their hands round an Aladdin heater in a shop near the bazaar to get down a *samāvar* that had caught her eye on the top shelf. The two looked at each other imploringly. Neither budged. "Come back tomorrow" they said and went back to their conversation. They had sold enough for that day's living and were certainly not going to leave the warmth of the fire for some fancy outsider.

The keys to two rooms in the basement to the apartment block in *Bāq-e Namāzi* had been entrusted to me by colleagues who had gone over to Switzerland and the US on sabbatical, respectively. It housed their furniture and increasingly my collection of banned oppositional literature, communist books, and of course large bottles of home-made wine. When you went to buy a crate or two of grapes, the grocer would wink knowingly. I had also tried cherries, persimmon and orange for wine. The last two were undrinkable until my colleague, Faramarz, always a true scientist, worked out how to distill them without danger. They made fairly drinkable liquor. The wine made from red grapes was pink and rather sharp, but still wine. The easiest brew was to add yeast to the alcohol-free *Mā' al Sha'ir* (literally barley water in Arabic – i.e. beer), which was sold legally, and leave them in the fridge for a few days. Even easier was to add absolute alcohol, which you could buy lawfully as a doctor, to fruit juice. Going in and out of those basements was tricky, as no one knew I had the keys and I had to slip in and out without being seen, like the star of a B movie. Luckily no one did. The heroic task of emptying the basements was left to the family and friends in my absence. Later, as conditions got worse, one of the professors, a colleague in the Association of Progressive Academics, panicked and gave away all his home-made wine collection. He was a real professional, and we drank our share of bottles in the veranda with Changiz, a veteran of the guerrilla movement and of the Shah's prisons. It was another sign of his iconoclasm. In left circles, drinking alcohol was frowned upon as being bourgeois. The common roots of the left and the Islamists appear in unexpected places.

The bombers began to fly over Shiraz as well. We blocked our windows with aluminium foil which had the added purpose of making the meetings in the

CHAPTER 38

basement more secluded. With Saddam's army bogged down in the plains of Khuzestan and the hills of western Iran, the war of attrition began. And with the novelty of the invasion gradually fading, the two camps within the country that had been stunned into a relative truce after the occupation of the embassy and again after Saddam's invasion, began to draw apart. You could feel it in the support people gave you in the street when the left managed a lightning photography exhibition or demonstration. Strikes in factories increased. Bani Sadr and his liberal allies alongside the Mojahedin increasingly expressed open opposition to the fundamentalists (*qeshriyoon*) in the Islamic Republic Party, though the person of Khomeini was still out of bounds. The Mojahedin staged large demonstrations in Tehran and there were daily demonstrations in the streets of most major cities, and increasingly the bystanders showed their support. The sale of illegal underground left papers and literature soared. The printing press in my basement moved to a different site to cope with the increased demand. The Mojahedin, Fadāi' and other left groups were recruiting in their thousands in schools. Even in factories their influence grew as did strikes and protests. There was little doubt in the mind of those of us involved down below that we were going towards another revolution. It all seemed like a repeat of 1978-9.

And then on June 21, 1981 there was an explosion in the *Majles* (parliament) building that killed many of Khomeini's closest associates and unleashed the first real wave of terror. Death began its dance in and with the sabre-rattling city (Walter Mehring).

39

Chapter 39

The night they came for me

Even the air was pregnant with shock. Though it was the first day of summer, the light was autumnal without the spark. A hush sat on the wards. People hardly spoke and when they did it was in a subdued voice. Even the patients were more silent than usual. The world I knew had died. The night before, the explosion in the Majles (parliament) building had ripped the heart of the Islamic elite, including Beheshti, IRP leader and Khomeini's closest advisor. It was 28th June 1981. The radio spoke of 72 dead, cynically choosing the magic mythical figure that had such significance for the Shi'a faithful. Seventy-two was the number of family members and disciples who perished alongside the prophet's grandson, Hossein on the banks of the Euphrates. What the true number was I never found out, but entering Sa'di, it was like walking into the wilderness of Karbela, the day after *Ashura*, so solemn was the silence. This was a collective *shām-e qariboon*. A close friend, Hatef, saw me doing my rounds and quietly sidled across. "Don't hang around," he whispered, fear narrowing his eyes piercing mine, "they came asking for Behruz earlier". I would be on their list. I called J and asked her to come home. We had to clean up.

We spent the rest of the day going through the house. It had accumulated

CHAPTER 39

six years of Shirazi clutter added to ten years of joint life in England. There was the basement which had doubled as the kids' playroom, a spare room for guests, a meeting place, and a makeshift printshop. The windows were blacked out with silver foil because of the Iraqi planes, giving a sense of quasi security. At *Eid* we had driven to Tehran to be with the family in the new year celebration, and someone had burgled the house taking away the gold watch given me by my father-in-law as a wedding present as well as our wedding rings. That could only have been the work of the Pāsdārān – the *bāq* had been so safe with regular guards covering all the entrances and also doing rounds. What else they had seen or taken we could only guess. Somehow, in the unreal atmosphere of almost daily demonstrations and clashes with the *hezbollāh* we had overlooked our vulnerability. The *bāq* had seemed like a fortress. I felt betrayed by the guards as only a few weeks earlier I had given them all their *eidi* presents, and they had smiled back. Naively, thoughtlessly, I thought of them as 'our' guards. So, the Pāsdārān had been inside my house. I felt uneasy. I felt violated.

We threw in all the leftist literature that were scattered around the house into the fireplace. But there were many books and pamphlets. Compacted paper takes time to burn, and time was beginning to flee. By afternoon we had filled an old brown suitcase with incriminating documents having carefully gone through them to make sure there were no real names. We then had to decide what to do with the suitcase. I did not want to drive out as there could have been roadblocks set up to search cars. A dry river runs alongside Namāzi – actually called by that name. I picked up the case, with J checking ahead to make sure no one saw us, climbed over the low wall that lined the south side of the river, jumped onto the riverbed which was covered with round stones and walked upstream in a river without water. I dumped the brown case in mid stream beyond the Namāzi complex. The crows were squawking to each other excitedly, perhaps anticipating a meal in that battered case. I dumped it and ran. It was dusk.

We rang our colleague Faramarz and asked if Nargess could stay the night there. I cleaned out the fireplace from paper ash and sat down to wait. Maryam went downstairs to her room. Why did we not send her away too?

Somehow, we had always seen her as grown-up. Years later she reminded me how in the UK we had left her babysitting Nargess, herself still a child, fearing, waiting, dreading in case her parents had an accident and never come home. Thoughtless.

The unusual quiet had infected the *bāq* as well. Normally our local pack of wild dogs would begin their nightly prowl and bark through the night. There were 50 to 70 dogs that homed in Namāzi. Many a time I had walked past that pack at night trying not to look scared. The city council refused to kill them, as that was said to bring bad luck to the killers. I had waited for the first rabies case. Tonight, they too were quiet, a black silence. Shortly after darkness had crept over the plane trees I felt, more than heard, shuffling outside. No cars, no boots just a feeling that the house was being surrounded.

And then a knock. A soft knock, like one the postman might do.

Ajalluyān, the third-year student, the same one who was on the Medical School *Shora* and who had chaired my working group rewriting the medical curriculum, walked in first dressed in khaki. He did not reply to my greeting but walked rapidly across the living room and straight down the stairs to the basement as if he knew what he was looking for. "Where is the printing machine" he asked angrily. There was none. He did not smile though the Pāsdār that followed him and did the searches on his command gave J and me one or two sheepish smiles. And then Ajalluyān picked up a pack of A4 paper. "What is this then" he pushed it at me triumphantly. "Paper" I replied, "to write up my research and articles". I felt utterly calm. I had expected them and had cleaned the house carefully. Any incriminating material was safe in the basement of the apartment block. There was nothing here to get me and in any case I, like many, thought the regime was on its last legs.

Ajalluyān, dressed in his Pāsdār outfit, started on my library. He picked out books and threw them in a pile on the floor. Books about other political organisations, Farsi books about history, English books on history. But we had already censored it twice, once when we came over from England and then once we had the key to the apartment block basements. Anything with clear Marxist links or any political group were stored there as were all the

CHAPTER 39

banned political newspapers. There was nothing at home that I could not buy off a shelf in the bookshop on the left in Zand Avenue. The pile, however, just kept growing as more and more books were thrown. "You could build a mosque with the books you have", he sneered at Maryam as he went through her bookshelf. He repeated this refrain again and again, like a prayer. At one point the *Pāsdārs* left their guns in the kitchen, so easy to have taken them. They clearly did not feel a threat, just disdain, class hatred almost.

The entire atmosphere of the house was alien to them. The design of the rooms and its contents were different to what they had been brought up in and they clearly resented everything about it. They felt foreign in their own town. They almost completely ignored J and me and addressed most their comments to Maryam. They chided her for living in such affluence, but there was nothing affluent there, no luxury, no special furniture, no ornaments they could point to. Only books, paintings and a gramophone – and rows of records. It was the entire space they detested, the atmosphere, nothing concrete, just alien and hateful. There was a deep anti-intellectualism in every comment. It was as if the books were the enemy, the impurity contaminating their land. It was the old traditional-modern antagonism superimposed on a perceived class war.

"What is that picture?" Ajalluyān, whose name had the ring of death,[1] said pointing to a picture of an old Russian man by Repin that was on the wall of the children's room. An old Russian man by the Russian painter Repin, I said. "Take that too" he instructed the Pāsdārs. My interrogator later accused me of having a picture of Marx on the wall. To Maryam, one of them said it is a caricature of Khomeini.

I only took a toothbrush. I will be back tomorrow I told J. That and the clothes I had on, a dark blue cotton shirt, and cream denim trousers. We kissed. The last memory I had was of Maryam's large black eyes looking up at me. The doors closed and I sat between two armed guards in a Peikan. It was a British designed Iranian manufactured Hillman that took me away.

As Maryam went out to get Nargess she saw the remaining Pāsdārs going into the house of our neighbour, Dr Qarib, for tea. Qarib had been one of the first to sign the manifesto of the National Association of Academics (SMD).

Now he was Dean. She came back, went downstairs and spent the entire night re-reading her collection of Enid Blyton.

[1] *Ajal* is the Farsi word for death and hour of death.

Chapter 40

Solitary

In that Peikan, sitting between the two armed men, I scarcely realised that I was about to enter a world for which I had no image, no concept and little preparation. It was an alien world that was so different from the world outside that for the next 13 months I almost totally switched the other one off. Selfish as it may appear, that was a survival strategy that helped me navigate the rapids and rocks that were going to be thrown up on my path almost on a daily basis. Roger Cooper, imprisoned by the same regime a few years after me, quipped on arrival at Heathrow how boarding school had helped him survive five years in Khomeini's prisons. It certainly did. But as an Iranian I needed other skills to manoeuvre the winding road.

The objective was to come out alive without losing one's identity, dignity and above all self respect. It was only made possible by the help of fellow prisoners who not only helped me steer the zigzags of the road ahead but helped me become a different person. It was both a university education and a psychological maze. And an obstacle course where any error of judgement could seriously jeopardise your survival. It is also clear to me that had I not got out when I did, I do not know what would have happened to me. I was interned at the right moment and came out at the right moment. To quote Don Delilo, true life is never reducible to words[1] and I cannot reduce that miracle to mere words. But I know that it was an amalgam of luck and comradery that transformed a potential disaster into a school for learning.

I was taken to a large room. There were perhaps forty of fifty men, most much younger than me, sitting around. All had been rounded up that day and were in their outdoor clothes. There was a pile of shoes by the door, and I took mine off and looked around. I recognised some of our students and went over. A young man, a stranger thirty years old or so, came over and started asking me who I was and why I was arrested. Before I could say anything, one of the students gestured. Don't say anything, his raised eyebrows conveyed. "I don't know" I replied and switched to a bland conversation.

We had only just sat down together when the iron doors opened and a Pāsdār poked his head in and called for brother (*baradar*)… to follow him. In that upside down world everyone was called brother or sister, even as they were being taken out to be shot. I rummaged round the pile of shoes, could not find mine, slipped on a pair of brown rubber sandals, the sort you use in your bathroom, and followed him. I was taken down the corridor and ushered into a smaller room with about 10 or 12 people. Mohsen Mahluji was there as was a young ophthalmologist, who looked like a frightened rabbit or, with his thick moustache and furrowed forehead, more like a racoon. We were the only members of the faculty, three generations, with me halfway between the two. Mohsen was dressed in his usual white *shalwār kameez* that was surprisingly untarnished. His calmness warmed me and reinforced my already unreal sense of security. I would be safe. That encounter was the beginning of a friendship that was to last his lifetime.

The room was a transit zone. People would come and go. We talked. We played. There was a game of *moshāe'reh,* a game where one person would recite a verse and another would have to recite one starting with the letter that ended the last, that Mahmud, a medical student had initiated. He was from somewhere in central Iran, perhaps Yazd, with the combination of the honesty, humour and shrewdness of people from there. With his thick black hair and big black eyes, the image that stayed with me was his permanent smile and his beautiful sad voice that seemed so uncoupled from the mischievous

CHAPTER 40

glint of his eyes. His game would start with his singing the first verse of Moulānā Jalāleddin Rumi's Masnavi,

beshno az nei chon hekāyat mikonad,
az jodā'iha hekāyat mikonad.[2]

And then each person would follow with a verse beginning with the last letter of the verse just recited. If they failed, then they had to bend over, and all the players would together bang his back like a drum singing another verse from the Masnavi. That was an adult variation on an old children's game – *ustā bedoosh.*[3] The next evening we were again playing the game of poetry. There was a middle-aged man with us, a Bahā'i. He had arrived earlier that day and we had exchanged a few words of welcome. He looked dejected in his grey suit and crumpled white shirt which had lost its earlier freshness. We had just finished drumming a back, incontinent laughter spraying everywhere, when the new arrival keeled over. He was pulseless, not breathing, clearly in cardiac arrest. I gave him a blow on the chest and began cardiac massage. Within a minute he was breathing again. His pulse was weak with occasional missed beats. But it was beating, and he was breathing and conscious. For the only time in my life that whack had been effective. It had restarted his heart. We banged and banged on the metal door until a Pāsdar opened it. "This man just died, and we revived him. You must take him to the infirmary" I blurted agitated. Someone then whispered to the obviously alarmed Pāsdar, if he dies, they will blame torture. They took him to the infirmary and from there to Namāzi. And beyond? Who knows? The entire room was infused with an optimistic glow – it was possible to cheat death. Twice. They were executing Bahā'is as apostates.

A day or two later the iron door opened again - '*baradar* .... collect your things'. I found another pair of slippers and went out with the Pāsdar down the corridor. Round the corner I saw two Pāsdars leading a young man who I immediately recognised as one of the leaders of the Mojahedin in their headquarters the day it was overrun by *hezbollāhi* thugs. We looked into each other's eyes, and with a flick of his right eyebrow he signalled to me not to acknowledge him. It all happened in a second. I later learnt that he had managed to fool his interrogators and was released two or three days later.

Mohsen later told me of another high-ranking member of the Mojahedin, who had feigned madness having been briefed by Mohsen on how real madness actually presents. Mohsen who had given up on modern psychiatry in the medical school rediscovered its usage inside the cage. Shouting and banging on the cell door, the young man had finally got his way when he smeared his faeces on the walls. For a Shi'a Muslim there is nothing more unclean than urine, faeces and blood.

At the end of the second corridor was an iron gate on the left which opened out to another corridor at a right angle to it. There was a row of cells on my right, each with a grey-painted solid iron door and a shuttered window. On the left was a largish room with two toilets on the far side, two grey concrete wash basins and a space with aluminium dishes that had been washed and were drying out in a pile. Beyond this room almost at the end of the corridor was the guard's room. There were, I think, six cells. I was ushered into the third or fourth and the door closed behind me with a clank. I had been taken to the solitary block. My situation was clearly more serious than I had imagined.

I was suddenly alone and unsure. But fear is a collective emotion and we had not yet reached that turning point. It was not a question of courage or even of a delusion. It was a collective feeling shared among thousands that we are on the winning side, the side of history, on a trajectory that could not lose. It is that collective feeling of invincibility that makes the individual fate much less important. In those early days of the terror unleashed on my country, terror had not yet been internalised. And so, the many encounters with immense courage that I was to witness over the next year has to be seen against that backdrop. You had no time to fear, only time to survive, awaiting victory. As someone later wrote, there are no fearless people, only fearless moments.[4] I was to witness this again and again.

In the next twenty-four hours, time became warped, stretched, twisted into a spiral and I forgot the clock. I wake-slept that night working out what possible questions they may pose, and possible answers. Going over them again and again. Thoughts going round in circles and spirals, refined, repeated, rejected, reappearing in new forms. What could they ask? Why was

CHAPTER 40

I picked out? Images from Koestler, Ginsberg and Solzhenitsyn[5] rumpled in a collage. In the morning the door opened and a boy, he could not have been much over 15, pushed in a metal plate with bread, a small packet of butter and five dates. The bread was fresh and the dates soft. They are giving out butter I thought and immediately felt less anxious. It is strange what signals one interprets. I had never eaten dates and butter and it was absolutely delicious. I had not eaten for hours.

Later, the door opened and the boy led me to the toilet. You can *vuzu* (ritual washing) for prayers, he said in an indifferent tone. His voice was like a child's – just cracking. I washed my face and plate. As I was putting it down, I noticed how he moved back so that none of the water might drip on him. I was unclean it flashed through my mind, and I flashbacked to grandmother *khānom-joon* who had made the same gesture when as a child, I passed her with a jug of water. Any wet contact with me, an unclean person because I do not follow the rituals or pray, would soil the recipient, requiring ablution. The Shi'a are very particular about what is *najess* (unclean) and what is *pāk* (clean).

A plate of green rice at lunch was pushed through the hatch. It had a strange smell. Must have been the oil. I took a few spoonfuls. I heard the doors of the other rooms open and close as their inhabitants were taken one by one to the toilet twice a day. I would see those housed beyond me fleetingly through a crack on the hatch. I was desperate for a pee and banging on the door persuaded the boy to let me out. On the way I saw a youth not yet twenty wearing a white shirt entering the room next to me. By the second day we were talking to each other in a low voice. The boy-guard would stop us when he heard us talking but he spent a lot of time in his room, out of earshot; maybe he was praying. Again, we did not tell each other why we were arrested but I understood that he belonged to a left group.

One day they brought a girl who would sing aloud communist songs and shout out slogans. She had a beautiful voice and if she sang a song that we recognised we would sing it aloud with her. That is how I found out that most of those in our block on that first week belonged to the left. Every few hours the *Pāsdārs* would open the door of her cell and we could hear them beating her. But she would resume her slogans and her singing. She was taken away a day or two later. I do not know what became of her. She was almost certainly shot.

On the second day I looked round my cell. Various names were hacked into the walls. In one corner was hacked the words *communistam communist, as to ey mortajeh-e past o palid bākam nist*. Written in rhyme it roughly translates as 'I am a communist, a communist; for you low, filthy reactionary, I have no fear'. At two o'clock the boy-guard would turn on the radio for the news. Right at the beginning they would read out a list of those they had executed as *mofsed-e fel-arz* (corrupt on earth) and *mohāreb* (someone at war with God). J would listen anxiously to this list every day, waiting for them to get to 'sh' which comes late in the Farsi alphabet. That is how I heard of the execution of Said Soltanpoor, the poet who had set the Revolution alight on day five of the ten-day poetry reading and arrested on his wedding day. And that is also how I heard of the death of my neighbour who had been taken out that morning. I cannot remember his name, but he belonged to Vahdate Komunisti, the same organisation as our young friend Yusef Yusefi who was to die under torture around the same time in an Isfahan prison. Yusef's badly bruised body was handed over to his parents the next day. We loved him like a son.

And so the days went by. The routine was unchanging, we were let out morning and evening and the boy-guard would stand well away as we washed the dishes. I was allowed a cold bath after two weeks. Breakfast was the delicious bread-butter-dates, a new combination for me, and lunch some rice dish, cooked in that smelly oil. The addition of butter was a truly pleasant surprise and to this day I adore bread-butter-fresh-dates. Once they brought us a thick soup, *āsh Shirāzi,* for breakfast which was so tasty I can still feel it on my tongue. The food was the same as that dished out to the Pāsdārs. They did not have a different kitchen for the detainees. When it was all quiet, I lay on the floor of the cell and reconstructed the first movement of Brahms' first symphony, bar by bar, in my head. I had first heard the piece when my neighbour in St Thomas' House, fellow student Andrew (Hottie) Jowell, lent me his entire record collection. Brahms was his favourite and it became mine. I was listening to Brahms while reading *The Rise and Fall*

CHAPTER 40

of the Third Reich[6] and forever associated his first symphony with the rise of fascism and its destruction. The movement begins with that ominous drumbeat, like impending death, and then the first subject, a three-note figure, no tune you could whistle, keeps reverberating throughout the movement. The finale begins quietly, threatening, almost fearful, ominously predicting doom... and then suddenly this joyous victorious tune, a debt to the *Ode to Joy* in Beethoven's 9th bursts through. The joy of liberation. I have no idea how successful I was with the construct, but it kept my brain in its box.

One day the door opened, and they let in another man. Apparently, they had run out of room and our solitary was to be shared. He did not say much and all I can remember is that he was tall and young. He was removed after two days. I never even learnt his name or anything about him. He may have thought I was a spy for the regime, which is a sensible attitude to take. I thought the same possibility for him but as he showed no curiosity, I dismissed it. Then a plastic bag arrived from the family with a change of underclothes, a shirt, toothbrush and paste and Harrison's textbook of medicine. What a wonderful present. Much later I heard from one of my students, Shojāi', who had become the head of Pāsdārān in Shiraz, that he "had kept an eye on me", their "very good teacher" as he put it. "Islam teaches us to respect our teachers, even when they are our enemy" he said. My profession was to come in handy all through the next years.

I was taken for interrogation about the fourteenth day. It was very early morning. My interrogator was Hosseini, a young man with the standard bristle, good looking and polite. The interrogation was remarkable for the paucity of the information they had, mostly hearsay, which he extracted from the three letters of denunciation that he lifted out of my file, one at a time. They were all written on both sides of A5 paper, the sort we used for prescriptions in the hospital. He lifted them up to read, he must have been short-sighted. And by turning them round to read the other side I saw the signatures, Ajalluyān who had arrested me, Faqihi, the one who had pointed me out to a left-leaning doctor as the sort of lefty he should emulate and the third who would later have a prominent position in government. The last one surprised me as he was one of our residents, and a good one at that, who had always been polite and correct with me, without ever showing any emotional bond with me which many of the Islamists had shown. After this amateurish exercise I felt even more secure. Nothing bad is going to happen to me and all I need do is keep my head above water. What I had not bargained for was how choppy the water was to become and the minor battles behind the scenes that were to determine whether I lived or died. After 21 days I was taken to the main prison block in the third army.

Through an iron door I entered a very large rectangular room that was divided up into four large sections lining the far side of the room, each approximately four by five metres, and fronted by iron bars from floor to ceiling, not unlike the lion's den in the London Zoo. As you entered the cell block, you faced the first of the four rooms. To the left an internal corridor about a metre and a half wide ran in front of the cages. Each cage was accessible through a large sliding gate, also made up of vertical iron bars, that were never shut – four open cages. To the right of the entrance was a large room with five basins, toilets and a shower room that was behind another locked metal door that was opened once a week on bath days.

The first thing that hit me as I entered was a huge pile of groceries, fruit, bags of tea leaves, melons piled up high at the far end of the inner corridor, like a grocer's. And the huge pile of shoes and slippers heaped haphazardly just inside the iron door. To the right of this pile was the 'dirty area', washing, toilets and all. To the left was the bedroom area kept scrupulously clean and washed daily by the inmates. I went to the first room but was immediately asked to go to the third room. The inmates, mostly political prisoners, had already established a system. All newcomers were put in the first room – with my old friend Mahmud, the medical student with the big black eyes and sad voice who had played *mosha'ereh,* in charge. It was nicknamed Mahmud's *fandoq,* the Arabic name for hotel. Mahmud would then evaluate each newcomer and send through those who were clearly political prisoners to the last two rooms, with Mohsen in charge. There the politicos could hold their ideological classes, their discussions, their morning exercises without being eavesdropped by potential spies. It was a naïve arrangement but essential to keep up militancy and morale. On the far wall of the last room was carved right across the room the arms of *Peikar* Organisation a beautifully executed piece of artwork. This was to be my home on and off for the next three months.

[1] Don DeLillo, Point Omega.

[2] The great Sufi poet and teacher. The verses that begin his *Masnavi*: listen to this reed/play out its plaint/unfold its tale/of separation (translated by Franklin D Lewis, Oneworld Publications, Oxford, 2008).

[3] The *usta* (master) would lift their index finger and in rapid succession name various animals and articles that fly or don't. The others would have to raise their hands if the object could be airborne. Anyone doing it wrong or is too slow to act would get the back-drumming treatment.

[4] Peter Hoeg, Borderliners.

[5] Arthur Koestler *Darkness at Noon* describing Stalin's purges of 1930's and Yevgenia Ginzberg's *Journey into the Whirlwind* and Solzhenitsyn's *One Day in the Life of Ivan Denisovich* of their years in the Gulag were the only books on prison experience I had read. I had not read Dostoyevsky's account of Siberia, nor the Fadāi' Ashraf Dehqāni's vivid portrait of her experience in the Shah's prison.

[6] William Shirer, Secker & Warberg, 1960.

Chapter 41

Ich liebe dich

How do you say I love you in German? My old friend Taqi and I were talking in the far room, by the barred frosted window. "Ich liebe dich" I replied. We were practicing German. It all came about when Hossein - Seyyed Hossein Musavi, to give him his full name, and no relation to the then prime minister – sat in a corner morose and despondent. We never found out who denounced him. As a first year resident in surgery he had set his mind on urology. Yes, he was vaguely sympathetic to the left, but he was not active in any of the political groups. Nor had he done anything when they closed down the University. Someone must have had a personal grudge against him. And Hossein just sat there withdrawn, morose, not participating in anything, not talking to anyone and hardly eating. His career, the only thing that had motivated him, had been ripped from him. The entire family had looked up to him as a budding surgeon. But he would not be able to resume his training after his six months prison sentence was over. Like the rest of us he had been expelled from the University.

It was then that Taqi and I hit on an idea. Don't worry I said. I have great contacts in East Germany, thinking of Kianuri's sister and Ezzy and Ensy's cousin, the midwife who had delivered my sister Mina for a fairly hefty fee,

CHAPTER 41

now exiled in Leipzig. "You can continue your training there, and I know some German, we can learn together". We started classes in German. 'Ich liebe dich' was what we were teaching, with a vague vision of love in Leipzig, when I saw a young man grinning from across the cell. He was a young engineer working in the Shiraz oil refinery who had been arrested with others a few weeks earlier as part of the crackdown at the refinery. They had initially been taken to Evin in Tehran but after their interrogation were brought back to Shiraz.

In Evin they shared a room with up to 80 people and had to sleep in three shifts. They were let out once a day to the toilets for half an hour during which time all eighty had to wash their hands, face and dish in 3 or 4 sinks and use the toilets in as many minutes. Yet piled up together as they were, they had managed to have drafting lessons, language classes etc. "I studied engineering in Germany" he said, smiling at our amateur efforts, and for the next ten days he led our German lessons. Soon we were able to talk about Die Beamten (guards) in Das Zuchthaus (prison) in broken German without fear of spies. It was liberating. And that is how Hossein was nicknamed Ichliebedich, shortened to 'ichlie'. Ichlie (pronounced *ishly*) began to smile as he imagined Leipzig and its tree-lined avenues, or even love. He never made it there. Years later he was readmitted to the Medical School and fulfilled his family's dream.

We regimented our days and our routines with military precision. And it was imposed on all, without exception, rigidly and purposefully. That was the only way to prevent demoralisation. Mahmud had control of the first two rooms. I was given room three with Mohsen in overall command of the entire cellblock. It was an assignment from below without any formal vote but accepted by everyone. We were, after all, the elders. Newcomers very quickly accepted the arrangement, including some of the non-politicals after some initial resistance, particularly when it came to sharing their belongings. Everyone had to get up at 7 am and all bedding was stacked away. No one was allowed to lie down or even be horizontal until the afternoon nap for two hours during which absolute silence was observed. Since I never slept after lunch it was left to me to keep the silence.

Morning exercise was voluntary and only the politicos took part, led by one of the boys. Meals were delivered in a huge vat by a Pāsdār (Revolutionary Guard) at the door. We asked, and ultimately got, a large pot of hot water that we used to make tea. Mahmud divided up the food with an obsessive precision, sometimes dividing the last bits with a teaspoon so that everyone got an exactly equal share. If he had scales, he would have weighed each portion. The process took so long that an already lukewarm lunch cooled to room temperature. No one complained.

Fruit, biscuits, tea and other groceries which were handed in during visiting time were also made communal and stored in at the end of the corridor. The huge pile was an object of ridicule to the Pāsdārs, who would taunt us for receiving so many goodies. It confirmed them in their self-image of defenders of the have-nots, conveniently ignoring the self-sacrifice and self-denial that was narrated in those packs of oranges and fruit sent in. The vast majority of the inmates came from poor families and each plastic bag of fruit would be a parcel of love and sacrifice, and also hope. It too was divided up with a precision that would have impressed the man leading the last supper. Since there were people who had special dietary needs, this was supervised by a *mas'ul,* literally 'someone responsible', selected from the trustworthy by Mohsen and later by me. There was also a *mas'ul* for the flat *taftoon* bread to make sure that the outer rim were eaten, something many Iranians hate. That is why they find the British loaf so strange, all that undercooked dough, the *khamir* in Farsi, ugh! The Pāsdārs insisted that all bread, a gift from God, had to be consumed otherwise our rations would be cut. That reverence for bread too is very Iranian. So, it was vital that none was wasted. The food too had to be eaten to the last bite. Waste was not allowed.

Our food ration was fixed regardless of how many inmates we had. Mahmud's hotel would fluctuate widely, ranging from as few as 20 to well over 150 inmates as prisoners were taken to court or to the main Ādel Ābād prison and new arrestees arrived. As I said before we had the same food as the Pāsdārān. Some days chicken. I will never forget when we got 20 chickens on a day when there were only 24 of us and we had to force down the lot. It compensated for the days we went short and slept hungry.

CHAPTER 41

The doctors were the only permanent prisoners here. Everyone else was in transition. This gave us a unique opportunity to gather information on interrogation practices and pass on tips and information. It was not long before *Die Beamten* got wind of this and eventually we were moved en mass to Ādel Ābād. Meanwhile it was accepted by all the prisoners that our position as regular inmates rather than merely passing through merited some privileges. This included having our own blanket and pillow and our own place to sleep by the window. Mohsen and I were also given the privileges of a flask of tea which we could drink after lunch. And each week books begin to arrive, ostensibly as medical books, but I sent messages that they could send me history books and even some novels. The *Beamten* either could not read English or could not care less. This is how I got histories of Joan of Arc and of ancient Rome and Greece, Prescott's The Conquest of Mexico and History of the Conquest of Peru, Anna Karenina and a Bruckner biography in German.

We were let out once a day for an hour to the central courtyard surrounded on all sides by building. There, under the eyes of armed guards pacing the roof above we walked up and down in pairs able to talk in a low voice without being eavesdropped. Mohsen would also referee a special game the boys from Khuzestan had introduced. Two teams would line up across the yard, a line dividing it into two fields. One person from one team would suddenly detach himself, take a deep breath and enter the territory of the other exhaling slowly, letting out a continuous sound all the time they were in the rival's territory. The aim was to try to touch one before returning to home territory without taking a breath, and all the time emitting a sound. The captured person would then be taken back as prisoner to his home ground. I was a regular loser and in the process, tore many Kurdish trousers which the family would have to find a substitute and send in. I wondered what they thought I got up to, tearing my pants once a week. The game was introduced by a young Abadani boy who we nick-named *zanbur* (the bee) since he used to emit a 'zzzzz' sound as he captured the enemy. He was executed soon after leaving our cell-block.

The courtyard also acted as the place when we saw our visitors. A month after my arrest I was called out. I had my first visitor, my mother they said.

But it turned out to be a patient who had used her contacts and some guile to come as see me as my mother. If I was angry, I tried to hide it. That afternoon my real mother had come and was refused a visit – I had already seen her they said. It was my sister Mina who ultimately persuaded them of their mistake. There they were behind the wire mesh, Mina, my mother and father, J's mother and father, but no J. She had prudently stayed away pending clarification of my situation. Mina passed on a message from a friend. *"E'telāst"* she said. She had to repeat it three times before I understood. There was a revolutionary upturn (*e'tela*), in Lenin's analysis the final stage before a revolutionary uprising. The message was from the old revolutionary Changiz. I felt warm. Yet another gross underestimation of the enemy.

Every day newcomers would come, and people would be called to interrogation or to court. A boy of around 19, tall and with a ginger hair which stood out among the sea of blackheads announced with pride, *barām hejdah sāl boridand*, they have cut 18 years for me. You discussed it like they cut a piece of cloth for a suit. He was a Paykar sympathiser. Javād a rather short boy with a round face and a permanent grin, a Mojahedin supporter, topped him with life. It is 17 years 364 days the ginger boy said the next day. Javād grinned his boyish grin that lit up his and our face. He didn't know how he could take a day away from life. Ginger-boy was to be a companion of another journey.

The door opened one day to let in 40 young men. Normally we would receive newcomers in twos and threes and Mahmud could cope in taming them, getting them used to the discipline, identifying and sending the politicos to the end two rooms. That day the Pāsdārs had attacked the village of Bolvardi, on the other side of the dry river, behind Hāfez Hospital, and arrested the entire young male population. They had had a riotous celebration when anti-government slogans had been heard. Mahmud reacted like lightning. He transferred the entire first room beyond, to the end two rooms and took the village into his 'hotel'. They were an unruly lot, over 40 young men from the same village, all friends. They point blank refused to share their fruit. Some pretended they had digestive problems and needed special diets. And they wanted to sing late into the night. The entire edifice of

CHAPTER 41

discipline we had created was about to crumble. Watching Mahmud skilfully and flexibly bring them to heel was like watching a tamer of wild horses. Within two days they were part of the team, only one person refusing to part with his oranges, which he insisted he needed for his stomach. By day four he agreed to have his special 'diet' delivered by the cheese *mas'ul*.

As part of the sudden shift caused by the Bolvardi gang we had to take in some non-politicos in our rooms. They had brought in this middle-aged peasant still wearing his brown felt hat made of tanned sheep skin, the sort Qashqāi' men wore with conical top and wing-like flaps reaching sunwards on either side. He looked truly bewildered. He had no idea why he was here. He was a man from another planet. He had come from his village somewhere near Firuzābād to Shiraz to buy presents for his forthcoming marriage. He had been to the bazaar and had brought some cloth and bric-a-brac and was about to board the mini bus back to Firuzābād when a Pāsdār had signalled to him with his Kalashnikov submachine gun to come out of the queue. He had panicked and ran. And here he was, incarcerated. He really had no inkling of what was going on, but a vague notion that there had been a Revolution and the Shah had gone. But that was it. He was like an innocent child cocooned in his village. He had never heard of Mojahedin, the explosions, the assassinations, the crackdown on dissidents. We confused him further when we told him we were doctors. Doctors? Prison? This is a trap, his incredulous eyes seemed to say. He just sat there and cried, lost, lonely, confused like a child, tears running down the furrows making an incongruous contrast with his sun-beaten face that looked much older than his real age. Taqi and I spent hours talking to him, calming him and reassuring him that it was a real misunderstanding that he would be released as soon as they discovered their mistake. That he would be able to go back to his remote village and get married. His entire village came to visit him with gifts of fruit and tea and pots and pans. He was given 3 months for resisting arrest. They took him away and I never saw him again. I hope someone realised how innocent he was.

There we were. In the morning the *mas'ul* for exercises would lead the boys on their morning exercise. All day long in our room there were clusters of people doing Qur'an classes, endocrinology classes, German classes, ideology discussions, Arabic classes. At lunch that day's *mas'ul* on the rota for *shahrdār*,[1] (mayor), would set down the tablecloth, distribute the food and later wash the dishes and make tea. The *mas'ul* for bread would make sure no crusts were left. The *mas'ul* for cheese would distribute cheese to those needing it for medicinal purpose – that was one of the weirdest beliefs I encountered. The inmates also had their own doctor, a doctor-in-the-house. We would take all the medicines that everyone was given at the infirmary, store it in the far room in our make-shift dispensary, and give out treatments as necessary. In the afternoon, the 'mayor'for the day would make tepid tea using warm water from the taps. At night the same 'mayor' would allocate people their places and distribute the blankets on a carefully thought-out combination of first-come-first-served and needs basis. There were times we had to use the corridor and even right up to the main iron gate, with its mountain of slippers and forgotten shoes, because of overcrowding. After lunch there would be a silent two hours when I was the only one awake, sipping my tea and reading. Lights out was at 9 pm and it was absolute. No one was allowed to talk until 7 am.

Then one day they came and ordered all the doctors to collect their things. We left in a bus to Ādel Ābād. There were no blindfolds. We could see the streets and it was exhilarating. I felt very sorry to leave the *Artesh 3*, the Third Army barracks. For us it had been a wonderful place. We had been left alone, cocooned. No one had bothered us. And we had been able to advise and help the hundreds of people who had moved through our cell-bloc-cage-home. By the end we had accumulated a wealth of information that we could pass on. And we had been a source of comfort to some, a doctor to others, a councillor, here and there. Mohsen had even taught elemental psychology to us in his famous talk on the Jo-Harry window which in Farsi, *johari*, could also mean window to the interior, to that quarter of the mind that was invisible and inaccessible to the self and others.

But we had been closely watched. Many months later, after our second sojourn in *Artesh 3* was over, I learnt that everyone that we had chosen as *mas'ul*, or who had shown themselves in any way as having initiative, if they

CHAPTER 41

had not been freed in the meanwhile, had been executed. The 'bee' was dead, Sa'id a quite, serious boy who had been savagely whipped on his stomach and took on the cheese allocation on my second sojourn in the same cell-block a month or so later was also shot. These are the two I remember but there were others. Mohsen's role as umpire was noted and was to cost him. Mahmud, surprisingly, escaped their wrath. On the whole, the Medical School got off relatively lightly. And an Ashraf Dehqani supporter[2] who had led the morning exercises in the first month had managed to get himself released. But those deaths will hang on my heart till I die.

[1] Literally mayorship, the name given to the person on the daily rota for cleaning and other tasks.

[2] The first split in the Fadāi' of those who still believed in the guerrilla armed struggle.

Chapter 42

The doctors room

We arrived at the *hashti*, the vestibule, the open area as you entered Cell Block number 3 (*Bande* 3) which was the section of Ādel Ābād run by the Pāsdārs. Majid Torābpour, the head of the block, came out of the guardroom to receive us. He was short, stocky, overweight, with a paunch, younger than his brother Khalil who otherwise looked like him. They had the looks, the walk and the swagger of thugs in the old regime, unlike the ideological Pāsdārs who were mostly thin and looked more intense. All that was missing was the blue-black velvet hat. Khalil, in that swaggering *jāheli* tone of his, an echo of his thuggish history, jeered at my plastic bag with a large textbook. This is not a library he sneered and took it away. But I was allowed to retrieve it in a few minutes.

We were herded into the first room on the left on the ground floor just opposite the guardroom. It was the detox room for the druggies. The room stank of urine. The walls and floor were smeared with spit, vomit and some brown stuff of dubious origin. "Can you get us some Dettol?" Mohsen asked Ali-Mohammad, his son who had earlier been arrested and was housed on the floor above. "Where the hell am I going to get Dettol here!" he quipped in his Shirazi lilt and got us some detergent from another inmate. It took us all morning to clean up what came to be known as the doctors' room.

CHAPTER 42

Ādel Ābād had been built by the Shah as a model prison and had housed a whole generation of revolutionaries on their rotational pilgrimage through the prisons of the monarch. It has three male blocs and a female bloc set a little apart. Block Three is at the end of the main corridor and furthest away from the entrance and the main prison kitchen. Each cell block is made up of three floors with ten or twelve cells lining each side being linked by a balcony which went round the block on each floor, linking up on the far side. Stairs climbed up at the *hashti* and also at the far end. Each cell contained three triple-bunked beds with a barred open unglazed window to the outside world at the level of the top bunk. The southerly rooms looked out into the large open area outside the cell blocks and if you were on the third floor, you could see the desert and the barren hills above and beyond the perimeter walls. The north-facing cells opened out to a narrow space which separated cell blocks two and three. Our block – *Bande 3* – belonged to the Pāsdārān. The other two blocks were run by the municipal police, and we did not meet the inmates, except when on kitchen duty we went to the common kitchen to collect the food.

On the ground floor, a central walkway separating the two rows of cells led to the concrete courtyard, about 15 metres square, which served as our exercise yard. At the time it was open for an hour a day when we played volleyball or simply walked in pairs. It was bounded by wire fencing topped with barbs. You got a glimpse of the block-two exercise yard, although you rarely saw the inside of their yard as they seemed to hang washed blankets and towels permanently on the wire-mesh courtyard wall to dry. There must have been a lot of vomiting going on over there. Surrounding the entire building were the grounds where some vegetables had been planted and where, out of sight on the right we could hear the firing squad from time to time, usually at dawn or dusk. Most the executions took place in Artesh 3, out of earshot, unlike prisoners in Evin who counted the coup de grace shots to get an idea of how many were executed, we only found out about the dead much later. We also used the central walkway for walking – 82 steps up, 82 steps back, which I did for an hour a day marching to the ricercare from Bach's musical offering playing in my head. It still does when I go for a walk.

In no time a routine somehow precipitated, crystallised out of random individual acts by individual prisoners, and life gelled into a habit, a pattern of behaviour. The doctors' room became a transit point for everyone on the way back from the infirmary. When we arrived there, there were about 150 political prisoners and twice as many ordinary prisoners under the custody of the Pāsdārs. They were there on *mavad* (drug charges), *lavat* (sex with a man)[1] or theft. *Mavati-lavati* we nicknamed them. Thieves too, but no murderers to my knowledge.

There was a shop on the second floor run by a drug smuggler serving a long sentence. A small wiry man with a thin moustache, he was remarkably friendly with Khalil and Majid, who may have taken their cut. We were allowed 100 tomans a week that we could spend in the shop. The barber too was on the second floor, open once a week and run by an Esfahani (Isfahani) man of 40 odd years who had two fingers on his right hand missing, chopped off by the regime for theft. He had been a barber and had been caught a number of times for theft in this and that regime. He was pretty nifty with the remaining three. "They said they will chop my thumb next", he smiled through his missing front teeth, a tell-tale sign of inhaling vapourised heroin. And there was Esmail, who had spent most of his adult life in prison on drug-related charges. He too had no front teeth and really bad gums. He was released while I was there but managed to be rearrested within a week. I have no one outside, he confided. Toothless Esmail spent a lot of time in our room. I knew he had an assignment and we fed him fodder to keep him sweet with Khalil. Coming back from the infirmary virtually all the prisoners would enter our room, tell us their complaint, and voluntarily hand over their tablets; mild tranquilizers, anti-acids and antibiotics dished out to everyone by the health assistant (*behyar*) regardless of their specific complaints. We treated each accordingly. Valium was in demand by the *mavadis* and we rationed it.

Morale was excellent. The Mojahedin would have their group exercises in the yard and conduct their classes in their cells. The left too would gather in their respective groups and hold classes. We continued with our German and endocrinology lessons. There was a library which astonishingly had not

CHAPTER 42

only books from Ali Shari'ati, but also novels such as Jean-Christophe, about a revolutionary composer by Roman Roland, in twelve volumes, beautifully translated by M. Behāzin (Mahmood E'temādzādeh).[2] It was in constant demand and all the volumes were out all the time. We never returned them for fear of confiscation. And so, I read this beautiful novel in a random order and only after having finished the last volume was I able to splice it together in my head. They took us to the gym, twice, and then gave up. They took us to the cinema, twice, and then gave up. It was there that I saw Ragbār (downpoor) by Bahrām Beizāi' the first Iranian film that showed illicit love. It had eluded the Shah's censors and now our Islamist guards. The other was a trashy Hollywood movie. The Torābpours had not yet totally discarded their previous existence but knew what to censor. Someone stood in front of the projector and covered up the girl's legs whenever they appeared below a miniskirt with his hairy hands. It was almost as if he was groping her.

It was Wednesday late in July, visiting day. We had been in the doctors' room about a week. It was hot outside. Maryam remembers that day clearly. It was the children's first visit. They arrived early morning and were made to wait in the scorching sun until late in the afternoon. There were hundreds of women, some men and scores of children running around. The children were thirsty. Mina went over to get some water from a tap, but it had been turned off. It was Ramadan. But what about the children, Mina protested. A shrug. They were allowed in around 4 pm, handed over the fruit, tea and a melon. Another long wait in the stifling hall. "It was over in a minute" Maryam remembered. "All that waiting in the sun just for a glimpse across dirty cloudy glass". I remember her big black eyes, loving. And 11-year old Nargess, another pair of beautiful eyes, anxious, questioning. Eyes let through a stream of words that defy the time it takes to articulate them in words. Looks can transcend time, stretching it into a narrative as long as life. In Maryam's eyes I read the stories that I had read to her in bed, teaching her to ride a bicycle, the emergence of a young women from the child, a fulcrum of two existences, the becoming. It was a sea of love ululating through the large black pupils. And in front of her, Nargess was always in front, the bewilderment of the why, the confusion of childhood interrupted, the anger for the scorching wait, and the love for a father who had abandoned them. We had little to say. But a life was being said in images, in glances.

Mina, calm, talked first across the dirty glass by telephone. J is fine. The phone cut off in the middle. Frantic shouting. The phone is off! The phone is disconnected! Reconnected. Then Ensy who could not find any words. Are you comfortable, or some such pleasantry? What do you say in such circumstances? Her eyes shimmered under the film of water stroking my cheeks across the glass barrier with words of regret. Regret for all that she should have done, regret for the child she had sent into the unknown, regret at the unknown she was witnessing, uncomprehending. Sarhang, my father-in-law, was there, Ezzy was there, mother-in-law Foruq was there. Puzzled disbelief. Little communication, but a world of interconnection. And then it abruptly ended. A moment of connection with the real world and we were back in the doctors' room. But not before I caught a glimpse of a boy, he could not have been much more than five, raising his fist in defiance, shout across the dirty glass to his brother '*Mohammad, Mohammad, moqavemat kon!* [3] Resist the 16-year-old did, and died for it.

In time I was to learn how to cherish time, the moments, and thus make them stretch. Time needs to be managed, massaged, nurtured, wooed, planned, folded into segments that can be run in parallel. Stretched like a concertina. Studded with hyper sensation. It is thus that moments can be expanded into hours and months contracted to an augenblick. I was left with those two sets of eyes. Naked love and baffled love.

A week later it was the last day of Ramadan – *Eide Fetr* – Islam's most important festival. Traditionally, people visit relatives and elders. All day long we had a procession of people coming to have tea and sweets with us in the doctors' room. Not just the politicos but also the two hundred or so *mavāti-lavātis* came, even the barber and grocer. The next day the tannoy called the names of Mohsen, Taqi, Ichlie, Mahmud, and all the other medics, all but me, to collect their things and go to the *hashti* (vestibule). The doctors' room reverted to its old role and I was transferred to the second floor to share a room with Esmail. I grew a moustache and watched a sunflower reach out for light through the barred window.

CHAPTER 42

"Seyyed", which was how everyone called me, "shave it off" the ginger-haired Peikari whispered. It will make you look less communist. I did and a few days later early one morning I was called over the loudspeaker. They took me and a number of prisoners, mixed politicos and *mavāti-lavātis* to the old SAVAK building. Another trip not blindfolded, exhilarating, seeing actual streets and cars and people able to walk. On the second floor, in three rooms the judges sat in judgment. The irony of the location! We waited in a landing at the top of the stairs into which the three rooms opened. At the end was a bay window opening onto a balcony. All morning the prisoners would be led in for a few minutes and would come out with their sentence. For *mavād* it was either prison, lashing, or fine. Beside me addicts were selling Valium at 25 tomans a pill. Eyes were running. The judgments seemed pretty arbitrary since it depended which room you went into. One mullah was harsh, one lenient and the third halfway. When I described this later to one of the boys, a Mojahed, he smiled a broad smile. "It's a lottery, this Islamic justice is" he whispered and grinned. "You can go in and get either *abad, abadā or abadiyyat*", life, nothing or eternity, meaning death. It was the most poignant summary of the justice system of the Islamic Republic I have ever heard. He himself drew the final straw.

It was early afternoon, and my brain was exhausted with conjuring up the questions I was likely to face and possible answers. "Do you realise" he said, "we can just walk out of the window on to the balcony and straight across to the house next door". He was another politico waiting with me, 24 or 25, with stubble and a moustache, very expressive eyes, I think belonging to one of the left groups. I had known of at least one person recaptured and instantly shot, I told him. "Goodbye" he said, "and good luck" and vanished through the window. There was no one guarding us and only two *mavādis* in the agony of withdrawal, too involved with their inner anguish to notice or care. I never saw him again. I have always wondered what would have happened if I had followed him and gone to Tehran. It was only later that I discovered how light my charge sheet had been. I might have got away with it. By evening my turn had not come and I was driven back with another disappointed prisoner. No one seemed to have missed him

[1] *Mavad* (slangified to *mavat*) – literally translates as stuff – was an allusion to drugs. *Lavat* was buggery – in most cases with an underage boy.

[2] A writer and excellent translator with Tudeh sympathies.

[3] Mohammad, Mohammad, resist! He was a Mojahedin sympathiser.

Chapter 43

Andalibi

A few days later the loudspeakers again called, 'brother …' meaning me, plus two more names. I was looking out of the window on the top bunk. There, a sunflower, patiently waiting with its one single sibling in the gap between cell block two and three for the sun to return for its short visit next morning. It too was a prisoner between walls. The orange-yellow petals radiating out optimistically from the seeds of its being was my only link to the outside, one that modulated the complex, complicating, one might say painful emotions of love and parenthood. I gathered my belongings in a plastic bag. The books I left behind. I would be back. I had rehearsed it all in the waiting room of the SAVAK building courthouse and felt confident. We joked all the way in the jeep. My fellow passengers were a young lad with an unusual light-coloured hair and a slightly older young man. I did not know either. The nightmare caught us totally unawares.

As soon as I re-entered the Atresh 3, the Third Army barracks, I knew that during my short sojourn in Ādel Ābād, life for prisoners had totally changed. It was like turning a chapter and finding a different book by a different author in different times and in different colours. This was burning red. This was a glimpse of hell. A world where sense was suspended, where words lost all meaning, where simple emotions melted into nonsense. Where life lost any links with existence. Where the illogic of nightmares put on the clothes of day. I was unprepared.

We were blindfolded and led down the corridor that I worked out was the one that led to the larger cells and the central courtyard. I had been too dazed to remember where exactly the solitary block was, but it was probably at the end of the same corridor, on the left. Or was it below stairs, as dungeons are meant to be? We were led to the left and ordered to take off our blindfolds. I found myself in the television room. I had been here before. It was on the opposite side of the corridor to the large four-roomed cell that had been home for a few weeks. The television room had fitted carpets and scattered all over the floor where about sixty young men, sitting or lying down in groups of three or four. The television was off or had gone. There was a strange silence. The air had died in that room. The place smelt of fear, that peculiar acrid smell.

The story was told in whispers. Andalibi, a young *mullah* had arrived from Qom as *Hākem Shar'*, *shari'a* judge. "He did not even have a beard", a boy of perhaps 16 or 17 who had been called to court whispered in awe, as if he had faced Ezrai'l, the angel of death. He had. Two days ago Andalibi had been to the city of Lār where he had executed 40 or 50 people. He then moved to Estahbānāt where another 30 or 40 had been shot. He had arrived in Artesh 3 and last night and overnight had sent about thirty-five prisoners to their deaths. He simply had two sentences, life or the firing squad. As we talked the names of four boys, they were mere boys, could not have been twenty, were called out. It was over in less than five minutes. All had received the death sentence.

One of them, aged 17, a beautiful boy with pale brown eyes and soft skin and a thin down of a moustache on his lips sat down next to me. "He asked me did you have a stone in your hand", he began. "Yes", he had replied. *Mofse-ed fel-arz*, Andalibi had barked his sentence (corrupt on earth) and went on to the next boy. "Please will you tell my parents when you get out", he asked me with a voice that had the musky smell of spring and eyes that combined intense sadness with the sort of courage that only comes from confidence of

CHAPTER 43

being in the right. How did he know that I would get out? "Please tell them that I was not afraid, and that I love them, and they should not cry for me, that I knew what I was doing". Yes, I thought, you held a stone in your young hands. Your tiny gravestone. "I love them and will always love them, always. Remember to tell them I was not afraid to die. Remember that," he whispered firmly, perhaps talking to himself. There are no fearless people, only fearless moments. This was one. They took all four away a few minutes later. We could not hear the shots. It was on the other side of the building. I never met his parents to pass on the love that was to last always, or his courage. The 'always' for the boy who held a stone had been less than a quarter of an hour.

And they kept taking them out in groups of two or three, for summary sentences. Only one question. The answer was irrelevant. Death or life was dished out at random, as you would throw crumbs to pigeons. As far as I could work out who lived and who didn't depended on a whim. On luck. On the utter stupidity of terror. The aim was to terrorise. And terror has no specific target. That is how Ja'far Zolqadr a 20-year-old Mojahed, who had already lost two brothers was given life. It was only a brief respite. Two months later when I was in Niriz on my way to a Jahrom prison, the same Andalibi happened to be passing by. He dragged Ja'far out of his crowded cell, two cells to the right of me, and had him shot. That angel of death had it in for young Ja'far, with his shy smile and one eye blinded following a childhood accident, who would always look down with his only good eye when he talked to you.

All day and all the next night I looked at death crouching beside me and kept telling myself that I would face it as these boys had done. It was to be my fearless moment. The test was not to come, the test never came. I would never know what it is like to face certain death a finger pull away. I never faced that test of fear. Next morning those still alive were taken out and lined up in the corridor outside. Blindfolded. I was pulled out of line and walked across the corridor. I never saw my two fellow passengers again.

Chapter 44

Jān-e Maryam

Later I found that the chief religious judge of Shiraz, Borujerdi, had taken my file from under Andalibi. He had insisted on personally judging the doctors. He was related by marriage to one or other of the many *mullahs* in my family. Earlier Ezzy had seen one of the ayatollahs in Tabriz, related by marriage to Borujerdi, and using family ties had obtained a letter of recommendation. Ezzy went on to knock on Borujerdi's home in Shiraz. A very beautiful blue-eyed woman in full *hejab* opened the door. He asked to see the ayatollah. He will not see anyone. But she had taken the letter. A visit by the other Jaleh, the other Mohsen's wife to the *Artesh* 3 had also been rebuffed. The Ayatollah Borujerdi will not see anyone. But who knows what had motivated the Ayatollah? Years later I was told that Tudeh chief, Kianuri, a cousin and childhood friend of Ezzy, had also interjected directly with Khomeini. But Khomeini had always refused to interfere with his religious judges even for close relatives, thus deflecting any blame. In the end Borujerdi acted as judge for both of us Mohsens.

The familiar grey iron gate opened and I was inside my old home, now reduced to two large rooms going across on the left from the door. *Seyyed khosh āmadi* (welcome), Mahmud said with a grin showing his youthful perfect

CHAPTER 44

white teeth, and we embraced like long lost family. All the medics from the old 'doctors room' in Ādel Ābād were there. I had been returned to our old four-roomed cell block, now shrunk to half its size. In my absence they had partitioned off the far two rooms. Only people who had passed through interrogation were allowed through to our side. Newcomers were shut up in the other half. Pre and post interrogations were cordoned off by concrete and it was now impossible to pass on experience to the newly arrested. The quasi comedy of June had run its course. The new play was more serious. Like everyone else, I had to readjust my expectations. It would be a longer haul.

Life went on in the now shrunken bay. Mahmud still ran his *fandoq* hotel with the first room facing the entrance continuing to act as a sifting bay. We even had two Pāsdārs imprisoned for crimes we never found out. You did not ask – you just took what was volunteered. They could have been plants and it became important to neutralise that by befriending them. I began the game of pretending that I was imprisoned by mistake. It was not that preposterous. So many others were. From prisoners transferred across the dividing wall we learnt that from the Medical School my colleagues Asqar, Faramarz and Khosrow had also been arrested. Clearly the University needed another whipping to tame it. I was looking forward to seeing them, but they were released after two months without making the transition across the concrete divide. But stories of how they had entertained the prisoners kept coming.

The mood was a little more subdued, but only a little. The news of Andalibi's bloody visits to the province had preceded my arrival. Mahmud went on with his obsessive dishing out although the grocery by the wall was less well stocked now. Mohsen continued to appoint *mas'uls*. One Said, a Left activist that I mentioned before, had been savagely whipped across his stomach and was left with much pain. He took on the cheese allocation.

I began an investigation of dreams, my own and other people's. My own dreams had a recurrent core theme through a variety of settings. I would be trying to get somewhere when I would suddenly be confronted with the choice of two roads. One road was entirely visible as far as the horizon while the other was obscured after a short distance, a bend or fog or an object obscuring the path. It may be two roads on a mountain side one of which looked impassable and disappeared round the corner with the other clearly visible to the crest, or I was flying a plane and one possible route was enveloped in cloud. In every case I chose the invisible road and after a frightening passage would reach my destination. The dreams seemed to be passing a message to trust my gut instincts and do as it dictates. As a young man I had read in a Pelican book about the problem-solving function of dreams. August Kekulé, a scientist puzzling on the chemical formula of benzine, dosed off one afternoon on a rocking chair in his veranda and dreamt of a snake biting its tail. The ring-shaped benzine molecule. In our cage everyone had a problem.

I had also had a strange experience of a premonition dream in Namāzi where Frances, the paediatrician Jurabchi's wife, had told us over dinner of a disturbing dream, in a very agitated state, that eerily predicted her death and that of both her children the day after she recounted the dream to us, including some uncanny details, that I had checked with Asqar before finding out the details of the car crash that killed the three of them. It had left an unanswered, indeed unanswerable question in my mind. Einstein's concept of a curved space-time presented intriguing questions regarding the circular nature of time.[1] One morning, one of the two imprisoned Pāsdārs recounted the dream he had that morning to a group squatting around him. It was about me. In his dream I had walked into a two-story building, then appeared from the upstairs window and prepared to dive into the pond in the courtyard below. "Don't jump *Seyyed*," he had shouted up in panic, "the pond is shallow!" Ignoring the warning, I had dived and disappeared under the cold water. I failed to appear for two hours, and everyone gathered around the pond worried. Then I popped out of the water smiling. We all laughed at the dream.

Just then the guards came in and unlocked the door to the baths. Everyone rushed in as we had not bathed for ten days. I undressed and turned on the tap, but the water was cold. Others called to the guard that there is no hot water. "Everyone out!" shouted the guard. But I had already lathered my head and was going to take a quick cold shower. Shades of boarding school.

CHAPTER 44

"Out! "shouted the guard. "Wait just a second," I said, "I'll rinse off the soap." Bang closed the door. I was locked in. They let me out two hours later to a clapping grinning crowd, so many teeth to greet me. I had dived from the second room of our two-roomed (two-storey?) home into a cool water only to emerge smiling two hours later. Premonition dream? Absurd constructs? Who knows?

And then I did go to court. Unlike Andalibi it lasted one and a half hours, an hour of which Borujerdi, the *sharia'* judge, expounded on the faultless nature of Islamic justice, a lengthy monologue justifying why he had passed a death sentence on Dr Narimisa[2] in Ahwaz, and why the doctor was guilty of major crimes against the state. It was as if he was trying to convince me that he was not a doctor killer. Was he trying to distance himself from the angel of death, Andalibi? Why me? He then turned to my file. "You have been a member of the National Association of Academics (SMD) that was set up by the SAVAK" he said and looked at me with a look that had an air of finality. I was struck by how handsome he was beneath his white turban. "If that is the case", I replied, "many people in government had made that mistake too. The martyr Abbasspour was in the executive and the martyr Ayat wrote its constitution" (both had been killed, the former in the explosion of the Majles building the day before my arrest and the latter by an assassin). Borujerdi, turned angrily to the only other person in the room, a scribe. "Why was I not informed of this?" The interview went on in the same vein. What had begun as descent into Dante's inferno, ended as a Jacobean farce. I was sure that I would get six months or so just like Ichlie and Taqi and virtually all the students arrested with me. It was the shortest sentence being given out and was as good as saying we were innocent of 'crimes'.

Then came Friday October 2. There were to be elections of a new president. In August the previous president had been assassinated, along with Mohammad Javad Bāhonar, the same Bāhonar in whose release I had participated in the hostage taking episode. That was the day we helped foil a plot by SAVAK to set the Bāhāi' and Muslim communities at each other's throat. The victory of Ali Khāmenei' was a foregone conclusion as Khomeini had endorsed his candidature. Those were tense times in the world outside with almost daily assassinations. Khāmenei' himself had one arm disabled by a bomb in a foiled assassination attempt.

The iron gate opened. We were going forour *havākhori* (literally 'eating air') break. As we went through the door into the central courtyard, white-haired Mohsen first as he was the most senior, a Pāsdār called out "anyone wanting to vote to the right the rest to the left!" Mohsen turned left without hesitation. I had a second or two to think and followed him, almost by instinct. A few other prisoners followed the two older doctors. We had been taken by surprise. Rather naively we had assumed that the voting booth would not be brought to the prison. Within an hour of going back into the cell Mohsen was told to collect his things and was moved to a smaller cell. That evening the television set was removed as was the daily Keyhan newspaper which we had read from cover to cover looking at obituaries and adverts to get a feel of what was going on out there. The kettle of hot water, a special favour which we had asked for, ceased. Thereafter we had to make tea with tap water. We banned the use of hot water from the beginning of the afternoon nap which gave us some tepid water which with a large handful of tea leaves made something barely drinkable. Iranians love their tea.

Prisoners kept arriving across the divide. Once a bunch of Fadāi' Majority were brought in. It was awkward at first as they were supporters of the regime. One of them had a beautiful voice and sang. Singing was now a regular part of the evening before lights out. There was an eighteen-year boy, belonging to the Ranjbarān. He was somewhat plump and was obviously spoilt by the family as he got huge bags of fruit and other goodies which of course was shared out. He had a very beautiful voice and used to sing the folk-song *jān-e Maryam* with immense passion. He too had been tortured by being whipped with electric cable on his feet and legs and could barely walk. Yet our nightingale sang for us. About a week or two after he had moved in, he was taken out and shot. Thereafter, whenever anyone was taken out to be executed, we sang *jān-e Maryam* just after lights out. We did the same when the men from the Fadāi' Majority were taken out to die a few hours after they had been brought into our cell.

Four weeks later I was allowed a visit by the family. J was there. She held

CHAPTER 44

two fingers up. What? Two fingers, two years. I had been given two years on a blank dossier and on the back of the voting boycott. Mohsen was given 5 years. No one bothered to inform me. That was my third personal encounter with the justice system of my country, totally arbitrary, utterly savage and for me, ultimately farcical.

A week later a number of prisoners were called. We were all asked to put blindfolds on, lined up in the corridor for what seemed hours as more and more people were brought. We were then led, each one clutching the man in front, ascended some steps and sat down on a bus. Keep your heads down, a *Pāsdār* shouted viciously. I heard a girl's voice at the back asking for something. Shut up, he shouted, and ran past and hit her hard and she let out a cry. The bus left. It was evening. Keep your heads down he kept shouting. "I feel sick", another girl's voice coming from the front of the bus. "Keep your heads down or I will shoot."

[1] For a mathematical-philosophical rejection of the possibility of circular time see *A World Without Time: the forgotten legacy of Gödel and Einstein*. Palle Yourgrau. Penguin Books 2007.

[2] Dr Narimisa was executed the previous year along with two other colleagues for his involvement in the defence of the Jondishāhpur University, Ahwaz, when thugs attacked the University as part of the 'Cultural Revolution' in the spring of 1980. At least 12 people died and there was a protest at the killing at the municipality offices which was led by Narimisa. The Pāsdarān fired on the protesters killing three. Previously Narimisa helped collect information that unmasked the hands of Islamists in the burning down of Cinema Rex in Abadan during the Revolution that had killed 600 people. He was a Fadāi' supporter.

45

Chapter 45

Niriz and Jahrom

Where were they taking us? Were we being driven to Evin? We knew what terror awaited us there. Why be taken in this clandestine way? "Keep your heads down!" Were the guards scared that people might react in the streets? I felt nauseous. Denied visual location, waves of retching rose and had to be pushed back. "Keep your head down!" they shouted. Keep your vomit down it echoed inwards. I peeked ahead from under the blindfold. A Pāsdār was facing us machine gun in hand. I felt a hard smack on the back of the neck. "I said keep your head down!" he shouted in a gruff voice. There was clearly one or more Pāsdārs at the back. There were at least four girls in the first row. I tried to work out the direction we were driven by imagining the route but soon got lost. Then I managed to peep sideways out of the window. It did not look like the road to the Qura'n Gate. We were not going north which meant we were going east. Then no more lights. No more houses. We were out of town.

An hour or so later we arrived and were led into our new prison. It was a row of cells, cages with open fronts looking out unto a corridor. There was a draught and it was clear that the corridor opened to the outside. There were five others sharing my cell which had a sort of platform at the back,

CHAPTER 45

raised about 20 cm above the entrance area – a kind of sitting-room-bedroom arrangement. We slept that night lying side by side. None of us could work out where we were. A *Pāsdār* came round with some food, bread and dates without the butter. He refused to tell us where we were. We only found we were in Niriz, a small town east of Shiraz, the next day. At dawn, a Pāsdār opened the door so that we could wash for prayer. It became immediately clear that I had to go through the motions. What was required is what Germans called Sitzfleisch – to see this all the way through without betraying yourself or your friends. "Seyyed', a young Mojahed nudged me smiling, "that is not the way to wash for prayer. You do the right hand first then the left." I had forgotten the rituals not having prayed since age of 18.

Next noon another prisoner, a local, was added to our midst. He looked frightened and we tried to comfort him but kept our own confidence. It was best to be safe. Now we had to sleep packed in like sardines. The only way to turn was if we did it all together. The second day we were communicating with our neighbours, a row of solitary cells now sleeping six to eight. On the third day we heard that young Zolqadr, the one with the one shy eye, had been taken out and shot. Andalibi, the beardless *Ezra'il*, a baby-faced angel of death in turban, was passing by and having heard he was here had called him out and had him shot, an afterthought. On the fourth day, we were on a bus to somewhere. It was clear that the authorities did not yet know where. The bus stopped a number of times and the Pāsdār, who was obviously in charge, spoke on a walkie-talkie with someone. We heard Estahbānāt and Lār being mentioned. In the end we were taken to Jahrom. Our destination had been decided at the last minute, on the hoof, so to speak. We were not blindfolded.

Mohsen and one or two of the junior medical students were on the bus and a number of people we knew well, including the ginger-haired Peikari who and been given 18 years, and a few lifers. But no Taqi or Ichlie, no little Javad. The girls were not with us. Mohsen was in great form. When we arrived at a converted school that was to be our prison, they were still sticking down the fitted carpets. Mohsen and I took the last room. The carpet was wet as if it had been flooded for some reason. Must guard against rheumatism, I thought, but best to be out of the way. I had no idea how long we would be there. It was best to plan for years.

And so began a relaxing interlude, through the winter months. Over the next weeks we persuaded our sole guard, Brother Mahmud, to extend the time spent in the school yard from one hour per day gradually to full time. It was clear that here you were in full view so the pretence to pray continued where necessary. Most of the time you just went to your room and did a bit of bending. The group prayer sessions were more difficult to fake. It would have been folly to refuse outright to attend and yet there were many atheists among us and keeping morale up was important. We two doctors were still the oldest and all the politicos looked to us for guidance. An unspoken compromise was agreed upon such that when they broadcast the *Doay-e Komeil*, a lament that took place every Thursday evening, you either sat it out in your room or in the corridor but did not lie down. And we would ignore the *doay-e shab* – the prayer that lasted most of the night.

Bathing was once a week but first we had to fix and then heat up the boiler. What had been its function when the place was a school? The water never got more than tepid but Jahrom is warm even in winter. It is filled with date trees and oranges and lemons. In earlier days I had come with Asqar, Faramaz and family to eat sweet oranges. There was a Zoroastrian fire temple dating from pre-Islamic days – now defunct. Now J came with Mohsen's wife Jaleh and our children, and we had face to face meetings in the garage. It was like paradise. Jahrom was a deeply religious city. But a number of the founders and leaders of the Mojahedin were from this city. Mahmud the guard had gleefully recounted how after June 1981 there was a massacre of the Mojahedin in the streets with their bodies dumped in ditches.

That no one should go to the official Friday prayers was an unspoken, undisputed, agreement among all the prisoners. The regime would film you, broadcast it and use it in its propaganda that the opposition had capitulated. Two captive doctors caught on camera in a Friday prayer meeting would have been an important propaganda coup. There had been many rumours circulating around Shiraz that we had been tortured, executed etc. Because of the central role of the Medical School in the Revolution in Shiraz, the arrest of us doctors had a prominence way above our actual importance. The

CHAPTER 45

unforeseen consequence of liberating the school courtyard and extending recreation time constraints was spending more time with Mahmud our sole guard. And he saw his job in persuading us to go to the Friday prayers.

I had spent every minute giving the impression to the prison authorities, either directly or through their stooges, that my arrest was some kind of mistake. That image was not difficult to convey as most of the Pāsdārs knew that the majority of arrests those days had been through some kind of guesswork or third-party report. Now I was even pretending to pray. What excuse did I have? Mahmud, the guard, was a typical young peasant boy attracted to the *Pāsdārān* through his faith and prospects of employment. Guile, particularly of the urban kind was unknown, alien to him. And the two doctors were almost certainly the only doctors he had ever spoken to on a one-to-one basis. And now they, these doctors, lived like him, ate the same food, slept on the same ground, used the same toilet. It must have been disorientating. Doctors have a special place in our society, a place that would make sense to anyone living in pre-war Europe. I was able to postpone the inevitable by inculcating in Mahmud the guard how dejected I was, how I could not face the people of the country, how upset my arrest had made me. My shame. I would postpone going to the Friday prayers a week at a time. Let me pluck up the courage, I would say. Maybe next week. And time was ticking. This was an ideological regime, and like all ideological regimes, they needed to mould society in their image.

The family visited and once even brought in a large box of cream cakes that fed the entire prison. The date trees fluttered freedom from over the wall. We had no other communication with the outside world. No radio. No papers. J and the kids had moved to Tehran as life in Shiraz had become impossible. No one would give her a job. They had been thrown out of Namāzi. "*Vila neshini bas ast,*" it is time you stopped living in villas, the new chancellor Mostafā Moi'n, an old friend of both of us, had sneered at the two Jalehs. The same Moi'n who later would become a reformist Minister of Higher Education in Mohammad Khātami's reformist cabinet. Those were days of 'radicalism, *hezbollāhi* style'.[1] My neighbour Qarib, the same Qarib who had been the first to sign the SMD manifesto and later fed the Pāsdārān after they had arrested me, now signed the paper throwing my family out. Even Āzādeh, the wrestling dervish, had walked past J on the street and pretended not to see her. Nargess, who had never liked his daughter, stared at him and decided there and then never to humour someone she disliked again. Revolutions shatter memories, shatter relationships, sometimes shatter what makes us human.

The family would now have to travel weekly from Tehran to Shiraz on a bus, an eighteen-hour overnight journey, and then to Jahrom. It was very hard on the two girls though Maryam had got a standing ovation from her new classmates in Tehran when the teacher had told them that her father was a counter-revolutionary in prison. It was hard on J too. She insisted on making these weekly trips to keep me in contact with life. In retrospect she should have cut it back to once a month. Why did I never suggest that? I was increasingly engrossed in ensuring my survival and the survival strategy became increasingly more complicated as the regime became more sophisticated and kept raising the bar.

To jump the hurdles and not flip the bar or fall down on the other side became a constant preoccupation. The outside world was shut off. You had to be able to predict the next move by the regime and have a plan in place in advance of that. You had to be one step ahead but think like them. This meant getting inside their heads. And more importantly, conferring only with trusted people at each step. We could not afford to be taken off guard a second time as we were when Khāmeneiʼ was elected president.

It became increasingly difficult to continue the same story. Even naïve, innocent Mahmud the guard was beginning to find it more difficult to follow the tale. I was beginning to think ahead to how I could change tactics. Fall ill. I did that one Friday but that could only be a one off. Break a leg. But they would just give me crutches. Maybe I could go and somehow hide behind the crowd. But I knew that in a small town like Jahrom I would be expected to get up and say something to the congregation. Then fate took a hand yet again. We were told to collect our things. We were all returning to Shiraz.

[1] The new regime pretended to be in a class war against the wealthy older

CHAPTER 45

class. Mo'in knew full well that I had not a metre of land in Shiraz or anywhere else and had actually turned down the piece of land offered by the University in Maliābād to the entire faculty.

Chapter 46

Living with tavvābs

The return journey was with eyes open. The Pāsdārs still needed lessons in maths. The Third Army barracks, Artesh 3, our old detention centre, refused to accept the prisoners because the numbers in the bus did not tally with the numbers on their paperwork. We parked in the barrack yard. Hour followed hour and our biological needs became critical. Mohsen was refused permission to leave the bus to urinate. I saw him gyrate, flush and then start a long discussion on the Qur'an with the driver. As he was interpreting a particularly emotive *sura*, serious and eloquent as only grey-haired white-bearded Mohsen could, expressively gesticulating with his right hand, his left hand disappeared. There was the crackling of plastic. Then he stopped fidgeting. Still deep in exposition he tied up the ends and gently kicked the bag under the seat in front. A master at work. I did mine my way. Smile, ask, and ask again. I was allowed out terminally exploding. Don't forget to squat, my neighbour whispered. It was a whipping offence to urinate standing up. The urine splashes about. Sprays of unclean body fluid, Shi'sm's nightmare.

That night they took Mohsen and me into a corridor with single occupancy cells unfamiliar to both of us. They were very polite, but no explanations. Where did the others go? Blank stare. One of the *Pāsdārs* that we had both known, a young man in his early twenties, thin like most *Pāsdārs* that we came across, and tall, came over to share our tea in Mohsen's cell. I had treated him for something or other during one of our stays. In the middle of a long conversation, I casually put a question to him "if the Emam [Khomeini] was to order you to kill one million people would you do it". He shrank into thought for a moment or two and then replied in a subdued, soft but determined voice "I wouldn't like to, but if the Emam orders me, I would" and his steely eyes told me that he would. It was the eyes of idealised fanaticism. The eyes of one who would commit any crime if ordered to.

That same evening, by coincidence, I witnessed another version of the relationship of the clergy and their henchmen. An old man, certainly over 70, was in the cell next door. They had not bothered to lock the individual doors to our cells as two middle aged doctors were an unlikely threat. The old man had been caught drinking. The guard in charge ordered one of the other Pāsdārs to give him 74 lashes. "Has the *aqa* (a deferential term for mullah-judge) ordered it?" he asked. "Yes", came the reply. "Can I see it in writing?" he retorted, determined. Only when the mullah appeared and confirmed the sentence was the old man taken and lashed at the end of the corridor in full view of us both. His screams became weaker as the lashing progressed. His fragile skin was denuded in multiple places, as if he had been burnt with a hot metal rod. Third degree burns. He moaned and cried all night. I don't believe he could survive the beating at his age. A death sentence for drinking alcohol, just as that student had told me on the Sa'di ward round.

Next day we were taken to our old Block 3 in Ādel Ābād. Majid and Khalil Torābpur were in the opening *hashti* (vestibule), their big paunches testimony to their former life in the *ancien regime*. The same sneers over the books. They took us to the third floor. In our absence the entire prison Block Three (Bande Seh) had been re-organised. The floors were segregated into degrees of seriousness of the 'offence', though with the usual confusion and muddle typical of the prison regime of those early days. The ground floor housed the *sare mo'zehi* (those who stand by their beliefs) prisoners. The old doctors' room was given to the Fadāi' Majority, somewhat incongruously, as they were staunch supporters of the regime. The middle floor housed the doubtful.

At the top were the *tavvābs*, those who had renounced, and in some cases denounced their previous opposition to the regime. It also housed the ex-SAVAK prisoners, the Bāhā'is, the innocent 'six-monthers', and others – a veritable hotchpotch.

Taqi came over quickly. Come and join us in the Savaki room. It was as astute decision as there you knew exactly who was going to spy on you. Mohsen and I joined Taqi, Keramat, a paediatric resident who I did not know from before, Ebrahim, and three ex-SAVAK prisoners including the deputy head of Bushehr SAVAK. The *mavāti-lavātis* and thieves had been removed *en mass* to the prison-blocs run by the police. Block Three was now an exclusively political prison holding five hundred or so, mostly young, men.

In the three months we had lounged in the relative paradise of Jahrom, prisons across the country were being reconfigured under the directions of the chief prosecutor Lājevardi, personally appointed by Khomeini and answerable to his personal retinue (*beit* – meaning household). Lājevardi, had tasted the Shah's prison and torture, had known most of the leaders of the left and Mojahedin and loathed them with an intensity difficult to convey in words. Years ago he told a friend of mine, who at the time was an Islamist sharing the *Qasr* prison with him, that "I would even work with the CIA to fight communists, and now the Mojahedin are asking me to sit down to eat with them!" he had sneered.[1] His mission now was to sort out the issue of political prisoners once and for all and break the opposition by instituting a reign of terror. He plunged into it with a passion wrenched away from its human roots by a hate only fanaticism can generate. Andalibi, the young harbinger of mass death in Fars province, was their first assault on the perceived 'soft touch' of provincial prisons across the country. The 'soft touch' was clearly patchy since right from the start in the prisonse of Isfahan, Qom, Shahsavar, and Kurdistan, to name a few, mass execution squads and systematic torture had been the norm. What the Lājevardi cabal brought was the systematic creation of *tavvābs* as a policy to be implemented across the entire country, a process that had began in Shiraz in Artesh 3 and was starting to be introduced into the main prison of Ādel Ābād. At the time of our transfer most of the *tavvābs* were still being held and used in the interrogation centre.

A *tavvāb*, which translates as penitent, was a person who had been forced through savage torture not only into revealing all his or her information but had also to surrender their mind. Their brain was to be cleansed of all the elements that made them what they were, to be restructured as devotees of the Islamic Republic. While in other regimes such goals of emptying and refilling were achieved by brainwashing[2] and similar techniques, Khomeini's henchmen followed Stalin and chose the naked whip. It is said that Stalin told the NKVD to forget about other more sophisticated tortures and just beat the prisoner until they break.[3] The prisoner of the Islamic regime would be beaten with wire cables on their back, legs, feet and sometimes stomach again and again … and again. Most people crack at some stage. The anti-Shah guerrilla movement recognized this and merely asked their members to hold out for 48 hours, later reduced to 24 and again to 6, until their comrades could clean out the hideout and move on. Later the more recalcitrant were placed in small wooden coffins, lid-less and back-less, blindfolded, sitting absolutely still, facing forward, in total silence, all day, day after day, week after week, month after month, no talking no movement, until they cracked. This living graveyard lasted up to ten months. Some cracked. Some went mad. A few survived.

The Shah's SAVAK, however, was uninterested in prisoners' minds, only their political cells and network. Khomeini wanted to swallow them whole. They were to repent, disgorge all the 'filth' that had been instilled in them, and cleansed to enter the fold of followers. A loathing for everything the left and the Mojahedin stood for was nothing new for the Islamists. In the prisons of the Shah, the followers of Khomeini had refused to share a meal with the left and had insisted that they take out their own food from the common pot first, before it became contaminated by faecally soiled heathens. As Lājevardi had once quipped to my friend Mazāheri in his inimitable lumpen style "what is the contradiction between shit and shit?" After they had betrayed all their friends and comrades, the *tavvābs* had to recant in public, at the Friday Prayer meeting, and for the more prominent, on television.

There was an unending soap opera of ex-this and ex-that appearing on television and asking for forgiveness from the 'forever present *hezbollāh*' (*hezbollāh hamisheh dar sahneh*)[4]. To go out with the Pāsdārs to entrap anyone they recognized on the streets. Later to act as interrogators and torturers. Even then the regime could never be sure that they had really capitulated. After all, there is the concept of *taqieh* in Shi'a teaching which allows the believer to simulate conversion while retaining their Shi'a belief deep down. *Taqieh* had kept the Shi'a flame alive in the ocean of Sunni dominance through the centuries. So even becoming a torturer may not be enough to be sure of repentance. Maybe if they executed their comrades and have their blood on their hands? There was no end to this cycle of suspicion and depravity. That is why many *tavvābs* were ultimately executed. Empty shells walking to their death, a pitiful sight.

But there was another side to the *tavvāb*. He or she would often try and keep one piece of information, a scrap of knowledge, to themselves. I didn't betray everyone, you can almost hear them murmuring inwards, I didn't give away so and so. It was this tiny spark, this miniscule morsel of self-respect that those of us who were captive but with relatively clean dossiers had to nurture. Kaveh, another academic had been tortured and when nothing significant could be beaten out of him, given 5 years mainly because of his role in opposing the regime's Cultural Revolution. He had been rather high up in his organisation and now shared a room with a young *tavvāb* who knew about his past in the real world. Enough to get him buried. The regime did not take kindly to information that had not come up in your trial. Everyone we knew who went on to a second trial was shot or hanged. That particular young man had cracked very quickly and brought in about 20 to thirty people most of whom had been executed. Now he was feverishly praying, getting up at night to do the *namāz-e shab*. He was totally broken. He spent hours over the Qur'an weeping. Kaveh had to play on the boy's fragile self-esteem to keep that tiny spark alive deep inside him. Like the Zoroastrian priests nurturing the fire and stopping it going out through the entire fourteen centuries of Islamic rule. Kaveh got away. The boy?

Another escape owed itself to a similar tiny fire. Abbās (his nom-de-guerre), who collected the printed newspapers and leaflets from the basement had

CHAPTER 46

been arrested and had been broken. He had brought in many comrades. Changiz was savagely tortured before being shot. Khadijeh, his wife, too was tortured and executed. The entire Shiraz structure had been blown apart by his betrayal. Abbās had gone out with the Pāsdārs on hunting trips of revolutionaries. But he had left one couple out from his confessions, his little spark of self-respect. Like many *tavvābs* he was executed after they had emptied his head. But that was still in the future. Changiz and the others were still active. I too had been well known in the University and there were a number of prisoners who knew more about me than my captors. As the possibility of collapse of the regime receded, more and more people began to question their previous beliefs. Cracks in their belief-systems began to appear in previously defiant young men. We were sitting on an exploding mine and had to get out as soon as we could.

One crunch point came when the Mojahedin leader, Massud Rajavi, fled the country, after his second in command, Khiābāni, had been killed alongside Rajavi's wife Ashraf, when their smart hideout in north Tehran was stormed. Lājevardi appeared on television holding Rajavi's child, a hypocritical pretence of fatherly care for the child, all the time showing his undisguised loathing for the entire family in the nauseatingly crude way he talked about Rajavi's wife Ashraf. There he stood, a detestable picture, with his sunken cheeks and hate-filled eyes, just as Abbas Mazāheri later pictured him in his memoires. The news broke the morale of the Mojahedin, just as the flight of the Shah had broken the back of his army. Taqi went to bed on the bottom rank, placed a pillow over his head and just lay there, immobile for three days. We would get him up to eat. He would eat with glazed eyes looking dead ahead and go straight back to his bunk. Something in him had died. He never recovered and a deep melancholy stayed with him even after he was released. He had given all he had to the Mojahedin. Their headquarters in Shiraz was rented in Taqi's name. He died a mysterious death, some say by his own hands, some say murdered by the regime. I miss his wise, angelic smile.

Cracks in the ideological edifice was another factor that determined the ability to resist the almost daily encroachment of the regime into the most private parts of one's existence and one's thoughts. There were those like the Tudeh Party or the Fadāi' Majority who painted the regime as anti-imperialist. To be arrested by such a regime created an incongruity and logical conundrum that made any rational thought problematic. The Mojahedin had a similar dichotomy. There was their Muslim belief and refusal to attack Khomeini; in fact a policy of sidling up to the regime while trying to goad it into taking a more radical line on land reform and other social issues, all the while arming and preparing for a coup. Their premature onslaught on the regime in June 1981, and the subsequent massive repression left their supporters in an impossible situation. A coup is a gamble that has only one of two outcomes, win or lose. They lost and their supporters were lost. For Peikar, the situation was more complex. Their entire organisation collapsed, as in a heap, leaving the individuals to fend for themselves.

The most resilient turned out to be those who, either through blind militancy had never had any illusions about the regime without necessarily a coherent explanation of its nature or place in history[5] or those who, like the two Kurdish organisations, Kurdistan Democratic Party and Kumeleh, were mass parties with deep roots and successfully resisting the regime, or like the Fadāi' Minority had a powerful presence in Kurdistan. Others had from the beginning a coherent explanation for the nature of the Islamists that had hijacked the Revolution (like Rāhe Kārgar and some other groups), one without overt internal contradictions. It helped to have your bearings when faced with an uninterrupted onslaught to your body and senses.

[1] Abbas Mazāheri was arrested as a member of *Hezb-e Mellate Eslāmi* (the Party of the Islamic Peoples). Much later he accepted Marxism and joined the Rāhe Kārgar organisation. His book is a vivid and truthful memoire of life in various prisons across Iran and also thumbnail sketches of various prisoners some of whom are ruling in Iran today.

[2] See William Sargent, Battle for the Mind. A physiology of conversion and brainwashing. Mailor Books, Cambridge, Massachusetts. Sargent was my professor of psychiatry at medical school.

[3] See Roy Medvedev, *Let History Judge* Spokesman Books 1971 or the

CHAPTER 46

memoires of Anna Larina, Nicolai Bukharin's wife, *This I Cannot Forget*, Pandora, London 1994.

[4] An allusion to Khomeini's calling on the entire country to act as the eye and ear of the regime.

[5] Such as the Fadāi' Minority and some supporters of Peikār and other smaller groups belonging to the third (Maoist) line, or some of the smaller Islamic organisations such as *Armāne Mostaz'affin* who believed that dictatorship of the proletariat was there in the Qur'an.

Chapter 47

Last months

Amazing how, within a day or two of arriving in Ādel Ābād, all those in whom the flames of resistance still burnt somehow knew we were not *tavvabs* despite being housed on the third floor. There was a game to play, melting into the earth, unobserved by the men with a scythe. They understood. In that television room no games were being played, just a hopeless desire to slip off the spiralling earth on its murderous trajectory, or not to betray your self to yourself. Now the game was to survive without extinguishing that inner flame of anger and vision. But life was so uncertain and erratic at a time when you needed to predict the unpredictable and stay one step ahead of it. It was like walking a tightrope in a storm with the rope slowly, inexorably, inescapably being slackened.

One day they banned all exercise inside the cell and in the exercise yard. A few of us would wake up in the dark to do half an hour of exercise in the cell taking care not to wake the Savakis. Exercise was a sign of resistance, of independence, of silent mutiny. Then one day, pre-dawn, they forced all of us out into the courtyard for some communal exercise, only to abandon it after two days. It was as if an idea popped up, like a bulb in a cartoon, and was implemented immediately. It became more serious when they applied

CHAPTER 47

the same methodology to prayer sessions. And unlike the exercise games this was an escalating demand. There seemed to be no end to the Shi'a ingenuity to concoct new types of prayer. To manoeuvre round it became daily more difficult. Initially we sat it out in our cells, but they then insisted that we must go out into the inner balconies and later downstairs into the ground floor sitting in the central corridor, the one I had used to walk my eighty times 82 steps to Bach. In full view. Like fish in a bowl. Easier to be observed. The ground floor prisoners were locked in their room, sealing us from contamination with resistance and unbelief. We communicated through bars in whispers when they were not watching.

One day they brought one of their young ideologues to talk to us. I sat at the back trying to be invisible to the cameras they had trained on us. You never knew how they would use the images. A thin man, with an ash-coloured five-day bristles framed by two deep furrows came in. He scanned the room with his dark eyes and then looked down. Beautiful, I seem to recall, like the eyes of the imams hung on walls of restaurants and shops, but with a steely, almost arrogant intelligence. He was enjoying himself. It was said he had been a Mojahed many years ago but split with them when the bulk of the organisation had embraced Marxism. He was frank about his understanding of where the regime stood. "We are surrounded by a world of corruption" he said. "If we don't export our Revolution we will be crushed in no time". That man had a greater understanding of the Islamic regime than most commentators then, and now. The export of the Revolution is part of the existential armoury of the regime. It is not an accessory, a choice. It was a life-sustaining necessity.

We had to find ways of mixing with the other floors. Ginger was on the first floor and Javad, with his cropped hair and round face now becoming obese from lack of exercise and the fatty prison food, was on the second floor. Opportunities came and went with the occasional cleansing sessions when the entire bloc was washed down from top to bottom, or when we passed the lower floors on our way to exercise yard or during the interminable *Komeil* prayer and when they mixed us up through their mixed-up programmes such as middle-of-the-night exercises. Prisoners also created opportunities.

The most versatile, in my experience, were those who had experienced the

Shah's prison. I have already alluded to one Mojahed who got himself released by pretending insanity those early days. Another, we will call him Ahmad, had been incarcerated in Ādel Ābād for many years before the Revolution. This time he had been caught on a bus with two copies of Rāhe Kārgar. You could explain one away, but two? He had given a false name and for the 18 months he was in Ādel Ābād he had not had a single visitor nor used the courtyard – the police guards in the prison-block next door were the same ones that had guarded him in the previous regime and no one who saw his distinctive features once would forget that face. Ahmad had endeared himself to one Rezāzādeh, a barber in Namāzi, an honest and decent man, who had close links with the mullahs in town. Rezāzādeh was allowed to visit and talk to selected prisoners, presumably to draw them into the bosom of 'real Islam'. After a while, Ahmad was given permission to move between floors and became a key link between them. So, when Mohsen and I were allowed a very rare face to face lunch meeting with our families, I was able to pass on a smuggled note, written in pencil in a miniscule script, Changiz's unmistakable handwriting, via Ahmad to all trusted prisoners. The note was an attempt to keep us up to date with events outside and also give us heart that we were not forgotten. A second face to face meeting with Ezzy was less successful. My father, who all his life had equated prison with criminals, was distinctly uncomfortable. He could not work out the why of me being there. He kept fidgeting to go. Looking at his watch. Uncomfortable. Short sentences for a man known for wit and eloquence. "I will miss my bus", he said again which was not due for another four hours. He left me after about fifteen minutes. I had so much more to ask him.

News was increasingly black. Peikar, the third largest organisation of the Left, had imploded. In an attempt to regroup the various sections of Fars and neighbouring provinces had organised a joint meeting. Unfortunately, the one person who was to make the links was arrested at the first meeting point and for some reason took the Pāsdārs to the second meeting point. Little or no resistance. Tens of revolutionaries were arrested, and the entire southern network destroyed. Such bad news was compensated by the regime being bogged down in Kurdistan. Then new year heralding spring. I was watching

CHAPTER 47

the movement of *Qashqai'* tribesmen across the barren plain south of Ādel Ābād from my upper bunk bed, smoking a pipe and blowing the aromatic smoke out of the window, when over the tannoy a voice announced that because of *Eid*, Khomeini had decreed an amnesty for some prisoners. Then followed the names of over 300 prisoners in Shiraz. Suddenly we heard Taqi's name and shortly after that mine. Taqi had already served his six months as had many of those on the list. For months no one had been released and hundreds were doing *melli keshi*, doing time for the nation, as we called it. We were to be released.

Many fellow prisoners not on the list came over and congratulated us. Some even had messages for the outside. Even one or two Pāsdārs who had become patients came over to congratulate us. As was now our normal habit a few of us sat and discussed what to do in case they wanted us to record a video of repentance or write a repentance letter. How to avoid siding with the regime without them noticing. But another five months was to pass. Clearly the Lājevardi cabal had objected to the list and ultimately whittled it down to eleven.

Meanwhile, the pressures increased daily. Having been shown a glimpse of the door, Mohsen, Taqi and I found ourselves being scrutinized more closely. We talked to Keramat. We conferred with Ahmad who through the friendly barber could get a feel of the land. Mohsen was able to persuade the guards to allow him to attend his private dentist outside, a friend and fellow academic Jāvid. Once he was taken to Namāzi hospital, where lying on a stretcher was one of the vilest *Pāsdārs* that we knew. With his cruel and cold grey-blue eyes, always unsmiling, a well-known torturer, he was hated by all. He had volunteered to go to the war and while squatting down in front of his motorbike was run over by a reversing car, crushing his spine and paralysing him from the neck downwards. There he was lying helpless on a stretcher in the corridor, his bladder full, deliberately abandoned by the emergency room doctors, when a nurse saw him. She had seen him kick her brother hard in the stomach one visiting day when he had asked for something trivial. Her brother was later executed. He looked up imploringly, recognising her. She turned away, with what she described to Mohsen as a wonderfully calming feelings of revenge and justice.

Over the months pressures to prove our submission to the regime by participating in its activities increased by the day. Life for me became very tense. If I claimed to support the regime, why then don't I go to the public Friday prayers? I had the same feeling that I had experienced in Jahrom of being boxed into a corner and would either have to capitulate or come clean. And once more I was saved by the bell. The names of 11 were read out on the tannoy, and mine was among them, and Ahmad's but no Taqi or Mohsen. I quickly conferred with Keramat and rehearsed once more what we would say on video, if asked, that would satisfy the regime while being unusable as a propaganda tool. It was not difficult to come up with a kind of bland talk that said nothing. But the fear was that the interrogator would not be content and push for something more concrete. In the event, we were given a sheet of paper to write something about not being against the Islamic regime. That made it easier as you had a few minutes to compose something that sounded good but in reality said nothing. Majid, the boss with a growing paunch, glanced at it and nodded his approval to all our papers. He was clearly glad to be rid of us.

I embraced my friends on the first (ground) floor for the first time since our return. Ginger was there as were a whole row of old comrades. We kissed. No messages though. Tears. And we walked the corridor to the entrance where we were handed over to the municipal police. One of them recognised Ahmad, looked at him, saw his false name on the list, gave a half smile of recognition and a knowing look, and let him through. We walked through the gate and said goodbye. Of the 11, four had been supporters of the same organisation. We had known how to play their cards. And we got out just in time.

I left the books – Anna Karenina with only five pages to go. A week later the guards raided the cells and confiscated all the books, and much more. A few weeks later the *tavvābs* were brought over from Artesh 3 *en mass* and took over the control of the prison bloc. Life became intolerable for the non-*tavvāābs* under constant surveillance and pressures. As in Evin prison, the *tavvābs* were given free rein to lord it over the block. And they in turn needed to ingratiate themselves with the jailors. It became difficult to breathe. Prisoners who could, pulled whatever strings they had to escape the suffocating atmosphere. Kaveh managed to get himself to the town where his father had been born and was released a few months later. Keramat was transferred to another city and also got out unscathed. Mohsen was released a year later. Ebrahim, our other cellmate was also released.

I do not know the fate of Javad and Ginger or many of the hundreds of others. Many of those on that initial list of over 300 were either executed that year, or if released rearrested and killed, or died in the massacre of autumn 1988. Conditions for those that remained behind, except for a brief interlude of relative relaxation, worsened and ultimately became intolerable for some and they joined the ranks of *tavvabs*.[1] Many died in the prison massacre of 1988.[2] Mohsen and Kaveh left Iran. It was not a good idea to stay in the town where your dossier was filed away. The Islamic regime had still some way to go before compiling a central data base. Some had made the mistake of staying in Shiraz. Maybe we are still alive because death forgot us.[3]

I took a cab to Dr Javid's house, the only place I knew. Everyone else had left Shiraz. He rapidly swallowed the look of surprise and understandable fear and smiled. A welcoming smile. I rang J. Next day, I walked on the pavement under the plane trees. It was 12 Mordād 1361, August 3, 1982. The burning midsummer sun threw sharp shadows of the broad plane tree leaves, like outstretched hands, on the pavement. I remembered the *khiābun kuchulu* and the little boy holding *baba* Ezzy's hands. As a child Ezzy would take me to Pahlavi Avenue where there were two streams, *jubs,* that carried water from the Karaj stream (*Nahre Karaj*). In between was a path shaded by plane trees where *baba* would cut a branch for me, and we would walk hand in hand. It was my little street – *khiābun kuchulu*.

It felt strange walking on a pavement. I had missed the sun for a year a month and four days. I took a bus to Tehran, never to see Shiraz again.

[1] There is a large and expanding literature from former prisoners who survived the ordeal of prison life in the Islamic Republic of Iran, virtually

all in Farsi. This witness to the suffering of a generation remains unknown to the outside world and awaits translation. The experience of a female prisoner who spent 9 years in various Tehran prisons, including the 'coffins' where prisoners were made to sit, still and silent, facing forward all day, every day for up to 10 months, and the five-times-a-day lashing that was meted out to non-praying Left prisoners until they cracked and agreed to pray, and the massacre of 1988 is described (in Farsi) in detail in *The Simple Truth* (*haqigat sadeh*) by M Rahā. Of the few published works in English see Behrooz Ghamari: *Remember Akbar*, OR Books, New York, London in partnership with Counterpoint Press, 2016, Nasrin Parvāz, *One woman's struggle in Iran: a prison memoir.* Victorina Press, 2018 and M.S. Kia, *Entangled Lives* in press.

[2] In the summer and autumn of 1988 after signing the peace with Iraq, which he called drinking the poison chalice, Khomeini personally ordered the massacre of prisoners who had remained true to their political beliefs or were not Muslim. Several thousands were hung in groups.

[3] Mahmoud Darwish. *Mural.* Verso 2009.

Chapter 48

The return

It was not easy, those months. It was like returning from the dead. I had been on one planet and J on another. And neither returned to the same world we had inhabited in the years before we were torn apart. It was not easy those months – like those first months of our life together, when we flipped and fought and tried to find the territory that the other had invaded. And to find the love that kept being obscured by the jockeying for position, for understanding, for filling in the gaps in experience without which the two cannot be one. Without which love is not meaningful. Love needs passion but it also needs a history. You move back into the other's past. You become like them, or more accurately you find yourself moving back in time, not on the road that you already know but one that feels like the one that the other trod. Now, we had to recreate history, only this time there were also two new, younger, historians who only knew part of the old history. It was not easy, those months.

    J had trodden a path of thirteen months of anxiety that I had scarcely thought about while inside. Prison was such a hermetic place that you just shut off the outside world just as you shut off time. Prison time is a different clock and prison space permits no intrusion. A glimpse of the sky, a solitary sunflower, a passing family of *Qashqāi'* trekking across the brown earth midway to the sky with their goats and sheep and pots and tent all strung up on the horse, and their layer upon layer of skirt in garish colours that somehow merge in beauty – that is enough of the outside to cope with. No. It is better to be on the ground floor. So even on the top bunk I spent most of my time looking inward, reading Anna Karenina, French, Bruckner in German, anything but the outside world. The occasional glance over the brown earth towards the horizon, the occasional thought of what went on in the few houses that were visible. But mostly inside, focused, safer. It was best to focus on navigating the narrow path that kept disappearing and the ground that was in continuous motion. One false step and you could fall of the edge. You read and you tried to work out what traps they could possibly set for you round the next bend. I had been in prison with the wrong dossier, and the other, the one that had not been opened, was filled with peril. There was little room for the outside world in that journey.

Except on Wednesdays, when the heart tumbled over with expectation. When a window opened to life. The ten minutes that brought the outside to within a metre of that dirty scratched window that kept the two worlds apart. In those ten minutes you renewed the pledge. Neither side of the glass barrier wasted precious moments digging deeper into experience. It was the eyes that told stories and the stories they told may or may not have been the real stories. The real outside was beyond that window, and it was best not to think about it too much. Even in the few face-to-face contacts we had, it had been like occasional visitors coming to your house. You did not dig deep. They smiled and you took that at face value.

The real knowing was to come in the first months of freedom. The air had been pumped out of my country and freedom had been warped and felt strangely dark. Then life intruded. It took decades for the four of us to fill the gaps in the same way we had filled the gap of childhood and adolescence in those early years. And of course, the two of us needed to revisit times of old. All history can only be understood in the light of the now and the now had been overturned by time. I was no longer the me of before, and neither was J, nor all the others around us.

CHAPTER 48

And like all gaps, there are always bits to be discovered and bits that remain hidden, maybe forever.

49

Chapter 49

Lost flowers, a reflection on the past

She died three days after her 23rd birthday her gravestone said. Years later, white haired, white brushes for eyebrows, I sat on a bench two graves away from my brother Ali's in London's Kensal Green cemetery. What was she doing on that birthday? Twenty-three is so indeterminate. You have passed a milestone and trip into a time limbo. Still young but hanging in that hiatus between the certainties of youth and the ambiguities that come much later. Still not enough memories to make a life, but enough to be nostalgic. The curtain had come down for her before the prologue was over. Did her young daughter who died with her cry on the night of her birthday? Did she keep the child up especially to share her joy? Did she know it would be her last? How could she? Death at 23 is so unnatural. It leaps around the corner, unannounced. The picture on the tombstone is smiling. Was she a single mother? Did death occur on the way to the nursery? Did she take her own life? Was it a crash? The tombstone is so silent on a life. The little girl in the picture looks disturbed. Death came to her also uninvited. He just walked in and snatched mother and child, unwanted, uncalled, premature, savage.

Latifeh and Khadijeh, two friends, two comrades, had lived with death, and disdained it. They too met death prematurely and alone, very alone. But it

CHAPTER 49

was not unexpected. He, and death is permanently male, always followed a few steps behind, an invisible shadow, like anti-matter. He was just uninvited. He broke into their young life brutally, savagely and unfairly.

Latifeh had walked unexpectedly into my office in North Tehran all those years ago, the last time I saw her. Her face was rounder than I remembered from a year or so previously. Maybe it was because of the creamy-white scarf she wore tightly wound round her head, totally imprisoning the hair. She was dressed in the prescribed loose-fitting manteau, light brown. It clashed with her big blue eyes, lighter than the blue jeans she wore beneath the manteau. But for the jeans, no one in the morality police, *jondollāh*, could have doubted her Islamic credentials.

"I came despite the ban on visiting you", she said and lowered her eyes, blushing ever so imperceptively. She herself would have felt the warm rush of blood on her cheeks. That was just like her. She was a true rebel, even to the organisation for which she would lose her life. The big blue eyes, flashing defiance and energy was the image that had suddenly entered that basement when she was first introduced to the group. Let me introduce comrade P, Changiz had said, using her assumed name. She will be in charge of students. That was two years ago. Sitting round in a circle were five others. Latifeh clearly came from the same background as me, a modern middle-class background, what was vulgarly called *motejadded*. The post-revolutionary arena was the scene of so many battles, rubbing shoulders, interacting, helping, and on occasion hindering one another. Superimposed and mixed into the class struggle was the historic battle between the traditional and the new, exemplified but not restricted to the traditional petite-bourgeoisie and the new middle class, the child of capitalist development in Iran. And like its creator, the roots of the modern on Iranian soil were very fragile. This battle could not and cannot be simplified as one between the religious and the secular, or even between defenders of the separation of state and religion and their opponents. It went beyond that into the struggle between two world views, *weltanschaungs*. There were intensely religious people in the modern middle class, while others, who believed themselves secular, exhibited deeply religious behaviour. The battle was part of the birth pangs of modernity, and modernity in Iran had been artificially injected from above, had not had time to develop deep roots.

Khomeini had used that battle to divide society into Islamic and other, them and us, (later called 'insider' and 'outsider' *khodi and qeire khodi*). So every institution, every office, every factory, every school and college was divided into the Islamic and 'other' - to paraphrase Nancy Mitford – to the 'u' and non-'u'.[1] And the 'other', the 'non-u', the outsider had then gone on to further divide themselves along ideological lines, Mojāhed, Fadāi', Peikar, Rāhe Kārgar, Tudeh down into the miniscule fragments of the minor sects, within each office, factory, school, and college. And thus, the two major battles along class lines of owner/producer and ideological lines of tradition/modernity, which metamorphosed into surrogates for totalitarianism and freedom, were not only confusingly interlocked but were also submerged amongst myriads of groups juggling for the leadership of the future. It was thus that the working-class gains were taken away one by one, and the main slogan of the Revolution, *esteghlāl, azādi* (Independence, Freedom) were subsumed by the dictatorship of the supreme leader disguised as a republic. And all these political groups who saw themselves as the future watched lamely, helplessly as, for example, 25,000 teachers were expelled as part of the *pāksāzi* (cleansing) of education, a priority for Khomeini, without any effective opposition being mobilised.

Latifeh had a north Tehrani accent. You could tell by her dress that she had been a member of the Fadāi' student organisation in universities, Pishgām, who had been recruited to this newly born organisation, Rāhe Kārgar, as had many who were looking for something deeper than the confused mishmash of anti-imperialist slogans that was the post-revolutionary Fadāi'. 'The Revolution is dead! Long live the Revolution!' the new organisation had announced at its birth and the cry was taken up by many who had seen the sudden death of their revolution that February. Her clothes were not shabby the way many of the left felt they should dress, a gesture to what they thought was working-class culture. That almost religious belief in asceticism was very deep in all the political organisations of the time, left or Muslim. The truly modern left was still struggling to be born from its traditional roots

CHAPTER 49

in the Tudeh party and beyond, and it remained entangled in the religiosity of the traditional petite-bourgeoisie. The battle between the two halves of society, somehow masked and obscured the battle the new had to do with the old within itself.

Latifeh too abided by that belief in asceticism but perhaps because of her stunning beauty the blue jeans and manteau combination would not have seemed out of place in a different time zone. What distinguished Latifeh from her background was her intense seriousness, her passion for what she believed in. That fiery passion somehow made her light blue eyes even more blue, and somehow more transparent. I was struck by that passion even on that first meeting. I hardly spoke, most unlike me. She spoke with confidence, as if she had been part of that cell for a long time. The passion remained with her although her earnestness softened. She had a wonderful sense of humour. But she remained puritanical. Alone among her family she had chosen rebellion and she had to bear that alone, in secret, clandestine and unobserved. She undertook some of the most dangerous tasks including setting up a photography exhibition in a busy thoroughfare.

All night, we gathered photographs of thugs attacking kiosks selling left literature and smashing them with clubs, beating people savagely and other atrocities being daily committed in Shiraz and other towns. The underlying concept for the exhibition was that people had an illusory concept of the regime and showing them reality would shatter that illusion. We wrapped the photos in cellophane and strung them up on two ropes. Latifeh and Roya were to carry these under their black *chador*, a loose-fitting single piece of cloth covering from head to toe, and to unveil them suddenly in crowded Zand Avenue. The boys were stationed discreetly around to protect them when the thugs attacked. It was another of those foolhardy escapades that preoccupied the populist left – propaganda by deed. Before the Revolution it was in the shape of armed guerrilla attacks, and now it took the form of daring provocations in the midst of enemy territory. It was like scaling the walls of an old castle in the Middle Ages to hoist a flag. Brave but utterly futile. The photographic exhibition was over in two or three minutes. Like a pack of hyenas, *hezbollāhi* thugs on foot and motorbike appeared from nowhere.

The two girls escaped by the skin of their teeth.

At the height of the repression after the 'Cultural Revolution' Latifeh organised the distribution of eight different leaflets in one day alone, over 120,000 individual sheets of paper across the city. It was an amazing feat of daring and organisation for a small group. That was the first time I had written a leaflet in a totally new eye-catching style, doing away with the bombastic opening statements and the endless repeating of the obvious. The political point was made in that first sentence, and I introduced another novelty, humour. You just hit the reader on the head with that sentence. If he or she chose to read further, well and good. If not, you had imprinted your message in the most effective way into the reader's head. I was praised for his innovation, but they went on to produce the same predictable dull leaflets. To my knowledge it was the first time humour had been used in a political leaflet in Iran. Iranian revolutionaries were such earnest people – another nod to the Shi'a tradition of weeping for salvation.

Strictly no alcohol, although Changiz, who had been a prisoner of SAVAK and endured its tortures, was uniquely not against alcohol. He was one of the most open persons that I had ever seen. The left, with its strict guerrilla ancestry, banned alcohol, and almost like the Islamists abhorred joy, except in the dumpty-dump mock-heroic version so beloved to Zdanov and the gauleiters of socialist realism in Soviet times, and made *de jure* by the Tudeh. Of course, you could like classical music, which rarely went beyond Beethoven's ode to joy or Amirov's *Shur*[1] and revolutionary songs. But popular song, the *tasnif*, was sniffed at. That was bourgeois. Not to Changiz. He was the kind of communist that was being born, phoenix like, from the ashes of the old. But the old retained a strong hold and this hold was not easy to escape in the atmosphere of the Islamic Republic where, as Khomeini kept reiterating, it was revolutionary to weep. It was in an atmosphere of weeping and lamentation that the struggles to win back the revolution, that had been snuffed out by the regime, were being fought. The Iran-Iraq war was slowly maiming and killing an entire generation and lamentation was what you breathed. The entire nation was drowning in tears. In this atmosphere, Changiz was teaching us to enjoy life.

CHAPTER 49

One day he turned to Khadijeh, who was the daughter of a village mullah, and said why are you wearing socks with holes? We are here to bring a better world into being, a world of joy and laughter. We should dress well. We on the left are an example to the poor of what they deserve, not the squalor they already have. Khadijeh had joined our cell before Latifeh. She had been a student leader in the university in Tehran where she was studying. Born into an intensely traditional family, her father a village *mullah*, she had broken with all its beliefs but retained the disdain for such frivolities as clothes and makeup. When she first came to the basement, she was wearing a long black skirt with thick navy-blue tights and a navy blue, somewhat shabby pullover. When she took her shoes off there was a large hole in her heels. That was what Changiz had been referring to. Khadijeh had joined the cell a week or two after Changiz was appointed to lead the southern region.

Earnestness and determination were part of Khadijeh's armoury. She had a more difficult climb than Latifeh. She had to renounce not just her parents, but her entire world view, her whole social being. It was a battle that she fought and won. And she too could laugh at herself. The road she had travelled from the stultifying, suffocating obscurantism of the village was not unlike the walk on water. History is made and moulded by these gigantic leaps into the unknown. How do you express in words the courage of such time-travellers? Picasso did it. So did Khadijeh. A cultural leap. Her passage and those of thousands of others like her fractured the way we see the world. Was their's less revolutionary than cubism, or a new vision of space-time or Giordano Bruno's cry? But their vision, their leap, their song, their immense courage, remains unsung.

Changiz stood out not just because of his open nature and strong personal pull. His whole being was unique. He stood out radiant in the southern sun. This was to be his road to death. There he was, walking upright, tall, with his gingerish head of hair, and his curious bobbing gait. He stood out. His whole demeanour, and even more so when he opened his mouth and spoke in his deep Azari accent, clashed with his surroundings. What were they doing sending this man to Shiraz where he would meet his death, broken physically but unbroken in spirit? I later learnt from a fellow prisoner how they had to carry him in a wheelbarrow to his interrogation, so savagely was he beaten. He would have smiled, he would, even as they pumped the bullets into his unbroken spirit. That was Changiz the eternal optimist. That same spirit that sitting on the veranda he would sip the home-brewed white wine which a fellow academic had given away in panic after the revolutionary tide faded, and let his voice soar upwards to a golden future in an Azari *ashiq* song. Latifeh would smile but decline. She too was entering the world of enjoyment but drew the line at wine. Khadijeh just smiled, maybe deep inside she too wanted to try the forbidden fruit.

One day, when I was in prison, Changiz went over to Roya. "I have a confession to make," he said shyly. "I'm in love with Khadijeh but don't know how to tell her. They never taught me the art of love in the school of SAVAK." He had been arrested by SAVAK in December 1974, his second arrest, and had been severely tortured, and he had spent the next five years in the Shah's prisons only to be released on the eve of the Revolution. The months and years after his release were too full of action to learn about love. But love strikes in unexpected ways and nearly always when you are not looking. He, who could see the beauty of a world without want or fear, who could express his love of man, woman and trees in poetic prose, stuttered to express his love for the girl in blue tights with a hole in her socks squatting in front of him in the circle.

He had no family in Fars and so Roya, pretending to be an aunt, went with him to ask for Khadijeh's hand in marriage. They travelled in her car that Changiz had borrowed earlier and crashed. Then, they had wriggled, improvised, danced their way out of the police station with a smiling Roya convincing the cops that the ginger-haired man, known and yet totally unknown to her, without name or surname, had not stolen her car. The trip to the village was another comedy in preparation for the tragedy that followed a few months later. The suspicious village mullah had asked awkward question and smiling Roya, as calm under the scrutiny of his tiny deep-set eyes as she had been in the police station earlier, had convinced them. Despite her Tehrani accent which clashed so with Changiz's Azari inflection, she pulled off the act of being his aunt. It was acting worthy of the stage. Their marriage was to last a few months. Both were arrested, savagely tortured and shot. Neither revealed my name or anyone else's. Heroism, there is no other term, that was not rare in Islamic prisons. Khadijeh was 23, Changiz 37.

Months after Latifeh had come to visit me in his office, she too was arrested alongside a large section of the central committee of Rāhe Kārgar. She too was tortured savagely and shot, her beautiful blue eyes clouding over by premature, but not unexpected death. She too did not reveal our name. She had married another member who never recovered from her death. It too was a match of love. She was 25.

How many deaths was I responsible for, I reflected later. Almost everyone I had appointed in our cell at the 3rd Army detention centre to such minor responsibilities as dividing out the bread and making sure it was all eaten up, or making tea, organising the exercise, giving out cheese, overseeing to the store of fruit were later executed. Someone had watched and reported. You must have some qualities if you were chosen to organise. You were dangerous. You had to be squashed. So many, so many had been wiped out. And I live with the thought that I was responsible, unwittingly, but still responsible, for those deaths.

Just as the woman on the tombstone in Kensal Green cemetery might have been responsible for the death of her young daughter. If she was not with her in that accident, who knows what would have become of that little girl with an anxious look staring out from the white stone?

[1] One of those folk adaptations so beloved of the Soviet cultural watchdogs.

Chapter 50

Hiding

My first act on arriving in Tehran was to report to the Pāsdārān headquarters to sign in weekly, a condition for early release. The Tehran Pāsdārān head office occupied one of the palaces in Kākh Avenue, the one that had been the office of the Shah's prime minister. As I walked down the tree-lined avenue the summer morning sun played music through the leaves of the plane trees, the trees of my childhood, already middle aged. A kilometre or so from here, just off North Kākh street, aunt Tāhereh, used to give me four rials a day pocket money on my way to school on that last year of childhood in Iran. We were using a room in her house in the year before leaving for Munich, a trip that for me brought nineteen years of learning and love. The Pāsdār on duty did not have a clue what to do with me – in the capital, the Evin jailor Lājevardi must have made sure none of his captives slipped out. He consulted a senior officer who proved equally baffled. "Go to the main headquarters in Pāsdārān Avenue", the senior one said hesitantly, as if unsure that I would make it there, turned his back and walked off. Like virtually all the Pāsdārs I ever saw he was in his early twenties.

More confusion followed at the national headquarters. Come back tomorrow, and tomorrow and again tomorrow. After a week of visits,

CHAPTER 50

perching hours on hard benches and being shunted from one courtyard to another, they gave me a sealed letter to take back to the Kākh avenue offices. At home I steamed it open and for the first time saw the crime for which they cut for me, like cutting a bespoke suit, the 'insiders' description of our sentence. Two years for possessing an insulting cartoon of Khomeini in the Guardian weekly, and propaganda against the Islamic regime at the University. It dawned on me that with a charge sheet so puny, no one would have missed me had I not bothered to report to the Pāsdārān. But now that I had, it was probably prudent to continue. After all they now had my Tehran address. Maybe that too was a mistake, who knows. It was not easy to guess, know how, organised their security apparatus had become. So, every week I would thump my blue-dyed forefinger in a book the *Pāsdār* at the gates of their Kākh offices would push towards me. He looked intensely bored.

Now the issue was to return to life. Family, once again it was family that came to the rescue. First upstairs at J's uncle and then downstairs at the rarely smiling Amu Sadri, the eternal bachelor 'married' to his sister. "Share my consulting office," aunt Tāhereh's husband Dr Qaravy had offered, and I was set up to work. Life apparently returned to normal.

Meanwhile some in the left who had survived last year's bloodbath woke up rather belatedly to the realisation that they were not merely meant to be doing propaganda in the streets and universities on behalf of the working class. They were meant to be part of the working class directly involved in its day-to-day struggles, and so planned a 'retreat among the working class'. It made sense ideologically; after all, what is the left without its class. It was also a sensible strategy, Mao's fish in the ocean, invisible and safe. Only what to do with the middle-class sympathisers? I helped to secure a job for Roya, a highly qualified girl who had trained in England, in a pharmaceutical factory where a cousin worked. He puzzled at the strange request but went ahead. They offered her a job in the laboratory. "But I want to work on the factory floor", she said to the manager's incredulous smile. She was chic even in her black scarf and loose manteau. He refused.

As for me, I answered an advert to work part time in a practice near Meidāne

Khorāsān, in one of the shanty towns in south-east Tehran. That was to be my ocean. I phoned the owner of the practice, and he gave me a lift in his Iranian made Cadillac. "I know you", the young doctor said as we drove into the poor southern suburbs, "you interviewed me for a job in Shiraz." and then added "I heard you spent time in prison". I took the job but after finding a copy of Das Kapital in his office drawer I rang one of my old residents who had graduated from Mashhad in the same year as my new boss. "He had been expelled after the Revolution on suspicion of being a Savaki" he said on the phone. I gave up, resigned the post, and took up Qaravy's offer to share his consulting office. There was really nowhere to hide. I had helped train over one thousand of Iran's doctors and was like a goldfish in a fish tank. But risk taking had become a cultural norm among the left. Roya, who had also left Shiraz for Tehran, was given a rendezvous in a large pharmacy in busy *Takhte Jamshid* (now *Beheshti*) Avenue by her immediate organisational supervisor. Her contact, who she later learnt was a member of the central committee, told her that he was well known to many in the present regime, as for years, he had lived alongside them as they were moved from one prison to another and seen the country, so to speak, from within high walls. Tehran, Zāhedan, Mashhad, Shiraz, Borāzjān, Karaj, the Shah's prisoners were well travelled. "But why risk your life, you with your huge revolutionary experience, for someone like me?" she told him, particularly in such an exposed meeting place? Why indeed?

A few months later, a number of people I knew in Shiraz, among them Changiz, Khadijeh, Latifeh, were arrested, tortured and shot. In Tehran eight central committee members, some of the best, wisest, most experienced cadres in the revolutionary history of my country were dead. Among them was Roya's pharmacy contact. It was a price they paid, and a risk they took, to stay behind and not abandon their comrades. It was a romantic notion and like most such notions a romantic error of huge magnitude. The real left in Iran had risen phoenix-like from within the country, unattached and non-reliant on any outside power and with little or no safe backyard to fall back on. They paid a bloody price for that independence. But meanwhile life went on in that twilight interregnum.

CHAPTER 50

On leaving home for the weekly forefinger thumping game, I would leave my house key somewhere else so that if I was detained there would be time enough to clean up the house. A sensible precaution, I thought. There were now many blue thumb-marks in the book at the Pāsdārān gate, an army of apparent illiterates on the loose. The office was beginning to pick up again; I had a new secretary, and I had enough earnings to be independent of the family. The kids were happy in uncle Sadri's ground floor flat. We invited the entire family, aunts and uncles and their offspring and grand-springs and all, to an *āsh reshteh* in our house, a thick vegetable soup with noodles usually given on celebrations, special occasions and before a trip. You have to cook *āsh reshteh* a long time and J put the huge pot on a slow heat, and we went over to my sister Mina's flat for dinner with a number of friends. The conversation was flowing when the phone rang. It was Bahrām. He had been frantically looking for us. They had arrested Hātef, my old comrade and student he told Mina. A cloud swooped on my head. I took J to another room out of earshot. "I cannot go back to the flat" I said. "There is no way we can know how far this would go. If I were to be arrested a second time, I would never see life again." The family? "What are we to do with everyone who is coming the next day?" "Get Mina to cancel it. We should all stay away from home until we have more information." What motivated her to refuse and insist on going back? Hospitality? Honour? Bravado? Or just simply her habitual risk taking; she loved risks. I can only imagine the gloom that surrounded that gathering next day. It was to be our homecoming, a happy reunion. "It was like a funeral", she later told me. And they don't eat *āsh reshteh* in funerals. Noodles represent the entanglement of life and the choices offered by life among the many that spreads before you.[1] They consume noodles before setting off on something new. Perhaps not that incongruous then, though I wasn't there to slurp them. I stayed with an old friend from Shiraz for a couple of nights, and from there my winter of hiding began. For the next three months there would be a lot of anxiety about.

It was a particularly cold winter with heavy snow that hung around for weeks. You followed certain simple precautions. Always use a public phone but don't have too many 2-rial pieces (the cost of a local call) in your pocket.

That gives you away. Always check behind you when you turn a corner. Never go straight to a place but take a circuitous route, preferably through deserted streets. If you are driving, and I did get the car after a week or two, always make sure there is no car following you for five minutes. That last was difficult in Tehran with its traffic. I used the residential suburb of Yusefābād where there was a chance of having a trail-free period. The dilemma was that during my internment the car had been crashed by Changiz. The chassis had been twisted to the right. On the icy roads of that winter, having to break when driving downhill on the steep hilly streets of Yusefābād became a nightmare as the car skidded rightwards towards the parked cars. I missed crashing by a whisper on many occasions. A dodgem car for grown-ups.

I had moved to my aunt A'zam's flat. Her husband Dr Mojtaba Sadjādi, a paediatrician and pathologist in Tehran University Medical School, had been imprisoned by Reza Shah as part of the famous '53' political prisoners, who were imprisoned by Reza Shah in Qasr prison. All had communist or social democratic beliefs. On release some helped inaugurate the Tudeh Party after the allied invasion of 1941. He was the only member of my immediate family sympathetic to my politics. I had closed my office once more on some pretext or other but felt that I could still continue with outside activities that did not tie me to any particular address. I had been asked by a colleague to do some teaching to the medical students in a Ministry of Health hospital. For some reason the government had transferred control of medical education from the Ministry of Higher Education to the Ministry of Health. I taught them endocrinology on a weekly basis. I also went to the Khomeini Hospital in Shah Abdolazim south of Tehran (formerly Reza Shah Kabir) and joined the ward rounds with Dr Sai'di, a highly esteemed surgeon who had earlier taught in Shiraz. There I witnessed the sorry state of medical education after the Revolution, when a recently qualified intern had not even heard of malignant hypertension – a not uncommon condition and a certain killer if not dealt with as an emergency. After a couple of weeks at my aunt's it became obvious that visitors to the flat would find my constant presence there rather odd. We therefore moved to their *bāq* (orchard) in Karaj, a city 40 kilometres west of Tehran.

CHAPTER 50

That winter was so cold that the outside pipes froze. Icicles dangled from branches. A metre or so of snow covered the alley, the other side of the walls of the dazzling-white *bāq*. Use of a car was out of the question. No news from Evin yet and I had not reported for finger-signing for some weeks. It was unclear how long I needed to remain in hiding. Best to ring up the Pāsdārān and come up with an excuse for non-attendance. Dr Sadjadi took me to the only public phones in Karaj, both outside the post office. I shared the queue with soldiers on leave from the war queuing up to ring home. It was fifteen degrees below zero. Getting through to any Pāsdārān headquarters was, well, like connecting to a call centre today, but without a computer talking, just a bored voice, and no muzak. They would either not pick up the phone or just shunt me to another number. The uniformed young men behind me were fidgeting uncomfortably in their boots visibly and miserably cold. I would let them through and stand at the back of the queue and try again. After about two hours I noticed that Dr Sadjadi, in his early seventies, was going blue round his lips. I abandoned the hopeless task. I spoke to J through Mina, our link, and she agreed that I go to the Caspian family holiday home, where I could contact the local Pāsdārs and use the cold weather as an excuse for not returning to Tehran.

The taxi trip across the frozen Alborz mountains was scary, dodgems again, with a deep crevasse or boulders for a wall. But we emerged on the other side of the long Kandovān tunnel which came out in Māzandarān province. The snow had simply evaporated. In the depth of winter, it was like a different country. I was the only person in the holiday compound. I remembered the week we had spent there with my fellow ex-prisoner Ahmad and his wife shortly after our release. I recalled the time Rahman (the Colonel) had insisted that he hated garlic and J and Parvin had fed him a *mirzā qāsemi*, a Māzandarān speciality made from aubergines, eggs and choking with garlic, pretending it is garlic-free, and he had finished it lip-smacking, wiping the last traces on the plate with bread. And then our trip to Siāhkal where the newly formed Fadāi' organisation had fought the Shah's armed forces for the first time in 1971, creating a legend and giving the initial impetus to the new Left movement in Iran. In those heady days after the Revolution, Siāhkal district had been taken over entirely by the Fadāi' while the Mojahedin ruled in the nearby town of Lāhijan, Māzandarān (where my aunt's husband, Dr Mojtaba Sadjādi had set up practice after his release from the old Shah's prison). For a brief period, we breathed the exhilarating air of freedom in that (and neighbouring province of Gilān) before it was brutally crushed by the Pāsdārān led by Rezāi', today a quasi-reformist. Now I sat in that small house alone, reading a novel. The local Pāsdārs in Noshahr, the nearest town, seemed not particularly interested but told me to come back every week anyway. It soon seemed to me that I would arouse more suspicion by staying in that holiday home in mid-winter, should they start looking for me, and resolved to go back to Tehran after a few weeks. I so missed being with J. Aunt or no aunt, being in hiding meant being a non-person. You did not exist for the world, and it is but a small step before you cease to exist to yourself. It is lonely and time congeals.

We moved in together with the mother-in-law of J's sister. It was a flat in Shemiran. I was not going to risk going back to my old house which was known to Hātef and the others arrested with him. I still had no news from Evin but took the risk and reopened the office. After a hesitant start a few patients, mostly referrals from old students including two from Taqi, arrived and I was soon able to pay my way. Maryam and Nargess stayed with Mina which meant a much longer trip to school. Mina was superb at keeping things normal. Sia, her husband, kicked out from his job in the state-owned radio television, dubbed films into Farsi for a living. The kids spent their evenings watching film after film and became film buffs. Nargess dubbed Tia in John Hough's *Return from Witch Mountain*. In that atmosphere of terror, many a family had to conjure up their coping strategy.

Uncle Sadri was furious when I told him that I could not return to his flat. I had never seen such hatred. "You had promised me that you would not get involved. You have betrayed me" he said with that particular steely look of hate that only he could muster. "But it is not me, it is the regime that has arrested my friends" said I sheepishly, dishonestly. He saw through my lies. I had involved him in my adventures, and he hated me, and for some reason he transferred that hatred to his brother Ezzy. And of course, he detested J

CHAPTER 50

intensely. I had taken a big risk in order to see him face to face but felt that was the least I could do after betraying his trust. We had taken particular security care when entering his house as it was above my old flat and if that was being watched, as often happened when they were looking for someone, the visit would have ended badly. Yet that was one of the most unpleasant encounters of my life, before or since.

Then in early spring I heard that Changiz, Azādeh and almost everyone I knew in Shiraz had been arrested. One of those arrested, known as Abbās to me, had become a *tavvab* and was leading the Pāsdārs to his comrades. He knew me well. And he knew of the printing in our basement. I had to hide again until things settled down and this time chose a different strategy. Doctors were given the choice of doing voluntary work in the provinces for a month in lieu of going to the war – *khedmate jebhe'* - 'going to the front' it was still called even though you may be working 1000 kilometres away. The entire country was a war zone. I went to Nezām Pezeshgi, the state organisation where all doctors are registered, and volunteered. I was offered the city of Kerman – in southeast Iran. I took it. I had come to realise that cross-country communication among the various security units was not that well developed as yet and if they were looking for me in Shiraz it would take them some time to trace me. By the time they had followed the trail from Shiraz to Tehran, to my old address, my office, Nezām Pezeshgi and finally to Kerman I would in all probability have been alerted.

I arrived in the flat of one of our ex-residents, Khorāsāni, gentle, devout, honest, very shy, with a particular passion for cream cakes which he called hand grenades on account of their round shape and lethal content. He was one of the first faculty members of a new medical school set up in this ancient city, recently devastated by a severe earthquake. It lay on the route of the opium trail which on its journey, left its slurry of addicts, like the sludge left in a sewage pipe. "If when taking a [medical] history someone here denies using opium, ask him or her when he or she had given up" he taught me on that first day. Watching him work he struck me as such an accomplished clinician despite his youth and lack of experience. We had been so fortunate in Shiraz in the choice of residents that applied to us. Khorāsāni, with his shy intelligence will remain with me forever.

On a ward round later that week I had another shock. Our intern was the ex-commander of the Shiraz Pāsdārān, Shojāi'. Short, beginning to bald and with the customary bristle, he had resumed his medical studies. He greeted me warmly. Later he told me how, as a respected teacher, he had put in a good word for me. I believe him, as I would not have got the books and pipe tobacco without a nudge from high up on the outside. He would not have been able to influence important decisions such as the prison sentence and release, but a good word would certainly have eased the amenities.

But my plan was in tatters. Shojāi' was a shortcut to oblivion. If they were looking for me in Shiraz, and if through any coincidence one of Shojāi's old Pāsdār colleagues should mention my name to him then my elaborately planned temporary hiding place was blown in a few minutes. I had to get back to Tehran, but my assignment to Kerman still had three weeks to run. It had to be done naturally. I told Khorāsāni that my father-in-law had been admitted to hospital with renal failure. That weekend aunt A'zam and her husband Dr Mojtaba Sadjādi had come over with my cousin Mojgān. My old cell-mate Mohsen had also come to Kerman. He had been released recently having witnessed the suffocating life of all my old friends under the rule of *tavvābs* in Ādel Ābād. We travelled together to Māhān, the shrine of the Sufi sheikh and *dervish*, Shah Ne'matollāh Vali. For Mohsen it was the most perfect architectures in the east. Sitting by the long, rectangular pond, the balancing of sky, the dark green cypresses, the blue dome and the shrine were near perfect, I was lifted into another world, a world of inner peace. The adjoining beautiful *bāq*, a classic Iranian garden, was closed to visitors. It was Friday, the guard explained, the Iranian sabbath! The Kerman tourist board had much to learn.

Later that week, I told Khorāsāni that my father-in-law had deteriorated, and I needed to go to Tehran. I took my things as "I may not be able to return". He was very understanding. I said goodbye to this gentle hospitable friend feeling, not for the first or last time, that I had betrayed a trust, and went back by bus. The bus trip travelled through the central Kavir desert, barren and beautiful in its dry majesty, and a number of stops with Pāsdārs boarding

CHAPTER 50

and checking passengers. I chose a bus as I needed to know the routines of road controls that were being used at the time. J had decided to leave the country with the children, and I could not let her go alone, though I would have preferred to go to Kurdistan. There was clearly no other hiding place in Iran for me. It was her sense that prevailed over my romanticism.

[1] See Najmieh Bātmānglij, *New Food of Life*, Mage Publishers, 2007.

51

Chapter 51

The escape

Bahrām had come to our rescue once more. He knew the smugglers who had smuggled Mani and Parvin across the Kurdistan-Turkish border. The barely audible gruff voice on the phone suggested we meet in a restaurant-tea shop in south Tehran on the 15th *khordad*, June 5, the anniversary of Khomeini's uprising against the Shah in 1963. The choice of the place, the date and his Kurdish outfit should have alerted us. His nervousness, fidgeting, eyes constantly darting around the teashop was infectious. We agreed to meet in a few days with the money and our passports that he would return to us once we were safely over the border. You would not want to be caught near the border carrying a passport issued by the previous regime. Each passenger was to pay 21,000 tomans, amounting to to nearly eight months of a salary I was no longer receiving. No discount for children but cheap when compared to what people smugglers charge today. Globalisation has inflated the market in human trafficking too. We were to pay half now and half after we had signalled our safe arrival in Turkey. I borrowed 100,000 tomans from my uncle Fazl without telling him why, orhim asking. Family trust again. Another furtive, fidgety meeting in a tea house and I passed over the documents. Just bring one small sac per person and no more, he

CHAPTER 51

instructed. We were to meet him at 8 in the morning four days hence in a *mosafer khaneh,* a poor man's hotel, in Khoi, a small town in Kurdistan.

Only Mina and Reza my cousin were in the know. It was important to keep the circle small. Reza would take us in his father's car, but someone had to return with him, as it would look strange if he were to be stopped on the way back from Kurdistan alone. We brought in Faramarz married to another cousin, a doctor, who had finished his postgraduate training in Shiraz. He had a friend in Tabriz and a visit to him would provide a good cover for the return journey, and also the journey to Kurdistan until the three-way junction where the road to Khoi turns left from the main Tehran-Tabriz-Turkey arterial road a few miles after the Azarbaijan capital. We also came up with an explanation if we were stopped at the junction. We were visiting the historic sites of Khoi, though what they were or if there were any historic sites around there, we had no idea. In all likelihood the *Pāsdārs* would not have a clue either.

My parents were due to leave for the USA for Ezzy's eyes that needed laser treatment after both his central retinal veins thrombosed – an extremely rare confluence with a real threat of blindness. On departure day, Mina brought Ensy, Ezzy, mummy Foruq and Sarhang to her house where she cushioned the pain of leaving by telling them she was pregnant for the first time – she was 38. We kissed, cried and said goodbye. For J's parents this was the second daughter they were to see off to the mountains; Shahla, J's sister and her husband Bahman had left in the autumn via a different route and had nearly lost their baby daughter from cold exposure in the swamps. It would not have made it easier for the old couple. It was early afternoon when we drove the beige Peikan to the children's school and picked them up. They too had not been told in advance. Why risk an unguarded comment. They both were in the middle of their exams and that afternoon Nargess had sat her end of year geography exam, but the timetables were now completely out of our hands. They changed out of their school uniforms as we drove west.

The children had of course known. When the grown-ups were crying in the next room they were watching *Gone with the Wind* and the anxiety next door diffused through brick-walls. Next morning, Nargess whispered in her friend Nikzad's ear that she was going to England and she immediately understood as she too was off to America. So Nargess just sat through the geography exam and dreamed of life in England - thatched cottages, green meadows ... the England of books and films.

Some hours later we were at the three-way junction. The revolutionary guards on the roadblock waved us by. Reza kept us amused all the way with his unique almost child-like humour. Faramarz sat soundless in the front. In Khoi we drove straight to the designated *mosafer khaneh* and booked three rooms, J and the girls in one, Reza with me in another and Faramarz on his own. The owner asked for our documents, but all we had was my Nezām Pezeshgi license to practice medicine card. A small detail that had escaped us. But the owner seemed happy with the card, smiled and signed us in. It was the middle of the night when Reza and I were catapulted out of our dreams into the world of the living by two Pāsdārs banging on the door.

They wanted identity documents. When all we had to show were driving licence and the permit to practice medicine, they separated us and questioned us individually. What were we doing here? What relation did we have with each other? Who were the women? That is my wife. And Reza? My cousin. I am divorced. Some people stammer when they talk. I stammer in my thoughts under pressure and Reza's ex-wife became entangled in my mental web. I simply could not remember Iman's name. Their eyes darted a shower disbelief. They then went to J's room. "How dare you barge in when I am not in my *hejab*", she said with feigned anger and shock, calm under pressure, as she has always been, an actress. Like the time, without licence or insurance, she had smiled at a policeman and asked him to look after her Mini in Piccadilly Circus while she bought a can of petrol. After an hour of interrogation, they apologised and left. In a regime obsessed by sex, they were after unearthing some sexual transgression between three men and three women in a hotel. The fact that Nargess was only 13 meant nothing when they married their sisters off at a younger age.

Early next morning, Reza and I went down to breakfast and ordered bread, cheese and tea. Faramarz was too nervous for food and went out for a walk. The boy who brought over our tea was none other than one of the Pāsdārs who had interrupted our dreams. That strange feeling of being trapped descended

CHAPTER 51

on me like a fog. But there was no choice but go through with this. By nine thirty our contact had not arrived. I went over to the proprietor and told him that my children were sick with diarrhoea and can he give me some tea and yogurt to take up to them in their rooms. We needed an excuse to stay in the *mosāfer khanāh* doing nothing. By noon I too became nervous and left Reza to keep an eye on things while I went out to scout the town, a town with two main roads crossing at a solitary set of traffic lights manned by a policeman and a bazaar nearby. There was clearly nothing of historic interest there, not even a decent mosque. I took some food for the girls upstairs and sweated it out in the tearoom. Once again time began to stretch like the bubble gums of childhood memories. Men would come in, smoke a *qalyoon* (water pipe) or light a *Marlboro*, the equivalent of the *Camel* cigarette of my youth, drink sweet tea and leave. We sat and waited. In the afternoon another young man took over from our Pāsdār who clearly needed his sleep. It was late afternoon when my smuggler came into the tearoom and sat on the chair next to mine. After a reasonable interval we began chatting, as if we had met for the first time. He looked more at ease in his own environment. We won't be going for another six days. "Something has turned up", he said, which I later found out were three more passengers. "You need to meet us at dusk on the road to Salmās in six day's time" he said. Then he walked away.

Salmās was beyond Khoi on the road south to Urumi'eh (formerly Rezai'eh). Beyond Salmās, roadblocks were set up by the Pāsdārān at night as you were entering liberated territory under the control of the Kurdistan Democratic Party Iran, KDP (I) at the time. We went upstairs and conferred with J. We would be driving south towards these roadblocks as night approached and needed to have a believable excuse and staying in Khoi for five days was simply out of the question as, at the very least, we would stand out as people poised to flee the country. Another former student came to the rescue. Milāni was a pathologist now, working in Urumi'eh's only hospital. "I will ring him tomorrow morning and propose a visit", I suggested. Faramarz had had enough and left by bus for Tabriz.

Milāni and his beautiful wife greeted us as dear friends and fed and bedded us over the next four days. There we also met another old student, now a successful surgeon, still with his Stalin moustache that betrayed his Fadāi' sympathies. He too feted us and even took us to a sumptuous wedding feast. The two were treated like khans in that town which at the time was barely under government control, ruled by the KDP from dusk to dawn. During a conversation, Milāni said something that I have never forgotten; that he was disgusted with all those doctors we knew who had fled the country. I felt my heart constrict in anguish. I had betrayed another trust. I so wanted to tell him, but it would have been sentimental folly. On the last day we had to devise another charade to have an excuse, should we encounter a roadblock, for driving back south along the same road from Khoi towards Urumi'eh at dusk the next day when we were to rendezvous with our smugglers. I dropped a bag full of some clothes behind a sofa in their living room just before we left for Khoi after lunch. "But why leave so late", Milāni and the friend with a moustache kept saying, "the roads become dangerous at dusk. Why don't you leave tomorrow morning", they added anxiously and then with mounting incomprehension at our insistence to leave that afternoon. "I wanted to stay the night in Khoi to visit a shrine", I said. He looked unconvinced and I believe he saw through my lie. I rang him from Khoi, from the same *mosāfer khāneh* who greeted us as old friends. Yes, we found the bag. "Don't worry" I assured him "I will come back for it another time, there is nothing important in it". That too was a lie. The bag contained one quarter of our entire belongings.

Next day, we drove out of Khoi immediately after lunch north toward Tabriz and away from our rendezvous site on the Khoi-Salmās road. It would have aroused suspicion if we had left the *mosāfer khāneh* later that afternoon. Dusk was clearly an absurd time for a rendezvous on a mountain road, although for the smugglers it made sense. A few kilometres outside Khoi we parked on the roadside and picnicked by a small lake waiting for the sun to start its descent, sharing the world with the mosquitoes and the choir of croaking frogs. They don't all have the same voice. When the sun was nearly set, our car returned to Khoi for the third time, hoping that the only policeman on the traffic lights at the sole crossroads would not notice us. It was such a small place even the rats would have been known by name. At each bend on the road my heart beat faster in anxious anticipation. It was almost night

CHAPTER 51

when we were flagged down by a torch just round a bend. Reza pulled to the roadside and put up the bonnet of the Peugeot. Run! The man who had flagged us said and pointed to a path. We ran, not even having time to say goodbye to my wonderful cousin. It was dark and we were running through fields. I took out my ophthalmoscope that I had brought with me along with my stethoscope. The smugglers apparently talked to later groups about a doctor who used his funny medical equipment to light up his path. J and the children let fly their chadors in an exhilarating gesture of liberty. That night we slept on hard rock in the open air on a hill overlooking the town. The lights of Salmās winked and flickered below. Up here was free Kurdistan. Down there, anxiety. I slept on that hard rock like the proverbial log.

The next four days are best pictured in images. First there was a river in a deep valley, beside which we waited out the day, snoozing, in and out of consciousness. Later that afternoon the other escapees arrived, a mother, in imitation mink and pencilled eyebrows, her son of about 20 – the boy ostensibly escaping being sent to the war, but almost certainly a Bahai' escaping a potentially more lethal outcome - and her younger daughter. Nargess later described how the girl had tried to convert her. The boy was quite pale and may have been hidden at home for some time, I thought. And a very mysterious middle-aged man who would reveal nothing. Only travelling at night, each of us sat behind a smuggler on a horse. Nargess, the youngest in the group, sat with the leader on a magnificent black Arab stallion. After a few minutes, for some reason, the horse reared up and threw rider and Nargess. In an effort to save her the leader, a very tall, distinguished Kurd, who by the way he talked made clear his superior status among the crew and beyond, broke his collarbone. He bore the pain until the end without showing it. Unlike all the others he had no moustache. I did not see him smile. Maybe the pain.

    Travelling by starlight, there being no moon, it is astonishing how much light remains from these few billions of stars and galaxies after they have travelled billions of miles over a few billion years. You could see the white lily-like flowers decking the slopes, the larger rock formations and the trees silhouetted against them. The only noises were the hooves of the horses, distant dogs barking and the occasional whispers of our smugglers. They spoke in whispers as if they expected the hills to carry their voices to an unseen enemy in an ambush. They were right.

On the second night we stopped between tall rocky hills and I heard the smugglers discussing something at length, arguing. The man who had been our contact seemed animated about something and trying to persuade the leader. I found out later that he had suggested taking a different valley to the usual route so as to avoid having to pay taxes to the KDP. We moved into a narrow valley along a small river. The road was rocky, and we kept criss-crossing the river and navigating round huge boulders. There were frequent stops and discussions as if they had lost the way. Suddenly we heard shots above our heads. There is a Pāsdār fort ahead my smuggler said in a voice that betrayed surprise and unease. We dismounted and ran towards a hill and climbed running and stumbling towards the flickering lights of a village. Halfway up that interminable hill Nargess simply gave up and sat down in tears. I tried to lift her but the leader with his broken collarbone picked her up under his good arm and carried her the rest of the way.

That night in that village, which we were meant to have circumvented, they gave us a delicious meal of chicken and bread. A mother brought a baby on her arms who was limp and listless. "How old is he?" I asked. "Two", his mother said. He weighed and behaved like a six or seven month baby. I could find nothing that explained his failure to thrive and then the mother said something that froze in my heart. A visiting doctor had persuaded her not to breastfeed but to use powdered milk and she was diluting it seven-fold. She had to make each tin go a long way, and after all, the mixture did look white. The child had been fed on not much more than white water. There was little that anyone could do. I wondered how much that doctor was paid by the powdered milk company to push for that instead of breast milk. How much was irreversibly damaging the body and brain of a child worth? We relieved ourselves, like the villagers, in the stables next door and slept the rest of the night.

And then there are the rags. J was on her period since the day after we

CHAPTER 51

left Khoi. She had endometriosis and would bleed profusely. Once her haemoglobin had dropped to less than half normal. This bleeding was not part of our calculation when we left Tehran expecting to be over the border in two days and she had brought no sanitary towels. On horseback her thighs had become red like raw steak. The men just looked blank when we tried to explain. Men and women live in two bubbles that overlap only in moments of social and other forms of intercourse. In the village, the women who served us food understood her need through the linguistic fog. Why do they not teach us the languages used by the majority of the people of Iran? That deep-rooted Fars chauvinism which the Shah perpetuated, and that the Islamic Republic had done little to reverse. Why can we not communicate with our fellow countrymen and women? They brought over a few rags, used, washed and reused many times. J smiled.

At breakfast of bread, fried eggs and delicious yogurt I learnt another Kurdish custom. If you put down your *estekān* (the small glass with a pinched midriff shaped like a female figure) they will fill it up until you lay it on its side, as if exhausted, playing dead. The boy on the samovar kept replenishing my *estekān* and the tea became weaker and weaker until it resembled the little floppy child's powdered milk, when I caught the weary glint in the boy's eye and suddenly understood. Just then we heard noises outside the house. It was a team of Jahāde Sāzandegi[1] (Reconstruction Brigade) bringers of electricity. We sat quiet, fairly sure that they would be unlikely to enter a home uninvited, catching the women unawares without their *hejab*. I do hope the smugglers paid our hosts for the food. We sat indoors till dark.

That night we just rode and rode on a path that went up and up. It is just round the corner, they kept insisting, but the corner had more corners. It is just over the hill, but there was another hill beyond that, and another, as promiscuous as my great grandfather. It was nearly 2 am when we arrived at a peak and dismounted. "We will stay here till morning", my smuggler-guide said, "until the border guards change over". We were on the Turkish border and the guards on duty were clearly not on the payroll. It was cold and J began to shiver. No one had told us to bring warm clothes and they had, sadly and understandably, discarded their *chadors*. The tall leader threw his long grey overcoat over J's shoulder. It was desperately cold. I threw myself over the two girls trying to keep them warm with my body. That mountain pass was the coldest night I was ever to experience.

And then the cold thawed at an astonishing speed, flying off to chase the vanishing stars. The rays of the sun peeked over the mountain ahead and we walked, no ran, downhill, down the mountain side, then over the threshold into exile. There was a large farmhouse in the valley below where an old man received us. He was a khan-like figure with a grey bushy moustache and a warm smile, living in a single long house with whitewashed walls with his extended family. Everyone was respectful to him. We had a king's breakfast where we met a statuesque girl of about twenty with big blue eyes that reminded me of the blue eyes of that young girl whose fingers had turned blue-black, one at a time. This was the second wife of the leader of our caravan that we had met. The other in the first house we came to above Salmās. He told me of another in Tatvan, our destination in Turkey, and a fourth in Mashhad, one at every stop. One night he asked me if I knew anyone in Tehran that he could marry. The three I saw were singularly beautiful. He had been smuggling sheep into Iran in the previous regime and had now switched to alcohol one way and human cargo on the way back – and I got a hint of heroin too.

After breakfast we took the girls to a mountain spring at the far end of the estate where they had their first bath in a week. I could not tear them away, particularly J who was soothing her raw thighs. She also got some clean rags from the wives. Finding out that I was a doctor, the khan's wife excitedly brought out a postcard that a lady from a previous group, also married to a doctor, had sent them from Istanbul to show J. They did not get much post out there in the mountains. It was from our old friend Parvin and conveniently she had written the return address – 24 General Yazgan Sok, Şişaneh, Istanbul.

Two days later we left in the evening in three taxis. The tall leader and our initial contact came with his son and another man from the farm. Our family was together in one taxi. There were two other taxis. Our driver, not much older than Maryam, must have learnt to drive that morning because

CHAPTER 51

he did not know how to change gear and drove most of the way in first gear until I showed him how to change, when he stuck to the second gear. After a few kilometres they ordered us to dismount, explaining that there is a police garrison ahead and we would need to walk across a shallow river. The taxis will pick us up on the other side. A horse was brought up and loaded with our bags and some other equipment. We took our shoes and socks off and waded into the shallow river. We were crossing the stream and I could see the three creamy white taxis ahead when I heard the now familiar crackling sound of gun shots very close by, felt its wind on my balding scalp, and shouted to the girls to run towards the taxis. We jumped in as the shooting continued. It was the same novice driver. He was desperately trying to get into reverse. The car doors were still open, J was still running and the gears were grating. I kept shouting and gesticulating to the driver who looked terrified, didn't understand Farsi and was looking death in the face. J finally made it to the stuttering car and the taxi hiccupped forwards in first gear, the driver having forgotten all I had taught him. As we left, I caught a glimpse of the horse turning back across the stream, led by the son of my contact. He had two of our bags. Nargess had kept hers. Through sheer chance it contained our passports and documents, without which life would be difficult in Turkey. A week later, the smugglers delivered both bags with news of our safe arrival to Mina, but minus a pair of new black shoes that I had packed for myself. That was their tip. We now had less than half our possessions.

Our driver, who by the end of the journey had discovered all the gears, was sure we are being followed. Every time a car approached from behind, they ordered us out and hid us behind the roadside ditch until the cars passed by. They seemed to be overreacting. The shots, in retrospect, were aimed above our heads and a warning to the smugglers to pay their dues. Tatvan by Lake Van, another apartment, another beautiful wife. We phoned Mina and she in turn phoned the family. It had been over two weeks since we had left Tehran. We did not want to linger there. There was a camp for Iranian refugees in Van, the other side of the lake and reports that some refugees had been returned to Iran. We needed to get to Istanbul to be as far away form the border as possible. Passing the police in the bus station was another nerve-racking experience, this time without the smugglers. They had delivered us two weeks late. The rest was our affair. The bus trip to Istanbul was a bumpy 24 hours. We arrived by taxi outside number 24 General Yazgan Sok, the address on Parvin's postcard.

By one of those strange co-incidences that makes up the tapestry of life, Mani was at that very minute telling Parvin "wouldn't it be good if M and J could join us". A few seconds later they heard their names shouted up from the street. "Come and pay this driver", I asked Parvin after a deep hug, "he is trying to cheat us". She sorted him out in Azari Turkish, close enough to their version to be mutually comprehensible. In any case I had no cash. My money was sewed inside my underpants. One hundred thousand Turkish Liras. We had improvised and stumbled our way through to Istanbul with one or two small spurts of adrenaline.

Parvin led us up the stairs to the first-floor flat and we were met by Mani, and their two children Pooya and Raha, together with Afsaneh and Said, Said's brother Sorush and his wife Parvin, and Farrokh. We did not know the others. We would be sharing the flat with them plus three young men who joined us later – twelve grown ups, two teenagers and two kids aged 2 to 4. That was to be our home for the next five months.

[1] The reconstruction brigade that the regime set up to bring the villages of Iran, who had been lukewarm or frankly hostile to the revolution, into the fold.

Chapter 52

24 General Yazgan

Cities exist in our imagination and wait to be discovered in the reality of our experience. Istanbul, Janus-like, sitting on the neck of Eurasia, looking both ways but not really belonging to either, resonated with J and me. We too faced both ways. It even felt like an island without really being one; you seemed to hit water whatever road you took. Watching the shimmering light on the Bosporus, inevitably choppy from ships, ferries and wind, was like watching free spirits bouncing up and down in abandon. Istanbul was ethereal despite the concrete chaos of a large metropolis. I loved, love, that city.

General Yazgan Sok was a small alley in Şişaneh, close to the US, British, French and many other embassies. Also close to the *karkhanehs*, brothels. It made us laugh and cry, this *karkhaneh*, since in Farsi it means a factory, an apt name for a low-class brothel. Nearby was a small covered bazaar with a dazzling display of fruit not seen in my war-torn Iran. In Istiqlal Avenue that led to Taqsim Square you could still find the sort of coffee houses that evoked childhood memories of Paris and Milan, brown upholstered pews and marble tables where you could order *qeimaq* (clotted cream), and ice creams that spiralled upwards from the bowl. And just up the road was Meşrutyet Street curving round the car park and looking down on what is now the

Erdogan Stadium, the blue waters of the Horn beyond, and where 28 years before I, a child on my first trip abroad, had walked over the smashed glass on the morning after the anti-Greek riots.

There was an English language bookshop, the only one in town. Otherwise, the city looked illiterate in an incongruous sense. Books spread out on the pavement were the combination of trash and aspiration that I recalled from our own pavements when the Shah whipped us towards the 'Great Civilization', long replaced by more serious stuff. Comics, Mills and Boon-like love stories, cowboys, cheap police novels, girlie picture magazines, living not-so bashfully alongside second-hand schoolbooks, technical books, improve yourself books. No politics other than Ataturk and occasionally Nehru and Gandhi. You could see the military censor's fist hanging over the spread. Even the English language shop was sanitized, though the British Council Office on the same street was a little better. I enrolled and took out some useful books. It was also there that I read of the new disease of AIDS for the first time in the *British Medical Journal*.

On that first day none of these interested us. We took the cable car dug into solid rock at the end of our road, the Bayoğlu Tünel, and got off at Karaköy near the Galata Bridge. There, under that bridge in one of its restaurants we lunched on fish caught right there from the Bosporus. And it was there that we had our first litre of beer for four or five years. It tasted as the rivers of milk in heaven are reputed to taste, ethereal. Mani then took us to a moneychanger not far from the spice bazaar in Eminönü, carrying the bunch of Turkish Liras I had unstitched from my underpants that morning. Enough for a thousand visits to the movies. We changed them for the more solid Deutsch Mark.

Living clandestinely in Istanbul was precarious. Police were regularly accosting Iranians in the street and shipping them to the special camp in Van with its threat of repatriation over the adjacent border. Mani, who had obtained an unpaid pathology post in Bayazid University, suggested that we go and see the Dean of the medical school. I spent 12,000 precious Liras on a beige suite, shirt, tie and a new pair of black shoes to replace the one that had vanished on horseback over the stream, and through Mani's English-speaking colleague made an appointment. The Dean, an overweight jovial man who

CHAPTER 52

spoke modest English, received Mani and me suspiciously. He had been to Shiraz and after I talked at length about the Dean, Dr Nasr, the 'fat man' to the taxi drivers of Shiraz, and gave enough details to satisfy him that I was an ex-faculty member he visibly mellowed. He picked up the phone and rang the Mayor of Istanbul and after a short conversation he rang the head of the Istanbul security police – the equivalent of SAVAK - and asked for an appointment for us.

The security chief received us in his office, situated in an imposing building. Icy, almost hostile. We had to pass several checks and body searches. This was still a military dictatorship after General Evren's coup in 1980. It was clear that he was unhappy to be asked for a favour by a civilian. He spoke only Turkish. Through Parvin, who come along as interpreter he told us to return the next day with the family. Next day with the children we were driven away in a blacked-out van that seemed to me to be making a complete circle. When we got out, the van was inside a building without windows. Was it the basement of the same building we had just left? A man in a dark brown suit, unfashionably cut, with a small paunch and a rich moustache came over and shook our hands. What language do you speak, he asked with a reassuring smile? We chose to communicate in a mixture of German and English.

After being told that I had left illegally because doctors were banned from leaving the country at wartime, he seemed satisfied. The remaining questions revolved round my entire family, where I had to detail the names and jobs of my parents and grandparents, every single uncle and aunt, and their children. He seemed to be only interested in links with the current regime in Iran. My beliefs did not interest him in the least. We were taken back the same, blinded, route. Next day I went to see the Dean, thanked him and sheepishly asked if he could ring the Chief of Security in person and thank him, which he did in my presence. My next visit to the security chief was full of smiles. Clearly, he did not want anyone to pull rank and the expression of gratitude had given him the respect he knew was due to him. We got the papers that gave us *Iltij'a*, a temporary permit to stay in Istanbul. The condition was to leave the country as soon as we got an asylum somewhere. This episode was the latest chain in that invisible network of the medical mafia that had woven a web of protection over me over the preceding five years. I was blessed by friends and profession.

Life in Istanbul had three dimensions. To enjoy life, to make the money last and to get out of Turkey – in reverse order of priority. Every morning we did the rounds of the embassies. The British Embassy ultimately gave us an interview. Margaret Thatcher had stopped automatic British citizenship for those born in the UK but even she could not pre-date it to before 1981. Maryam and Nargess ultimately got their dark blue British Passports and flew to England in late August to stay with J's brother Massoud and his wife Fereshteh. The French embassy did not even see us, though we initiated a request for asylum through the help of the exiled lawyer Abdolkarim Lahiji in Paris. I wrote to everyone abroad that I knew, or even vaguely knew; among them a paediatrician in Pennsylvania, Brian Creamer who during his year in Shiraz had become a friend and was now Dean of St Thomas' Hospital Medical School and Martin Hartog my old boss in Bristol. We filled out a request for refugee status in Canada and proceeded to the second level which would have involved an interview in another European City. Through contacts of our flat mates, we also initiated asylum application to Sweden which at the time was receptive to Iranians. We even tried the Finnish embassy, which would not let us in and told us to push our application forms under the gate. It must have been the way they fed plague victims in the Middle Ages.

Then one day, walking the street housing the UN office, J met my old friend and resident Behruz, one of the brightest brains among a lot of bright people. We have met him before when he attacked Mohsen during the Congress of Traditional Medicine.[1] He had got to Turkey after a particularly traumatic escape during which his wife had been caught and imprisoned for a month. He had settled in Ankara and had learned Turkish. He joined us in the flat, as did Mohsen's son Ali-Mohammad who fled after us - another hair-raising escape through Pakistan - and later Parvin's brother Keyvan. Farrokh, the only one among us who had left Iran because of military service and to pursue higher education, had relinquished his small room to our family, where J and I shared a single bed and the girls slept on the floor. The master bedroom was given to Mani who had two small children. The other two families used the other bedroom. The four bachelors had to sleep in our sitting room.

We recreated the strict discipline of the prison, no sleeping after 8 am and no lounging about. There was a lot of grumbling. Money control was easy. We allowed ourselves the equivalent of one British pound per person per day and started a strict rotation for cleaning, cooking and shopping. Maryam's obsession with charts led to a wall chart that recorded the expenditure for the day, which she kept diligently. Parvin regularly exceeded the limits and ignored the gentle rebukes. Parvin even had an order of priority of those who she gave the choicest pieces of meat: Pooya her son, followed by me. She was the exact opposite of my old cellmate Mahmud in the Third Army (*Artesh* 3) Detention Centre with his obsessively meticulous division of food, an unruly team player of the Yazgan commune. The wall chart, which took on the appearance of a fever chart at the end of a patient's bed, would exhibit a sudden spike of fever on her day, once almost falling off the top edge. We rationed water, which was cut off daily for hours at a time. And there was bossy Said, guardian of order and water. Ali-Mohammad had a ditty for him that went something like this: 'I am afraid of those eyes; afraid, afraid, afraid of those two black eyes',[2] sung with a strong Shirazi accent.

Mornings we hunted visas. Afternoons were leisure time, idyllic days. Regular trips to Büyükada, the largest island in the Sea of Marmara loaded with a big bottle of *sharabi qermizi* (red wine), bread, tomatoes, cheese, and boiled eggs, and travelling with *doroshgeh*[3]to the sea. There, the large colony of mussels that we cooked over a fire with red wine gave us more protein. And the cool blue water of Marmara on Büyükada or Flory beach touching our dried-out skins momentarily froze time and the uncertainties of the road ahead. The children loved it. When she first arived, Nargess, after some initial hesitation put on her bathing clothes. After the strictures of the Islamic Republic during the most formative years of her life, she felt a little naked even with short sleeves. But new environments create new body images. And within days she was plunging into the sea with the rest. The two newlyweds in the flat next door had their real honeymoon there. The Black Sea though, lived up to its name and we ended up cleaning tar off our feet and clothes all night. Life was good. There was the beautiful castle on the Bosphorus, there was the beer and the ubiquitous fried mussels, there was fish, fresh cheap fish, and Emek cinema off Taqsim showing films in the original language once a week for 100 liras.

The departure of the children relieved our main anxiety. We could now stay as long as it took. They stayed in Massoud and Fereshteh's flat with 2-year old son, Jabiz, she heavily pregnant. The girls' first impression of London was shock. England was not cottages and green fields and meadows but yuppies, punks, men with earrings, and dyed hair. They had expected Suffolk and got Kings Road and Camden Market. Maryam found the posturing of the chic Iranian left difficult to swallow at first and wrote at length about it. Nargess spoke next to no English, and Maryam's linguistic skills were mainly from reading. The first months of Hendon Comprehensive must have been tough, especially for 13-year-old Nargess. "We had the wrong clothes and the wrong hair" she said later. But 13-year-olds learn fast, and my 16-year-old girl skipped over 'teenagerland' altogether. And the adventures of the escape gave them 'street cred'.

Ensi and Ezzy arrived in Istanbul on their way from the US where Ezzy had his retina lasered to stop him going blind and Ensi had been admitted to a coronary care unit (CCU), the same one that had apparently looked after Eisenhower earlier, having collapsed in the street. They had monitored her all night, charged her 1,000 dollars and said she may have had a cardiac arrhythmia. Over the next week I noted her occasional pallor and shortness of breath. I took her pulse and found she was in atrial fibrillation – irregularly, irregular heart beat. In the flat I listened with my stethoscope and heard the murmur of mitral stenosis. She had rheumatic heart disease, was going in and out of atrial fibrillation and no one in that illustrious CCU had bothered to listen to her heart. That in essence was what was wrong with US medical care then and now.

I was offered a post at the American Hospital in Istanbul, another perk of the old medical Mafia, with a monthly salary of 17,000 lira of which I would have to pay out 10,000 to an interpreter. The remainder would have been

CHAPTER 52

enough to keep us well within our needs. Canada, France and Sweden would have taken us in due course though I preferred the UK since I could work as a doctor there. Farrokh was the first to leave us. We all collected outside the door to bid him goodbye. He had been sent 1,000 DM by his father, a single crisp one thousand Deutsch Mark note in an envelope, a vast sum squashed into that brown-red rectangle, and with that he bought a ticket to Germany via Belgrade. We wept. Said-with-the-fearful-eyes went with him to the airport. The smugglers had promised that they could get him through; unlike us Farrokh was an illegal in Istanbul. He got through to the inner desk and was returned. A couple of weeks later and another 1,000 DM note and this time he made it to Belgrade. Late that evening he knocked on our door. He had been turned back as he was boarding the plane for Germany. The third attempt, same price, he got as far as Vienna, his new destination, but was repatriated after a day. Farrokh was still there when I left in October.

[1] See chapter 16: Congress of Traditional Medicine. Mohsen never had a good word for him.

[2] *Man as oon cheshha mitarsam, as oon do ta shemaye siah mitarsam, mitarsam, mitarsam.*

[3] Horse drawn carriage which was our mode of transport when I was a child. Cars were banned in the islands of the Sea of Marmara.

Chapter 53

Revolutionary court

We had a practical problem to contend with in Istanbul. Afsaneh was pregnant with her first child. She had the congenital blood disorder thalassemia minor. Her haemoglobin started to fall slowly as her belly swelled with the child I nicknamed Roqieh - a very old-fashioned name. I never doubted it was going to be a girl. Her haemoglobin dropped to 5, well under half its normal value, despite all the kebabs Said-with-the-black-eyes gave her and she found it difficult even to walk. Through our links with Bayazid University we found one of the world's experts on thalassemia. Medical mafia again. Our Roqieh was born under his care in late October and given the name of Solmaz and grew up to become a poet.[1]

Political debates alternated with singing. Behruz had a wonderful way of singing street (*koocheh-bazari*) songs while Afsaneh and Parvin possessed a huge repertoire of revolutionary songs. None of us talked of our political affiliations though we all knew. Two young newlyweds belonging to another left group joined us in most activities, as did some students studying in Istanbul who were either Fadāi' or supporters of various Maoist leanings. It was almost as dangerous to be politically active in Turkey under military rule as in Iran under the ayatollahs. We met people who had been in Turkish

CHAPTER 53

prisons and torture was routine there. It was in this light that the tragicomedy of the general took place.

We were sitting cross-legged at breakfast around the cloth. There was butter, feta cheese and *halvardeh* (halva) with its subtle blend of sweetness and nutmeg. The cook of the day had made some fried eggs. Breakfast was an elaborate affair in General Yazgan Sok. There was a knock on our door. It was an unusual time for friends and neighbours to arrive. On the far side of the door were two middle aged men and a young girl who turned out to be the daughter of the thinner man with greying hair and a trimmed moustache. Elegant. They must have known we lived on the first floor. After the usual pleasantries the girl handed us a letter. It was from Bahrām, the same Bahrām who had found us the people-smugglers - asking us to look after these very close friends of his. The girl was a little plump, and rather plain, not much of her rather distinguished looking father in her. Despite his humble politeness he held himself like someone in authority, used to being obeyed. He sat down on one of our two chairs, erect, perfect posture. He introduced himself as Salari. The other man was younger but had a pronounced paunch. The daughter declined to sit and stood beside her father, a little behind, like a guard. They had fled Iran and arrived the previous day. They politely declined an invitation to join us for breakfast but asked for help in finding a hotel. We invited them to supper and found them a hotel nearby.

During supper it transpired that Salari and his daughter had fled Shiraz and had been hiding in a flat in Tehran for the last two and a half years. Then the man with a paunch said almost out of the blue "Mr. Salari has rendered great services to our country, services that will one day be recognised". It was a strange thing to say and set me thinking. After they had left, I went to my room and pulled out my driving licence. It was issued in Shiraz and signed by General Salari, head of the Shiraz police. This was the same Salari who had ordered the shooting from the citadel of Shiraz on that last day of the Revolution. He had been responsible for the brain spilling out of that boy's skull and all the other shattered corpses I had seen in the mortuary of Shahrdari Hospital. I felt physically sick. Why had Bahrām sent this butcher to our house and appealed to my hospitality? The more we looked at the circumstances, the name, the hints of the man with a paunch of the 'great service to the country', and the subtext of Bahrām's letter, the more we became convinced that it was him, now looking so meek.[2]

We conferred with the rest of the flatmates and next morning with some of the students who were studying in Istanbul. The two young couples in love also came. A Fadāi' student suggested we set up a revolutionary court on behalf of the people of Iran, sentence him to death and carry out the sentence. She was deadly serious and was supported by a few others. It took Mani and I some time to dissuade them from such an absurdity. What right did this bunch of refugees have to speak for the people of Iran? That was the way the left then, and to some extent now, behaves – as guardian for the people, not at all unlike Khomeini and his absolute unquestioned and unquestionable power over the country enshrined in the concept of *velayate faqih*.[3] It was turning into a farce, but I have no doubt that they would have carried it out. But here also was the tragedy of the Revolution exposed in all its nakedness. All three sides of the triangle, the monarchists, the Islamists and a big chunk of the left were willing to impose their vision on society by any means.

In the same way as I cannot hate the Pāsdārs because nothing binds me to them, I could not hate the butcher, but understood that tribal urge for revenge, or as Seamus Heaney so beautifully put it:

I
   Would connive
   In civilized outrage
   Yet understand the exact
   And tribal, intimate revenge[4]

General Salari, his daughter and his minder fast-tracked the refugee process, were taken to the UN transit camp after three days and were in the US within a week. I wonder if his 'services' to the country will ever be justly judged.

In early October, Martin Hartog, my old boss in Bristol, called me on our upstairs neighbour's phone. His senior registrar had gone on sabbatical leave for six months and he could offer me the locum post. Within a short time, I had obtained a Laissé Passé from the British Consul who handed it over with a typical British half smile. We gathered outside the house for the goodbyes. Said accompanied me to the airport, as he had done for all the other hopefuls. Each desk was a nerve-racking experience. Each look by a uniformed man or the military personnel scrutinising every traveller was a potential rejection. Then the plane and that was that. J joined me a month later having seen the birth of Solmaz (Roqieh). All the others left Turkey by the following spring. Said's brother Sorush, his wife and her brother ended up in France. The remainder went to the US, via a few months in the UN transit camp in Italy. Farrokh was the last out, just as he was the first in among our group.

And I flew into London. I had grown up, rather late. But I had grown up, ready to work on the geography of volcanoes.[5]

[1] Solmaz Sharif is a prize winning poet currently teaching in Berkley, California. Among her many publications is the anthology, *Look* (Graywolf Press, 2016).

[2] Later in the US, Bahrām confirmed our suspicions.

[3] Article 5 of the Iranian constitution states: "…the *vilayah* and leadership of the *ummah* devolve upon the just (*'ādil*) and pious (*muttaqi*) *faqih*…" and goes on to give the leader, Khomeini, absolute power over the entire civil and political society in Iran.

[4] Part of Seamus Heaney poem *Punishment*.

[5] I have work to do on the geography of volcanoes, Mahmoud Darwish.

54

Appendix 1

APPENDIX 1

Family tree

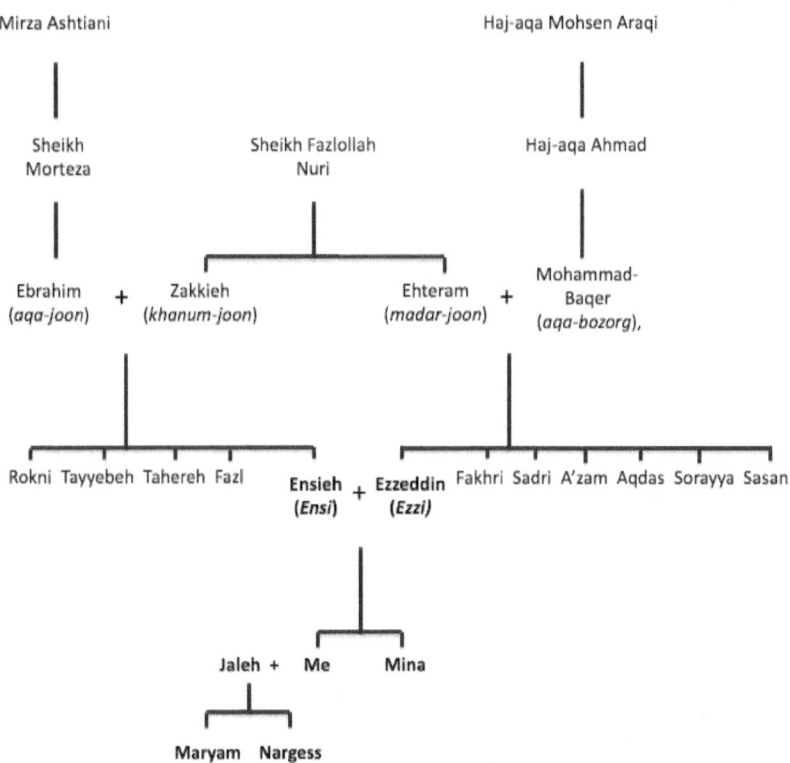

Appendix 2

Main opposition parties and groups to the Shah and Islamic Regime

Tudeh Party: formed in 1941 and became one of the largest official communist parties in the Middle East. Tudeh, with its trade union base and having infiltrated the armed forces, played a major role in the nationalisation of the Anglo-Persian Oil company during the premiership of Mosaddeq and was highly influential in the intellectual life of the country. After the CIA-organised coup in 1953, the party, including its extensive network within the military, was all but destroyed inside Iran and its leadership was exiled to the Soviet Bloc. After the Sino-Soviet split in 1956 the Maoist faction split calling itself the Revolutionary Organization of the Tudeh Party - later renamed Ranjbaran Party. During and after the Revolution, Tudeh supported Khomeini and his regime until it, in turn, was brutally suppressed by that same regime in 1983.

Ranjbarān Party (originally, **Revolutionary Organization of the Tudeh Party**), the Maoists split in the Tudeh that had taken place in the late 50's which also supported the Islamic regime, although a different faction of the regime to that of Tudeh. It too was suppressed in the bloody crackdown of 1981-3.

Organisation of Iranian People's Fadāi Guerrillas (OIPFG) - **Fadāi** for short. Created in 1971 after the amalgamation of two guerrilla groups following the attack on Siāhkal police station. It suffered a number of near lethal blows from the Shah's SAVAK but survived to emerge on the eve of the revolution. After the Revolution the Fadāi became the largest left organisation in the country with tens of thousands of supporters. The occupation of the US Embassy by the Islamic regime caused the Fadāi to split into the Fadāi (Majority - so called because it included the majority of the Central Committee) which allied itself with the Tudeh Party and supported the regime, and the Fadāi (Minority) which continued in opposition to the regime.

Fadāi (Majority) supported the Islamic regime alongside the Tudeh Party until 1983 when it was suppressed along with the Tudeh Party. It consistently mirrored the Tudeh line.

Fadāi (Minority) after the split with the Fadāi (Majority) went underground, but fought alongside Kurdistan Democratic Party (I) and Kumeleh in Iranian Kurdistan. In the rest of Iran, the Fadāi (Minority) inside suffered severe blows in the bloody crackdown of 1981-3.

Organisation of Iranian Peoples Mojahedin (PMOI) created in 1965. It initially had links with the religious section of Mosaddeq's National Front (Nehzat Azadi). It espoused a revolutionary interpretation of Islam, strongly influenced by the Shi'a thinker Ali Shari'ati, but also by a Maoist version of Marxism. It joined the armed struggle after the Fadāi' attack on the Siāhkal police station in 1971. In 1975 a large section of the Mojahedin converted to Marxism and emerged after the Revolution as the Peykār Organisation. In the aftermath of the Revolution the Mojahedin became the largest opposition group in Iran. While initially supporting Khomeini, they prepared for an uprising and suffered severe blows in the crackdown of 1981.

Peykār (full name: Sāzmān Peikār Barāye Rahāi' Tabaqeh Kārgar - Combat Organisation for the Liberation of the Working Class) originated as splinter group from the Mojahedin (1975). Originally known as the Marxist Mojahedin, it adopted a Maoist interpretation of Marxism, and was strongly against the Soviet Union. In 1978, on the eve of the Revolution it adopted the name of Peikār. After the Revolution Peikār became the second largest left organisation in the country, after the Fadāi'. Under the blows of the regime Peikār imploded and many of its activists and cadres were executed or imprisoned.

Rāhe Kārgar (full name: **Sāzman Kārgaran Enqelabi Iran - Rāhe Kārgar - Organisation of Revolutionary Workers of Iran - Rāhe Kārgar**). Originally created inside the Shah's prisons by a number of cadres from various opposition groups, both Marxist and Islamic, who had escaped execution. It was formally launched in 1979. Rāhe Kārgar was unique in that it rejected the reformism of the Tudeh, the reliance on the armed struggle of the Fadāi' and the 'third worldism' of the Maoists. It attracted members from many opposition forces and rapidly grew to become the third largest force on the left with an influence on the radical left wider than its numerical strength. In 1982-3 the Organisation, including large section of its leadership suffered under the blows of the regime who were either executed or received long prison sentences.

Vahdat Communisti (Communist Unity) was a Marxist offshoot of the Mosaddeq's National front (Jebh-e Melli Four). Despite its small size it had a substantial influence on other left organisations because of its ideological sophistication.

Ettehādieh Communisthā (League of Communists) was created in the

Confederation of Iranian Students abroad and later changed its name to **Sarbedāran.** The Sarbedāran organised an uprising and brief occupation of the northern city of Amol in 1982 which was brutally put down.

Razmandegān, a Maoist organisation, also with roots in the Confederation of Iranian Students, continued until its dissolution in 1981 as a small but very active organisation.

Regional and National Organisations

The above list excludes the two mass Kurdish parties that are active in Kurdistan - **Kurdistan Democratic Party of Iran (KDPI-I)**, a mass party with a social democratic ideology with particulary strong base in rural areas of Kurdistan and **Kumeleh** with Maoist ideology and with a strong urban base. Both were, and remain, predominantly Kurdish organisations. Kumeleh later merged with some left groups as the nation-wide Communist Workers Party of Iran. Kumeleh later underwent a number of splits.

56

Appendix 3

Bibliography

Ervand Abrahamian, *Iran Between Two Revolutions*, Princeton University press 1982. A good historical background to the period between the Constitutional Revolution and the Revolution of 1979.

Fereidoon Ādamiyat, *tārikhe bidari Irāniān* – History of the Awakening of Iranians, a classic history of the events leading up to the Revolution of 1906 (Farsi).

Hamid Algar *Religion and State in Iran*: 1785-1906. Berkeley: University of California Press, 1969, for the role of Shi'sm in Iranian history.

Jahangir Amuzegār, *The Dynamics of the Iranian Revolution: The Pahlavis' Triumph and Tragedy* SUNY Press, 1991. The revolution from the royalists' view.

Assef Bayāt. *Workers and Revolution in Iran*. Z Books, London and New York 1987.

Lois Beck, *The Qashqai' of Iran*. New Haven, Yale University Press 1988.

Dr Ali Behzadi's memoires, *shebh-e khāterāt*, Tehran 1996 (*in Farsi*) gives a moving account of the fall of Mossadeq and the trial and execution of his Foreign Minister, Dr Hossein Fatemi.

de Bellaigue, C. *Patriot of Persia: Muhammad Mosaddeq and a Very British Coup*. Bodley Head 2012. A good description of the central of role British intelligence in the overthrow of Mosaddeq.

James A Bill, *The Eagle and the Lion,* Yale University Press, 1988 and E. Baqi, '*Figures for the Dead in the Revolution',* Emruz*, 30 July 2003 (in Farsi) who give high estimates of the numbers killed in the Revolution; and Charles Kurzman, *The Unthinkable Revolution in Iran*, Harvard University Press, 2004, for lower estimates of the casualties of the Revolution.

Edward G Browne, *The Persian Revolution 1905-1909* (1910), New York 1966. The first account of the Constitutional Revolution in Iran in English.

Cosroe Chaqueri, *The Left in Iran* 1941-57, Merlin Press, 2011, p 45-54 for the Autonomous Government of Azarbaijān.

Regis Debre, *Revolution in the Revolution? Armed Struggle and Political Struggle in Latin America,* translated by Gregory Elliott and Bobbye Ortiz, Verso Books, London 2017. The classic book that proposed a novel form of revolution using the Cuban Revolution as a model.

Franz Fanon, *The Wretched of the Earth*. Translated by Richard Philcox, with a foreword by Bhabha, Homi K. and a preface by Sartre, Jean-Paul. New York: Grove Press 2004.

Robert Fisk, *The Great War for Civilisation: The Conquest of the Middle East,* Fourth Estate 2005. For an account of the war see Dilip Hiro, The Longest war, Paladin 1990. For a moving eye-witness account description of the battlefield during those early days.

Thomas L Friedman, Foreign Policy May-June 2006.

Mark Gasiorowski, *U.S. Foreign Policy and the Shah.Building a Client State in Iran,* Cornell University Press, 1991, for a description of the fall of Mosaddeq and the extent of the blows to the Tudeh Party.

Cyrus Ghani, *Iran and the Rise of Reza Shah,* IB Tauris, London 2000. A somewhat sympathetic account of the reign of the first shah in the Pahlavi dynasty.

Shusha Guppy, *The Blindfold Horse: Memories of a Persian Childhood*, Minerva, 1992, Describing the village of Damavand in the 1940-50's where the family had a *bāq*.

Fred Halliday, *Iran: Dictatorship and Development,* Penguin books Ltd, London 1979. A good summary account of Iran under the Shah and the opposition,

Dilip Hiro *Iran Under the Ayatollah's,* Routledge 1988. A sympathetic account of the post-Revolutionary Islamic regime.

Dilip Hiro, *The Longest war,* Paladin 1990. An account of the Iran-Iraq war.

Michael C Hillman, *A lonely woman: Forugh Farrokhzād and her poetry*. Mage publishers Washington, 1987. One of the greatest and most courageous modern poets in Iran.

Ryszard Kapuscinski, *Shah of Shahs.* Quartet Books, London 1985.

Homa Katouzian, *The Persians,* Yale University Press, 2010. A brief history of Iran from ancient times to the present.

APPENDIX 3

Homa Katouzian, *The Political Economy of Modern Iran 1926-1979.* London Macmillan, 1981.

Nickie R Keddie, *Roots of Revolution*, Yale University 1981. Good standard account of the Revolution of 1979.

M.S. Kia *Entangled lives, in press.* A semi-biographical story of three interlocking lives in their struggles against two totalitarian regimes of Shah and Khomeini.

Nureddin Kianuri's *memoirs (in Farsi).* He was General Secretary to the Tudeh Party and wrote his memoires after he was imprisoned and tortured by the Islamic regime, despite the support Tudeh Party gave to the regime.

Stephen Kinzer, *All the Shah's men.* John Wiley and Sons 2003 and 2008. A journalistic account of the CIA-engineered coup against Mosaddeq.

Afshin Matin-Asgari, *Iranian student opposition to the Shah.* ISBN:1-56859-079-2. An authoritative account of the Confederation of Iranian students abroad.

Abbās Mazāheri: *The blossoms of pomegranate tree: memories of 4791 days of imprisonment under the Shah's dictatorship* (in Farsi). An eyewitness account by a long-term former political prisoner giving a vivid account of the relationships between Islamic and left prisoners.

Ardeshir Mehrdad and Yassamine Mather, *Political Islam's relations to capital,* Critique 36-37 Routledge, Taylor & Francis Group. A comprehensive and perceptive account of the effects of Khomeini's policies on ordinary life and the country.

Sheikh Fazlollāh Nuri's refutation of the idea of constitutionalism in *Religion and Politics in Modern Iran: A reader* Edited by Lloyd Ridgeon. IB Tauris

London 2005.

Younes Pārsā Benāb, *One hundred year history of the Iranian political parties and organisations* (1904-2004), Rāvandi Publishing House, Washington DC 2004 (in Farsi). A detailed history of all political parties in Iran.

Nasrin Parvāz, *One Woman's Struggle in Iran: a Prison Memoir.* Victorina Press, 2018. A personal account of the experience of female prisoners under the Islamic regime.

M Rahā, *Haghighate Sadeh (simple truth).* A young girl's story as political prisoner for nine years in the prisons of the Islamic regime including a personal experience of the coffins and an eye witness account of to the massacres of political prisoners 1988 (in Farsi),

Ali Rahnema (ed), *Pioneers of Islamic Revival.* Zed books London and New Jersey 1994. An excellent review of the main thinkers behind the Islamist movements in the Middle East.

Geoffry Robertson QC, *The massacre of political prisoners in Iran,* 1988. Published by Abdorrahman Boroumand Foundation. June 2011. http://www.irantribunal.com/PDF/Iran%20Massacre%20of%20Political%20Prisoners%201988.pdf.

Siavash Randjbar-Daemi: *The Tudeh Party of Iran and the land reform initiatives of the Pahlavi state, 1958–1964*; 2021 https://www.tandfonline.com/doi/full/10.1080/00263206.2021.1976157

Sirus Sa'dvandian and Mansureh Ettehadieh, Eds: *amāre Dār al-Khalāfeh Tehran* (Statistics for the capital Tehran), Tehran 1368 (1989) in Farsi for a description of the social make-up in Qājar times.

Jack Shenker, *The Egyptians: a radical story,* Allen Lane 2016. The story of the

APPENDIX 3

Arab Spring in Egypt.

Annabelle Sreberny, Ali Mohammadi, *Small Media, Big Revolution*, University of Minnesota Press, 1994, for the role of media in the Iranian Revolution.

Peyman Vahābzadeh, *A guerrilla odyssey Modernization, Secularism, Democracy and the Fadāi' Period of National Liberation 1971-79.* Syracuse University Press 2010. A history of the left in both the Shah and Islamic Republic.

Story of the Revolution. BBC. Published in Farsi as *The Writing of the Verbal History of Islamic Revolution of Iran*, Tehran Spring 1994.

Afterword

Reflections

Those months in Istanbul we, silently, inwardly, tentatively, within ourselves, unable yet to articulate it in an open discussion, began thinking through where it went wrong. We avoided confronting our past openly, still wary of revealing too much of ourselves. The prison that was Iran had created a mesh of self-censorship that was to some extent subliminal. And the look-back came, like the ticks of a clock, in little jumps, and like that clock needed constant rewinding. It was only over the subsequent years that I began to formulate a clearer picture of how the left, which in my lifetime until the Revolution had been central to the very idea of change in Iran, had failed. And where it had succeeded. It was the left that had articulated the vision of change through Iran's entire contemporary history. It was the left that had shaped the throbbing cultural life of the country over that time. And it was from the left that the resistance to the Shah in the 60's and 70's had sought inspiration – whether the Marxist guerrillas, or the Mojahedin. Even such radical anti-Marxist religious innovators as Ali Shari'ati had been influenced by it.[1]

So, what went wrong? Why all that sacrifice in vain? What was missing in that historic narrative? How had the left failed in the tasks it had set itself a century before and deposited the country into the hands of those whose compass pointed to a bygone era bounded by the sandy hills of marauding tribes and caravans of merchants crossing deserts?

Was it our history? Our national psyche? Our collective historical maladjustment? Social schizophrenia? Marx's class analysis of history needs to be adapted here. Never through the centuries did we have a proper landed aristocracy, one with longstanding roots. Our landowners were suicidally dependent on the whims of the latest strongman on the throne. In a land of tribes, the only continuity was discontinuity. And then there were the invasions through time: Alexander, Arabs, successive waves of Turkish-speaking tribes from the Central Asian steppes, Changiz (Genghiz) Khan, Holagu, Timur, Afghans. Our ancestors on the Iranian plateau had only one defence against these waves – retreat into yourself and to those you are closest. The only defence against wave after wave, century after century of bloody conquerors from all points of the compass was to withdraw into the safety of the tribe, the family, or inner thought. Did survival impose fragmentation of any existing social cohesion as we withdrew into smaller and smaller units? Is that not how we retained our culture by bending to the new power, to Iranianise it from within?[2] When could we, we Iranians, ever learn to work in larger groups? Individualism was, is, deeply ingrained. Even Shi'sm individualises religion by its emphasis on the *marja' taqlid*,[3] where, as a believer, you are free to follow the Shi'a authority of your choice.

In more recent times, an Iranian bourgeoisie was implanted from above by Reza Shah and his son on this rock-hewn, invasion-swept land. A new middle class with few roots in society, without a cultural heritage, a sterile middle class. An illiterate, shallow bourgeoisie gave birth to an equally shallow opposite, whose understanding of its own history was as superficial as its knowledge of Marxism. Its models were either the ossified Tudeh with its regurgitation of what came from Moscow academics, whose golden boy was Ehsan Tabary. Or, equally sterile, the peasant revolutionaries of East Asia. Tudeh's naive concept of socialism by osmosis,[4] so busy looking up to whoever was in power, they kept tripping over their shoelaces, was one model. Maoist voluntarism and the utopian idealism of Che Guevara were others. We on the independent left had an almost comical belief in the power of our reasoning with a nod or more to imam Hossein's heroic martyrdom. We would guide, persuade, and perhaps drag people into the beautiful world that awaited them, if only they could see it our way. In miniature, the tiny underground group a handful of us had created to 'direct' the struggles in the University. On a larger scale, the top-light Fadāi'.[5] A binary vision of the world, divided between good and bad, no shades of grey, no paths, no clear routes to our goal, impatient with the pace of history. Khomeini had a definite goal and knew how to get there. And patience.

Mesmerised by the 'anti-imperialist Imam Khomeini', a large part of the left inside and outside Iran ignored the second of the two key revolutionary slogans of *esteqlāl, āzādi* (independence, democracy) and pathetically clung to a quasi-independence that had a very limited application within the constraints of global capitalism. We too on the new left, the independent left, abandoned by most of our potential allies the world over, did not fully appreciate the life force of democracy. That you need to breathe in order to fight. And all the while criss-crossing the ever-present class fractures, we also had to side-step other ravines more typical of societies of our type: the widening gulf between tradition and change. After the Shah was deposed, we had to manoeuvre on a landscape of crevasses, dodging death, only vaguely aware of the organisational ability of the clergy. Just as the Polish communists would underestimate the ubiquity of the Catholic Church a decade later. No wonder we kept tripping up. Or dying. But do not blame the dead for their deaths – they did not ask to be killed.

Should we repent our role? No. The New Left had fought in the Shah's graveyard when no one else was prepared to utter a sound. Those boys and girls of the New Left had raised the banner of revolt with their blood, contemptuous of the ridicule of the Tudeh leadership who cynically, and I would add maliciously, called them 'radishes' (red on the outside, white inside) and demanded the overthrow of the monarchy years before the ayatollahs.[6] And after the Revolution was stillborn, we on the left desperately kept the flag of revolt aloft, remained faithful to both parts of the key slogan of Revolution: independence and freedom, even though our understanding of the latter was incomplete and our defence fragile.

Could we have changed the course of history if we had fought better? Who knows? We fought, but fought badly, and against an opponent who was a tactical genius, had excellent organisational ability and deep roots. This scattered, poorly trained mishmash that opposed both Shah and the Islamists, ignorant of its history and poorly equipped by its theories faced Khomeini and the entire structure of the clergy. A clergy that had been left relatively untouched by the dictator Shah, who, with his western allies, saw them as a bulwark against communists. Whether Khomeini's strategy is lasting history will decide.

Yet our call for freedom and independence has echoed through time resurfacing again in the Arab Spring in Egypt. That too was started by secular forces and highjacked by the better organised Islamists once the weakness of the dictators was revealed.[7] And many thousands lost their lives for these ideals. Ideals that are not utopian but achievable in the here and now. 'Was it needless death after all' or 'was a terrible beauty borne' (Yeats)? Ideals are what make us human, our unique signature. Stamped on our forehead. I thought, I think, we can hold our head high - we fought, fought with faulty theory and faulty organisation, but we fought. And lost. Perhaps the next generation will learn from our mistakes. It is better than not fighting at all. There is no victory in inaction.

[1] For example, that of the Algerian radical revolutionary Franz Fanon.

[2] Alexander, the Arabs, the Moguls, the Turkish invaders all adopted Iranian culture and structure. Iranians ran much of the administrative apparatus of the Arabs, the Moguls and the Mugals of India. Farsi became the language of courts and government in many places.

[3] The Shi'a can emulate (*taqlid* i.e. follow) whichever religious authority they choose. Shi'a clergy are organised in a totally non-hierarchical, even anarchic structure. See Hamid Algar *Religion and State in Iran: 1785-1906*. Berkeley: University of California Press, 1969.

[4] The non-capitalist road to socialism was a theory cooked up by the Moscow academics to theorise Soviet support for such despotic allies as Saddam Hossein in Iraq, Hail Maryam in Ethiopia and Moammar Qaddafi in Libya.

[5] The Fadāi' themselves claimed they could mobilise a million supporters

at a time when they only had 100 members. The true figure was probably less, at a guess 250,000 – 500,000, still a huge multitude. The left candidate in the only election they were allowed to participate obtained 150,000 votes in Tehran and over 50,000 in the provincial city of Rasht. The Mojahedin probably had more than a million supporters. Khomeini did not allow us to see how many by blocking their leader Massoud Rajavi standing for the first presidential election. Yet Bani-Sadr, supported by the Mojahedin got 10.7 million of the 14 million votes.

[6] Khomeini only targeted the monarchy as an institution late in the Revolution.

[7] See Jack Shenker, The Egyptians: a radical story, Allen Lane 2016.

About the Author

The author is a medical doctor who trained in the UK and went back to Iran to teach in Shiraz (formerly Pahlavi) University. He participated in the revolution that overthrew the Shah and was later imprisoned by the post-revolutionay regime for his defence of freedom. After release he returned to the UK to work as a medical doctor in the National Health Service. He is now retired.

Also by M.S. Kia

Entangled lives, in press
The interlocking lives, loves and prison experience of three young revolutionaries in their struggles against two totalitarian regimes of the Shah and the Islamic Republic.

Reflections on life and love
Collection of poems (in press)

www.ingramcontent.com/pod-product-compliance
Lightning Source LLC
Chambersburg PA
CBHW022000160426
43197CB00007B/204